WITHDRAWN
HARVARD LIBRARY
WITHDRAWN

ONE HUNDRED YEARS OF PHENOMENOLOGY

PHAENOMENOLOGICA
SERIES FOUNDED BY H.L. VAN BREDA AND PUBLISHED
UNDER THE AUSPICES OF THE HUSSERL-ARCHIVES

164

DAN ZAHAVI AND FREDERIK STJERNFELT (EDS.)

ONE HUNDRED YEARS OF PHENOMENOLOGY
Husserl's *Logical Investigations* Revisited

Editorial Board:
Director: R. Bernet (Husserl-Archief, Leuven) Secretary: J. Taminiaux (Centre d'études phénoménologiques, Louvain-la-Neuve) Members: S. IJsseling (Husserl-Archief, Leuven), H. Leonardy (Centre d'études phénoménologiques, Louvain-la-Neuve), U. Melle (Husserl-Archief, Leuven), B. Stevens (Centre d'études phénoménologiques, Louvain-la-Neuve)
Advisory Board:
R. Bernasconi (Memphis State University), D. Carr (Emory University, Atlanta), E.S. Casey (State University of New York at Stony Brook), R. Cobb-Stevens (Boston College), J.F. Courtine (Archives-Husserl, Paris), F. Dastur (Université de Nice), K. Düsing (Husserl-Archiv, Köln), J. Hart (Indiana University, Bloomington), K. Held (Bergische Universität Wuppertal), D. Janicaud (Université de Nice), K.E. Kaehler (Husserl-Archiv, Köln), D. Lohmar (Husserl-Archiv, Köln), W.R. McKenna (Miami University, Oxford, USA), J.N. Mohanty (Temple University, Philadelphia), E.W. Orth (Universität Trier), P. Ricœur (Paris), K. Schuhmann (University of Utrecht), C. Sini (Università degli Studi di Milano), R. Sokolowski (Catholic University of America, Washington D.C.), B. Waldenfels (Ruhr-Universität, Bochum)

ONE HUNDRED YEARS OF PHENOMENOLOGY

Husserl's *Logical Investigations* Revisited

edited by

DAN ZAHAVI

University of Copenhagen

and

FREDERIK STJERNFELT

University of Copenhagen

KLUWER ACADEMIC PUBLISHERS
DORDRECHT / BOSTON / LONDON

A C.I.P. Catalogue record for this book is available from the Library of Congress.

ISBN 1-4020-0700-0

Published by Kluwer Academic Publishers,
P.O. Box 17, 3300 AA Dordrecht, The Netherlands.

Sold and distributed in North, Central and South America
by Kluwer Academic Publishers,
101 Philip Drive, Norwell, MA 02061, U.S.A.

In all other countries, sold and distributed
by Kluwer Academic Publishers,
P.O. Box 322, 3300 AH Dordrecht, The Netherlands.

Printed on acid-free paper

All Rights Reserved
© 2002 Kluwer Academic Publishers
No part of this work may be reproduced, stored in a retrieval system, or transmitted
in any form or by any means, electronic, mechanical, photocopying, microfilming, recording
or otherwise, without written permission from the Publisher, with the exception
of any material supplied specifically for the purpose of being entered
and executed on a computer system, for exclusive use by the purchaser of the work.

Printed in the Netherlands.

In meinen LU habe ich uralt ungefüges Gestein der Erkenntnislehre wie mit Dynamitpatronen zersprengt. Es giebt viel rohes Geschiebe u. Gerölle, aber Mancherlei ist an den Tag getreten, was verborgen war, an Problem[en] u. Ergebnissen.

Letter from Husserl to Willliam Ernest Hocking, September 7, 1903

TABLE OF CONTENTS

ACKNOWLEDGMENTS	9
ABBREVIATIONS	11
PREFACE	15

PART I. PROBLEMS OF LOGIC

Rudolf Bernet: Different Concepts of Logic and Their Relation to Subjectivity	19
John J. Drummond: The *Logical Investigations*: Paving the Way to a Transcendental Logic	31
Jocelyn Benoist: Non-Objectifying Acts	41
David Woodruf Smith: What is "Logical" in Husserl's *Logical Investigations*? The Copenhagen Interpretation	51

PART II. REALISM AND IDEALISM

Dallas Willard: The World Well Won: Husserl's Epistemic Realism One Hundred Years Later	69
Richard Cobb-Stevens: "Aristotelian" Themes in Husserl's *Logical Investigations*	79
Dan Zahavi: Metaphysical Neutrality in *Logical Investigations*	93

PART III. CATEGORIAL INTUITION

Ullrich Melle: Husserl's Revision of the Sixth Logical Investigation	111
Dieter Lohmar: Husserl's Concept of Categorial Intuition	125
Frederik Stjernfelt: Categories, Diagrams, Schemata: The Cognitive Grasping of Ideal Objects in Husserl and Peirce	147

PART IV. SEMIOTICS, ALTERITY, COGNITIVE SCIENCE

Robert Sokolowski: Semiotics in Husserl's *Logical Investigations*	171
Bertrand Bouckaert: The Puzzling Case of Alterity in Husserl's *Logical Investigations*	185
Dieter Münch: The Relation of Husserl's *Logical Investigations* to Descriptive Psychology and Cognitive Science	199

APPENDIX

Dorion Cairns: The First Motivation of Transcendental Epoché	219
INDEX	233

ACKNOWLEDGMENTS

Most of the articles collected in this volume stem from a conference on Husserl's *Logical Investigations* which was held at the University of Copenhagen in May 2000. The organization of the conference would not have been possible without the generous support from a number of individuals and institutions. For financial support we wish to thank the Danish Research Council for the Humanities, the Carlsberg Foundation, the French Embassy in Copenhagen, the Goethe Institute in Copenhagen, and last but not least the University of Copenhagen (Department of Comparative Literature, Department of Education, Philosophy, and Rhetoric, and the Faculty of the Humanities). Eva Hjelms was of invaluable assistance in the preparation and holding of the conference. We are also indebted to Gerol Petruzella and Berit Brogaard for their help with the proofreading of the manuscript. Finally, it was as always a pleasure cooperating with Maja de Keijzer from Kluwer Academic Publishers.

ABBREVIATIONS

References to the writings of Husserl have often been included in the text according to the following abbreviations.

The Husserliana edition

Hua I — *Cartesianische Meditationen und Pariser Vorträge*, edited by S. Strasser (Den Haag: Martinus Nijhoff, 1950, rpt. 1973).

Hua II — *Die Idee der Phänomenologie. Fünf Vorlesungen*, edited by W. Biemel (Den Haag: Martinus Nijhoff, 1950, rpt. 1973).

Hua III/1-2 — *Ideen zu einer reinen Phänomenologie und phänomenologischen Philosophie. Erstes Buch. Allgemeine Einführung in die reine Phänomenologie*, edited by K. Schuhmann (Den Haag: Martinus Nijhoff, 1976).

Hua IV — *Ideen zu einer reinen Phänomenologie und phänomenologischen Philosophie. Zweites Buch. Phänomenologische Untersuchungen zur Konstitution*, edited by M. Biemel (Den Haag: Martinus Nijhoff, 1952).

Hua V — *Ideen zu einer reinen Phänomenologie und phänomenologischen Philosophie. Drittes Buch: Die Phänomenologie und die Fundamente der Wissenschaften*, edited by M. Biemel (Den Haag: Martinus Nijhoff, 1952, rpt. 1971).

Hua VI — *Die Krisis der europäischen Wissenschaften und die transzendentale Phänomenologie. Eine Einleitung in die phänomenologische Philosophie*, edited by W. Biemel (Den Haag: Martinus Nijhoff, 1954, rpt. 1962).

Hua VII — *Erste Philosophie (1923/24). Erster Teil. Kritische Ideengeschichte*, edited by R. Boehm (Den Haag: Martinus Nijhoff, 1956).

Hua VIII — *Erste Philosophie (1923/24). Zweiter Teil. Theorie der phänomenologischen Reduktion*, edited by R. Boehm (Den Haag: Martinus Nijhoff, 1959).

Hua IX — *Phänomenologische Psychologie. Vorlesungen Sommersemester 1925*, edited by W. Biemel (Den Haag: Martinus Nijhoff, 1962).

Hua X — *Zur Phänomenologie des inneren Zeitbewusstseins (1893–1917)*, edited by R. Boehm (Den Haag: Martinus Nijhoff, 1966).

Hua XI — *Analysen zur passiven Synthesis. Aus Vorlesungs- und Forschungsmanuskripten 1918–1926*, edited by M. Fleischer (Den Haag: Martinus Nijhoff, 1966).

Hua XII — *Philosophie der Arithmetik*, edited by L. Eley (Den Haag: Martinus Nijhoff, 1970).

Hua XIII — *Zur Phänomenologie der Intersubjektivität. Texte aus dem Nachlass. Erster Teil: 1905–1920*, edited by I. Kern (Den Haag: Martinus Nijhoff, 1973).

Hua XIV	*Zur Phänomenologie der Intersubjektivität. Texte aus dem Nachlass. Zweiter Teil: 1921–1928*, edited by I. Kern (Den Haag: Martinus Nijhoff, 1973).
Hua XV	*Zur Phänomenologie der Intersubjektivität. Texte aus dem Nachlass. Dritter Teil: 1929–1935*, edited by I. Kern (Den Haag: Martinus Nijhoff, 1973).
Hua XVI	*Ding und Raum. Vorlesungen 1907*, edited by U. Claesges (Den Haag: Martinus Nijhoff, 1973).
Hua XVII	*Formale und transzendentale Logik. Versuch einer Kritik der logischen Vernunft*, edited by P. Janssen (Den Haag: Martinus Nijhoff, 1974).
Hua XVIII	*Logische Untersuchungen. Erster Band. Prolegomena zur reinen Logik*, edited by E. Holenstein (Den Haag: Martinus Nijhoff, 1975)
Hua XIX/1-2	*Logische Untersuchungen. Zweiter Band. Untersuchungen zur Phänomenologie und Theorie der Erkenntnis*, edited by U. Panzer (Den Haag: Martinus Nijhoff, 1984).
Hua XXI	*Studien zur Arithmetik und Geometrie*, edited by I. Strohmeyer (Den Haag, Martinus Nijhoff, 1983).
Hua XXII	*Aufsätze und Rezensionen (1890–1910)*, edited by B. Rang (Den Haag: Martinus Nijhoff, 1979).
Hua XXIII	*Phantasie, Bildbewußtsein, Erinnerung*, edited by E. Marbach (Den Haag: Martinus Nijhoff, 1980).
Hua XXIV	*Einleitung in die Logik und Erkenntnistheorie. Vorlesungen 1906/07*, edited by U. Melle (Dordrecht: Martinus Nijhoff, 1984).
Hua XXV	*Aufsätze und Vorträge (1911–1921)*, edited by T. Nenon and H. R. Sepp (Dordrecht: Martinus Nijhoff, 1987).
Hua XXVI	*Vorlesungen über Bedeutungslehre. Sommersemester 1908*, edited by U. Panzer (Dordrecht: Martinus Nijhoff, 1987).
Hua XXVII	*Aufsätze und Vorträge (1922–1937)*, edited by T. Nenon and H. R. Sepp (Dordrecht: Kluwer Academic Publishers, 1989).
Hua XXVIII	*Vorlesungen über Ethik und Wertlehre (1908-1914)*, edited by U. Melle (Dordrecht: Kluwer Academic Publishers, 1988).
Hua XXIX	*Die Krisis der europäischen Wissenschaften und die transzendentale Phänomenologie. Ergänzungsband. Texte aus dem Nachlass 1934–1937*, edited by R. N. Smid (Dordrecht: Kluwer Academic Publishers, 1993).
Hua XXX	*Logik und allgemeine Wissenschaftstheorie*, edited by U. Panzer (Dordrecht: Kluwer Academic Publishers, 1996).
Hua XXXI	*Aktive Synthesen: Aus der Vorlesung 'Transzendentale Logik' 1920-21. Ergänzungsband zu 'Analysen zur passiven Synthesis'*, edited by R. Breeur (Dordrecht: Kluwer Academic Publishers, 2000).
Hua XXXII	*Natur und Geist. Vorlesungen Sommersemester 1927*, edited by M. Weiler (Dordrecht: Kluwer Academic Publishers, 2001).

Hua XXXIII	*Die 'Bernauer Manuskripte' über das Zeitbewußtsein 1917/18*, edited by R. Bernet and D. Lohmar (Dordrecht: Kluwer Academic Publishers, 2001).
LI	*Logical Investigations*, translated by J. N. Findlay (London and Henley: Routledge & Kegan Paul, 1970).
Hua Dok III	*Briefwechsel.* Husserliana Dokumente III/1-10, edited by K. Schuhmann and E. Schuhmann (Dordrecht: Kluwer Academic Publishers, 1994).
EU	*Erfahrung und Urteil*, edited by L. Landgrebe (Hamburg: Felix Meiner, 1985).

PREFACE

Husserl regarded *Logical Investigations* (1900-1901) as his 'breakthrough' to phenomenology, and it stands out not only as one of Husserl's most important works, but also as a key text in 20. Century philosophy. The work had a tremendous influence on the subsequent development of phenomenology, and it also left its mark on disciplines such as linguistics, comparative literature, psychology, cognitive science, and mathematics. By predating the split between 'analytical philosophy' and 'continental philosophy', *Logical Investigations* remains of particular interest to those concerned with the possibility of a rapprochement between the two traditions.

One of the most striking features of *Logical Investigations* is its incredible richness. It is a work that is literally brimming over with new, fresh, and in many cases, revolutionary ideas. Not only does it contain Husserl's first treatment of a whole range of phenomenological key-concepts, it also contains some quite devastating criticisms of a number of traditional views. The following are some of the most important analyses found in the *Logical Investigations*:

- A refutation of psychologism
- A defence of the irreducibility of ideality
- A sketch of a general 'theory of theories'
- An outline of the process of eidetic variation
- A presentation of the program of descriptive phenomenology
- A rejection of the mental-image theory of meaning
- A criticism of nominalism and empiricist theories of abstraction
- The outline of a general mereology
- A new interpretation of the synthetic a priori
- The distinction between material (or regional) and formal ontology
- A theory of pure grammar
- The introduction of the concept of foundation
- A revolutionary theory of intentionality
- A criticism of representionalism
- A distinction and analysis of different modes of givenness
- An introduction and analysis of notions like 'adumbrational givenness' and 'bodily presence'
- A description of the process of constitution
- An introduction of the concept of categorial intuition
- A theory of truth and justification based on the notion of intentional fulfilment and evidence
- A distinction between synthetic and ideative acts

After its publication, *Logical Investigations* quickly gained in reputation, and received positive reviews and mention by thinkers such as Mach, Schuppe, Natorp, Stumpf, Dilthey, Wundt, and Lipps. As to its *Wirkungsgeschichte*, its most obvious impact was of course to be found in the subsequent development of phenomenology, be it in the "eidetic" and "realistic" phenomenology of the Münchener phenomenologists and of Husserl's Göttingen students (Lipps, Daubert, Reinach, Geiger, Stein etc.), or in Husserl's own development of a transcendental phenomenology. But even for post-Husserlian phenomenologists *Logical Investigations* remained a work of crucial inspiration and importance, as is testified by, e.g., Heidegger's *Prolegomena zur Geschichte des Zeitbegriffs* (1925) and his *Zur Sache des Denkens* (1969), Sartre's *La transcendance de l'ego* (1936), and Derrida's *La voix et le phénomène* (1967). This in some sense 'official' line of influence leading from the fountain of the *Logical Investigations* to the many later works of Husserl, to the works of his personal students, and to the works of the post-Husserlian phenomenologists is relatively well known and well documented, but in fact the influence of *Logical Investigations* reaches much further. Another legacy is to be found in linguistics, primarily via Roman Jakobson who very early on read Gustav Spet's Russian translation of the *Logical Investigations*. Even though Jakobson did not himself conceal this inspiration, for a long time it passed largely unnoticed that the very founder of linguistic structuralism imported crucial parts of his conceptual apparatus from the *Logical Investigations*, especially from the First, Third, and Fourth Investigations. Jakobson used, among other things, the idea of foundation in his phonology (the "distinctive feature" as a moment of the phoneme). From Jakobson, this inspiration passed—often unnoticed or via inscrutable connections—into mainstream linguistics and semiotics; thus it is striking to see Husserl's three basic dependency relations between parts surface in exactly identical form in Louis Hjelmslev's *Prolegomena* of 1943. The Third and Fourth Investigations also inspired and influenced the Polish logicians—in particular Lesniewski's idea of a formal mereology, which was initially formed in order to dismantle Russell's paradox, and Ajdukiewicz's idea of categorial grammar, defining word classes by dependency relations. Through Roman Ingarden (*Das literarische Kunstwerk* from 1931), the idea of describing the structure of the intentional act by means of a series of interrelated moments proved highly influential in phenomenological theory of literature and, later on, in reader-oriented criticism (Jauss, Iser, Eco). The same parts of the work also influenced Gestalt psychology through the main philosophical figure in the Berlin School, Max Wertheimer. As for the flourishing Cognitive Science such debts are all over the places, though often tacitly present in second or third hand forms.

There is plenty of reason to immerse oneself in a close reading of the *Logical Investigations*. This volume celebrates and commemorates its centenary by subjecting the work to a comprehensive critical analysis. It contains new contributions by leading scholars addressing some of the most central analyses to be found in the *Logical Investigations*.

I

Problems of Logic

RUDOLF BERNET
Husserl Archives—University of Leuven

DIFFERENT CONCEPTS OF LOGIC AND THEIR RELATION TO SUBJECTIVITY

In secondary literature, Husserl's *Prolegomena to Pure Logic*[1] has aroused surprisingly little attention. Several circumstances might be responsible for this inattention, the first being that the problem of *psychologism* is considered to be resolved. With this in mind, it no longer seems worth the effort to reconstruct Husserl's meandering and repetitive lines of argument. The fact that the text of the *Prolegomena* essentially stems from a lecture delivered in 1896 is another reason to turn directly to the more mature discussions regarding the relation of pure logic and phenomenology in the Second Volume of the *Logical Investigations*.[2] Finally to some readers, Husserl's extensive discussion of literature contemporary to him seems dated and irrelevant. This is supported by the work of merited scholars, such as Dallas Willard,[3] which has shown that one cannot always trust Husserl's presentation of opposing positions.

Nevertheless, in the following contribution I want to limit myself entirely to the *Prolegomena*. This decision requires an explanation especially since I want to deal with the question of the connection between logic and the subjective consciousness of logical objects. Concerning this question, the Second Volume of the *Logical Investigations* has made significant progresses in comparison to the *Prolegomena*. Apart from the fascination the multi-faceted text of the *Prolegomena* has always had for me, there are, however, at least two motives for my procedure: First, Husserl's tentative attempts to bring logic together with descriptive psychology, in the midst of the discussion with logical psychologism, seem to me especially instructive for understanding the difficulties connected with this endeavor. Usually, these difficulties are not sufficiently accounted for when reading the Second Volume only. Second, the role of logic as a theory of science (*Wissenschaftslehre*) comes into clear relief in the *Prolegomena*, and this in all formulations of logic, i.e., apart from pure logic, in normative logic, and in logical technology (*Kunstlehre*). Therefore, in this paper I will inquire into the question of the relation of objective logic to subjective consciousness

---

[1] E. HUSSERL, *Logical Investigations, First Volume: Prolegomena to Pure Logic*, transl. by J. N. Findlay, London and Henley: Routledge & Kegan Paul 1970 (*Logische Untersuchungen I*, Husserliana XVIII, Den Haag: Martinus Nijhoff, 1975). Quotes without further indications are from Findlay's translation of the *Prolegomena*; the German pagination is given in brackets. In certain cases our translation of Husserl's text differs from Findlay's. In this case, D. CAIRNS' *Guide for Translating Husserl* (Dordrecht/Boston/London: Kluwer 1975, *Phaenomenologica* 55) has been consulted.

[2] E. HUSSERL, *Logical Investigations, Second Volume*, transl. by J.N. Findlay, London and Henley: Routledge & Kegan Paul 1970 (*Logische Untersuchungen II*, Husserliana XIX/1-2, Den Haag: Martinus Nijhoff, 1984).

[3] D. WILLARD, *Logic and the Objectivity of Knowledge. A Study in Husserl's Early Philosophy*, Athens: Ohio University Press, 1984.

in each of these three formulations of logic. Needless to say, the *objective* foundational connection, which unites pure logic, normative logic, and logical technology, will also be examined.

I. PURE LOGIC AND ITS RELATION TO SUBJECTIVE
LIVED-EXPERIENCES OF EVIDENCE AND OF IDEATION

From the most acknowledged Eleventh Chapter of the *Prolegomena* it is known that Husserl attributes three tasks to pure logic, which essentially persist up to *Formal and Transcendental Logic.*[4] 1. The doctrine of primitive apophantic and formal ontological categories and the laws concerning their complication; 2. the doctrine of the connection of these categories in terms of a logic of consequence, which on the side of meanings has developed into independent theories such as syllogistic, and on the side of formal objects into arithmetic; 3. the apophantic theory of possible forms of theory and its corresponding formal-ontological, mathematical theory of manifolds (*Mannigfaltigkeitslehre*). It is also well known that the clarification of pure logic, achieved in the Second Volume of the *Logical Investigations* under the title of a "phenomenology and theory of knowledge," deals especially with the first task of logic.

However, little acknowledged are the definitions of "knowledge," "knowing," and "science," as well as the determination of logic as "theory of science" (*Wissenschaftslehre*), which at the outset of the first chapter of the *Prolegomena* are programmatically introduced. Knowledge or knowing differs from "baseless opinion" (*grundloses Meinen*) owing to its insight into truth. Husserl calls this insight, constitutive for knowledge, "evidence." The object of this subjective lived-experience of evidence is a truth, which concerns the reality of the state of affairs (*Sachverhalt*) asserted in a judgment. Now, truths or true states of affairs can be of an empirical nature, as in the case of a judgment pertaining to natural science, or of an a priori nature, as in the case of a logical or mathematical judgment. The latter truths are supertemporal, general and absolutely valid; one might characterize these sorts of truth as *vérités de raison* in Leibniz's sense. Regarding these, Husserl mostly speaks of "truths in themselves" (*Wahrheiten an sich*). Furthermore, one still has to distinguish these "truths in themselves," as propositions (*Sätze*) or laws from the "being in itself" of the states of affairs to which they refer. In both cases, however, one deals with ideal objects, whose being, referred to as "validity" (*Geltung*) by Lotze, is intuited in an act of "apodictic" evidence. Matters are different for facts of empirical experience: their existence depends on all kinds of changing circumstances. Assertions and laws, which refer to them, involve forms of truth, which are, properly speaking, mere probabilities. Therefore, empirical judgments and the empirical objects to which they refer cannot meet the demand for apodictic evidence.

---

[4] E. HUSSERL, *Formal and Transcendental Logic*, transl. by D. Cairns, Dordrecht/Boston/London: Kluwer 1978 (*Formale und Transzendentale Logik*, Hua XVII, Den Haag, Martinus Nijhoff, 1974).

The difference between a knowing that refers to ideal objects and a knowing that refers to empirical facts persists in the difference between the sciences of essences and the sciences of facts. Logical psychologism, which Husserl battles against, implies a crude misjudgment of the fundamental difference between these two forms of science. However, in both cases we are dealing with genuine sciences or theories, i.e., sciences or theories that systematically order a manifold of known objects under the perspective of a "unity of the foundational connection" (*Einheit des Begründungszusammenhangs*).[5] This unity of the foundational connection is constitutive for the construction of a scientific theory and has its basis in the things themselves. However, the way in which different things are arranged in relation to each other also has a formal-logical aspect. For most essential sciences (except for phenomenology itself!) there arises the possibility of constructing this logical foundational connection under the form of a formal deduction. Such an axiomatic foundational connection does not apply to the causal relationships investigated by the empirical sciences, unless, as Husserl already asserts in the *Prolegomena*, by way of "idealizing fictions" (e.g., by employing mathematical models in natural science). It goes without saying, however, that the causal judgments of the empirical sciences remain subject to the essential laws of formal logic.

Thus, the difference between the sciences of essences, such as logic, and the empirical sciences, such as psychology, must not make us forget that pure logic applies to all sciences, i.e., that it is a *universal* doctrine of science (*Wissenschaftslehre*). Every science utilizes categories of meaning and objectivity as well as forms of inference (*Schlussformen*) and every science instantiates one form or another of theory. Pure logic owes its regulative relevance to all sciences (including itself) to the fact that it deals exclusively with the forms of possible meanings and possible objects. However, since the logical doctrine of science is itself a science, it strives for a systematic order of its own knowing under the form, for example, of an axiomatic-deductive theory. Yet, the success of this endeavor has less relevance for its function as a regulative doctrine of science than for its own scientific character.

The theoretical core of the logical doctrine of science (in the double sense of a doctrine of all other sciences and of a meta-logic) lies in the fact that pure logic formulates the laws concerning the possible connections between ideal objects. These ideal objects are either simple or complex *forms* of meanings or of objects. The apophantic and formal-ontological categories are ideal objects just as are the logical laws founded upon them. I have already mentioned their relation to subjective lived-experiences of apodictic evidence. That the validity of these ideal logical objects is, however, in no way dependent upon the lived-experiences, in which they are evidently given, is a basic insight of the *Prolegomena*. For according to their doctrine, the validity of logical objects is independent of *any* (evident or non-intuitive) givenness. In this sense, the being-true (as truth in itself) of hitherto undiscovered logical principles is not in principle different from the truth of those principles already known. Further, this also

---

[5] Findlay translates this as "unity in the whole system of grounded validation" (cf. e.g., p. 62).

means that each factual subjective givenness of the validity in itself of an ideal object is an act of radical subjective *self-transcendence*. For example, the subjective insight into the validity of the principle of non-contradiction brings consciousness into connection with something essentially *alien* to it, i.e., with something that is neither consciousness of any sort nor reducible to something like consciousness. In light of this reflection, logical psychologism is nothing but the attempt to bridge the gap between the being of consciousness and the being of ideal objects by making ideal objects subjective. This subjectivation is a reduction of the transcendence of ideal being, and such a reduction can be interpreted as an appropriation or annexation of the *alien* by one's own consciousness.

Therefore, Husserl's doctrine of the *subjectively evident givenness* of logical laws in the *Prolegomena* (§§ 27, 32, 39, 50-51, 65) stands in the middle between the extreme positions of psychologism, on the one hand, and of a "logical absolutism"—which contests any possible relation of logical objects to consciousness—on the other. With the logical absolutists, Husserl shares the conviction that logical laws, according to their own sense, have nothing to do with subjective lived-experiences of consciousness. The propositions and laws of pure logic refer exclusively to ideal objects that are either forms of meanings or forms of objects. The validity of a logical law, however, can be consciously given in a subjective act of evidence. Conditions of validity of ideal objects are thus *eo ipso* conditions of evidence, and logical laws are thus "equivalent" to propositions regarding possible evidence. According to Husserl, though, one has to pay heed to two points: 1) "equivalence" does not mean "identity"; 2) the equivalent transformation of logical laws exclusively concerns acts of evidence according to their "ideal possibility." Hence, the validity of a logical law implies the "ideal" possibility of the "real" performance of a conscious act, in which either the (analytic) necessity of the law itself is grasped or in which this law is instantiated.

How, then, is one to understand more precisely this "singularization" (*Vereinzelung*), which Husserl calls "application," of logical laws in an individual act of knowing? Husserl writes:

> Obviously, these laws may undergo self-evident transformations through which they acquire an express relation to knowledge and the knowing subject, and now themselves pronounce on real possibilities of knowledge. Here as elsewhere, a priori assertions regarding ideal possibilities arise through the transferred application of ideal relationships ... to empirical instances. (§ 65, p. 233 [Hua XVIII, 239]; cf. also ibid. §§ 29, 50-51)

This transference or application of the logical law onto an act of consciousness, however, is an *exemplary* singularization, which says nothing about the empirical-psychological determination of the act (i.e., the circumstances of its performance by a certain person etc.). Husserl does speak of a "psychological utility" of logical laws but at the same time denies any dependency on the empirical-psychological determination of consciousness (§ 50). Anticipating his later characterization of eidetic psychology or phenomenology, Husserl insists time and again that this consciousness in which the logical law is applied is a consciousness "as such" (*überhaupt*). The application of logical laws to exemplary acts is not a psychological process. This also becomes clear through the fact that such a possible application entails no psychological-causal necessity of the performance of any act whatsoever. Logical laws, while being applicable to acts, do not cause such acts.

However, this account of the application of logical laws leaves open how precisely one must understand the "singularization" of an ideal object in an individual act of knowing. Does not Husserl himself repeatedly assert that a logical essence can only singularize itself in a subordinate species, but never in an empirical fact (cf. e.g., § 46)? How can he then write at the same time: "Truth is an idea, whose peculiar case is an actual experience in the evident judgment"? (§ 51, p.194 [Hua XVIII, 190]).[6] The solution is surprisingly simple: under the form of a formal apophantic, formal logic deals exclusively with ideal meanings of judgments. As such, none of its assertions refer directly to acts of judgment. Its task consists entirely in the determining of such laws that ideal propositions and their connective forms must follow when logical nonsense or contradiction are to be avoided. Now, when one understands these propositions or ideal meanings, as does Husserl throughout the first edition of the *Logical Investigations*, as act essences (*Aktwesen*), then one understands that the relation of the ideal content of judgment to the respective act of judgment can again be conceived as a process of singularization. More precisely, one would have to distinguish, on the one hand, between an objective-logical singularization of a formal-logical law in ideal propositions or meanings and, on the other, a subjective singularization of ideal meanings of judgments in an act of judgment. With this it becomes clear that the "application" of a logical law to an act of judgment always occurs via the singularization of the law in an ideal content of judgment.

It seems as though the process of "*ideation*" or of "ideational abstraction," in which logical concepts and laws are gained (cf. §§ 29, 46, 67), is essentially nothing but a reversal of the explicated process of application. In the framework of the *Prolegomena*, ideation is dealt with more in details than in application precisely because logical psychologism is especially active in this field. Thus, Husserl takes pains to distinguish ideation, in which logical laws are apprehended, from the process of "induction" or empirical generalization, from which natural laws of physics or psychology stem. As a science of essences, apophantic logic deals with meaning formations as formal essences. Therefore, the connections of meanings that it establishes have the character of super-temporal and absolutely valid analytic necessities, and certainly not, for example, of probabilities of the highest dignity as in the case of the laws of natural science. The ideal meaning formations or "concepts," with which pure

---

[6] The word "inwardly" has been omitted in the above quotation. Findlay translates "*evidentes Urteil*" as "inwardly evident judgement".

logic deals, are established by "ideational abstraction," i.e., by way of generalization and formalization from the equally ideal meanings of concrete acts of judgments. These ideal "contents of judgments" or meanings are in turn grasped in an intuiting of essences (*Wesensschau*) called "ideation," which rests upon an actual act of judgment. Yet in the *Prolegomena*, more concrete information regarding the structure of this "ideation" and "ideational abstraction" is not given. Husserl obviously does not yet dispose of the doctrine of categorial intuition and intuition of essences, which will be presented in the Sixth *Logical Investigation*.

Moreover, other principal questions regarding the relation of purely logical objects to subjective lived-experiences remain unanswered in these passages of the *Prolegomena*. Husserl does assert that the "logical" origin of purely logical concepts must be distinguished from the "psychological questions as to the origins of the conceptual presentations". (§ 67, p.238 [Hua XVIII, 246]). However, in the second edition he replaces the expression "logical origin" by "phenomenological origin." Certainly, this in no way changes the fact that Husserl, in his determination of the process of ideation or of the formation of concepts, does not refer to factual circumstances, to spiritual dispositions of an empirical person, nor to hypotheses regarding evolutionary theory, as empirical psychology does. It is also clear that the logical formation of concepts occurs in an act of ideational abstraction, and that this act rests on the meanings of judgments, which are already ideal objects. However, since Husserl at the same time conceives of these ideal meanings of judgments in the first edition of the *Logical Investigations* as act essences (*Aktwesen*), an act of reflection is required in order for them to be grasped. Brentano's model of the formation of concepts by a reflection on psychic acts becomes amended in the *Prolegomena* by insisting on the ideality of meaning, but it is by no means given up. Thus, the "logical" origin of the formal concepts remains a subjective, or even "psychological," origin (albeit in the sense of "descriptive" psychology).

Obviously in the first edition of the *Prolegomena*, the specter of psychologism made Husserl circumvent the insight into this identity of logical and (rightly understood) psychological origin of logical concepts. For the same reason, Husserl mentions nowhere what utility logic draws from such an analysis of the subjective origin of its basic concepts. From reading the second volume of the *Logical Investigations*, one knows that the utility of an (eidetic) psychological or phenomenological analysis of origins consists in a *clarification of concepts*, which is most important for any science. Ultimately, the fear of falling back into psychologism as well as the absence of a clearer perception of the difference between empirical and eidetic-descriptive psychology are the obstacles that prevent Husserl from understanding that a full-fledged subjective insight into the validity of logical laws can only be achieved by way of the analysis of origins mentioned above. For, if logical laws can be reformulated equivalently into conditions of subjective lived-experiences of evidence, and if there is also evidence which refers to the ideal validity of logical laws themselves, then this intuitive givenness of meaning and validity of logical laws can only be achieved via the long path of an ideation and ideational abstraction starting from an exemplary act of judgment. This long path of an intuitive forming of a logical law would then have the same status of a subjective grounding or justification of this law's validity. In the *Prolegomena*, however, there is no talk of this. Furthermore, Husserl seems to stick to the conception according to which the evident insight into the validity of a logical law has nothing to do with analyses of subjective origins, i.e., with the performance of acts of ideation and of ideational abstraction. Evidence pertaining to the validity of a logical law is, in the *Prolegomena*, apparently set as equivalent with the subjective insight into the *objective-logical* grounds of this validity. The evident givenness of the validity of a logical law is thus nothing but a special case of the application of this law.

II. Normative Logic and its Relation to an Ideal Subject of the Ought

Apart from the presentation of a *pure logic* in its ideal basic concepts and laws according to the different levels of its tasks, according to its function as doctrine of science, as well as according to its secondary relation to subjective lived-experiences of evidence and ideation, one also finds in the *Prolegomena* a mature presentation of the idea of a *normative logic* on the one hand and a *logical technology* (*Kunstlehre*) on the other. In these last two logical disciplines the interest in a theory of science is even more prominent than in pure logic. We will discover that with them the relation to the knowing subject will also gain importance and concretion. This is not surprising when one takes into consideration that every ought based on norms, and especially every practical instruction, is addressing a subject and possibly takes into account factual potentialities of this subject.

Husserl's theory of a *normative transformation of pure logic* is preceded by a remarkable and concise characterization of the basic structure common to all possible normative sciences (§ 14). It is shown in particular that normative sciences—unlike theoretical sciences—owe their unity not to a foundational connection (*Begründungszusammenhang*) achieved by logic, but rather to their relation to a unitary "basic norm." This basic norm is the expression of what counts as the highest good in a particular normative science. This highest good is in turn grounded in a "basic value taking" (*Grundwerthaltung*).[7] This basic value taking can be expressed in a predicative sentence such as "X is the highest good". However, unlike in theoretical expressions such a statement is grounded in an axiological form of evidence. According to Husserl, this *subjective* act of a basic value taking and its axiological evidence can and must be *objectively* justified. This objective justification of the rational character of the basic value taking is, however, a matter of a specifically axiological reason, and it is accomplished by referring to an objective order of values. Next to the absolute basic value there are thus relative and lesser values. The scientific foundation of a particular act of axiological value taking involves a logical operation in which this value taking

---

[7] Findlay translates "*Werthaltung*" as "valuation".

is measured against the basic norm of the relevant objective system of values. Whether my act of taking-for-good, taking-for-beautiful (etc.) a specific action, person, or matter is justified depends on the possibility or impossibility of its being subsumed under the basic norm in question. It is thus clear—apart from the possible transformation of pure logic into a normative discipline, to be discussed subsequently—that each normative science has a theoretical-logical core, which concerns the "measuring" relation between manifold acts of subjective value taking and a basic norm. Whether a particular value taking complies with the basic norm or not is a theoretical, i.e., logical matter (§ 16)—even if the norm, which has to be complied with, can no longer be founded theoretically but only axiologically.

This excursion into the essence of normative science as such has a double function in the *Prolegomena*: first, it demonstrates that pure logic plays an indispensable role also for normative sciences; i.e., that pure logic is indeed a universal theory of science. Second, it shows that pure logic itself can be transformed into an equivalent normative discipline (§ 16). This last point is important given that the a priori fundament of logical technology, which Husserl puts forward against psychologism, consists essentially in such a normative formulation of logic. Now, the transformation of *pure* logic into *normative* logic, seen from the standpoint of linguistic analysis, consists in the transformation of predicative "is"-propositions into "ought"-propositions. The purely logical or theoretical principle of non-contradiction thus is transformed into a normative proposition, which asserts how one *ought* to or *must* not formulate expressions. The purely logical law thus becomes a basic norm of value estimation or, as Husserl says, an "end" (§ 15). Such a possible transformation into a normative discipline actually applies not only to pure logic but also to every other theoretical science (§ 42). A normative transformation of pure logic, however, in no way means a renunciation of its function as a doctrine of science. For normative logic forms the normative conditions to which every science ought to adhere. Furthermore, it judges concretely whether a given assertion or a scientific theory adheres to these norms (§ 11). However, one cannot deny that this normative logic and theory of science, which have come about by a transformation of pure logic, present an atypical axiological science. For, its basic value is not an originally axiological but a theoretical value. It is constituted through the transformation of a purely logical condition of scientific knowledge into an end to be pursued.

Reflecting again on the connection between normative logic and subjectivity, one must first of all pay attention to the "ought"-character of its assertions. It seems plausible that there can be no ought without subject, i.e., without a subject that ought to (do something) and without a subject that formulates the demand or the end to be striven for. However, Husserl's detailed definition of the ought implied in normative logic (§ 14) rightfully asserts that we are dealing here with an *impersonal* demand in which the demanding subject as well as the demanded subject remain necessarily undetermined. *One* ought to judge this or that way if *one* wants to comply with the demands of scientific knowledge. This "one" is an "anybody" (*jedermann*) and as such it is an ideally possible subject and not a real, empirical subject with personal qualities, intellectual dispositions and individual interests. Hence one can in no way say that normative logic owes anything to empirical psychology. In Husserl's own, pointed expression this means that logical "normative laws of thinking" are distinguished *toto coelo* from psychological "natural laws of thinking" (§ 19).

Now, unlike in pure logic, "one" apprehends *normatively* expressed logical laws no longer as something *absolutely* alien, that is in an experience, which we have described as a form of *absolute* self-transcendence. This change, however, is brought about in the first place not by the attitude of the subject towards the law, but rather by the normative formulation of the law itself. Normative logic transforms the logical law, which expresses necessary connections between ideal conceptual forms, into an imperative. This imperative has by necessity an addressee. Thus, it essentially belongs to the meaning content of a normatively formulated logical law that it refers to a subject, which ought to comply with it or obey it. This necessary connection between the normatively formulated pure logical law and an ideal form of the subject, however, implies no loss of the law's transcendence and sovereignty. The subject subjected to a normative law is addressed or called upon by this law, but it does not itself stand at the origin of this law; it meets the law as something alien. Thus, just as in pure logic, in normative logic there can be no talk of adaptation of the law to the subject or, vice versa, of appropriation or assimilation of the law by the subject. This is the crucial point in which normative logic differs from logical technology. Only in the guise of technology does logic or the logical law adapt itself to the potentialities of the subject. This adaptation implies also with necessity a use of empirical psychology. Hence, logical technology is a further and entirely new step in the process of relating logic to the knowing subject.

III. Logical Technology and its Relation to the Empirical Subject of Psychology

What Husserl calls "technologies" are essentially scientific methodologies and "auxiliary devices" (such as, e.g., arithmetic calculus) (§§ 9, 42). Unlike normative sciences one does not only judge if an assertion fulfils the conditions of the basic norm; rather, a technology formulates *precepts* or *prescriptions* for correct conduct or action (§ 15). In accordance with this, the meaning of logical assertions also changes in logical technology: The norms functioning as "ends" in normative logic become "goals" of action, which can be achieved more or less efficiently. As instructions for the correct or best possible way of acting, these prescriptions of practical technology essentially refer to future action, whereas the main task of normative science consists in the judging of the rational character of value takings accomplished in the past. This means, tersely put, that in technology logical laws are transformed into "rules" of correct thinking (§ 40). However, these practical rules of correct thinking or acting are always and necessarily founded on normative laws in such a manner that there can be no rational technology without one or several founding normative disciplines. Contrary to this, it is possible that a particular normative discipline does not allow for the formulation of a practical technology corresponding to it. This is always the case where an "ought" cannot be realized for some reason in a corresponding action. Husserl exemplifies this with Schopenhauer's ethics, which, according to him, is a genuine normative science, although the impossibility to change the empirical character of a human person makes Schopenhauer doubt whether it can be practically realized. Thus, from Schopenhauer's normative ethics there does not follow a practical ethics, which would be a technology of moral activity (§ 15).

As far as the specifically *logical* technology is concerned, it strives for the realization of logical laws in factual acts of thinking. Husserl in no way rejects this "ortho-pedagogical" use of pure logic. Quite to the contrary, he considers it to be an integral part of a logical doctrine of science. The meaning of logic does not concern itself exclusively with the construction of formal theories and forms of theory. It also endeavors to formulate prescriptions or rules for correct thinking and for the "production" (§ 6) of scientific knowledge. The latter enterprise can be successful only when it does not demand something from human subjects they cannot accomplish. In other words, logical technology must adapt to the limited human capacities. In order to do so, knowledge of the nature of human thinking is necessary. Yet such a reference to our factual manner of thinking is alien to the genuine sense of logic. Therefore, *empirical psychology* is, alongside with pure logic, a necessary theoretical ground for logical technology. If logic does not content itself with the adequate formulation of pure logical laws or with the transformation of these theoretical laws into normative ought-propositions, and if it deals with how one has to actually think in order to adhere to these laws, then this practical technology of correct thinking has to consider the empirical circumstances and factual limits of human thinking. This collaboration of pure logic with empirical psychology, aiming at achieving a practically effective instruction for correct thinking, only becomes problematic when the essential difference between the respective contribution of both sciences is overlooked. This occurs when one concludes—with psychologism—from the *necessary* contribution of empirical psychology to logical technology, that psychology also supplies the *sufficient* theoretical foundation for this technology. Husserl writes in the *Prolegomena*:

> Not all rules which set standards for correct judgments are on that account *logical* rules. It is, however, evident that, of the genuinely logical rules which form the nucleus of a technology of scientific thinking, only one set permits and demands a psychological establishment: the technical precepts concerning the acquisition and criticism of scientific knowledge, *precepts, which are especially adapted to human nature*. The remaining, much more important group consists of normative transformation of laws, which belong solely to the objective or ideal content of the science. (§ 41, p.171 [Hua XVIII, 158])[8]

---

[8] The crucial passage set in italics is missing in Findlay's translation.

When we again reflect on the relation to the *knowing subject* implied in this logical technology, we find in the above quotation the key term "adaptation." To be sure, this "adaptation" of practical logic or logical technology to "human nature" must not be confused with the "application" of *pure* logic, for example, to an ideally possible lived-experience of evidence mentioned above. The subject, to whom logical laws must be adapted if they want to determine or reform our factual ways of thinking, is the empirical subject of psychology. At the same time, this adaptation of logical technology to human nature can be legitimate only when it does not contradict the laws of pure logic. Each "adaptation" of logic to a factual human subject is thus already a case of an "application" of a purely logical law to an ideally possible "consciousness as such." This means, concretely, that practical instructions for bringing about an evident insight into a scientific state of affairs may not come into conflict with the ideal, i.e., purely logical conditions of evidence. Of course one cannot deny that there are psychological conditions of evidence, which are bound to circumstances such as concentration, mental freshness, experience, etc. These empirical conditions add something new to the purely logical conditions of evidence (§ 50). However, the conditions of evidence derived from empirical psychology must necessarily be complemented by the conditions derived from pure logic and especially from normative logic. Psychology alone does not suffice to ground the validity of a logical technology.

Thus, the subject to which logical *technology* refers is not only and exclusively the subject of empirical psychology, it is also the "ideal subject" ("anybody") of *normative* logic as well as the subject of an "ideally possible lived-experience of evidence" determined by the laws of *pure* logic. Thus: Husserl's refutation of psychologism in the *Prolegomena* does not disregard any relation of logic to any kind of subject; its core lies, on the contrary, in the insight that the subject of thinking, far from being a one-dimensional entity, is given different meanings by different logical disciplines. Psychologism consists in a conflation of the different meanings and approaches of the subject of knowledge, while Husserl's own phenomenology will be a lifelong endeavor to both distinguish and unify different forms of apprehension and self-awareness of the subject in science and natural life from a "higher" point of view.

Translated from German by Cristina Sophia Ramirez Albott, Sebastian Luft and the author.

JOHN J. DRUMMOND
Fordham University

THE *LOGICAL INVESTIGATIONS*: PAVING THE WAY TO A TRANSCENDENTAL LOGIC

> Soon after the publication of the *Logische Untersuchungen* the reproach was cast that the phenomenological investigations demanded there under the name of the "clarification" of the fundamental concepts of pure logic, investigations which the second volume attempted to block out in broad outline, signified a relapse into psychologism.... The obscurity still generally prevalent today concerning the problem of a universal epistemological psychologism... is something that, at the time, I myself had not entirely overcome; though precisely the "phenomenological" investigations in the second volume, so far as they paved the way to a transcendental phenomenology, opened up at the same time the necessary avenues to the setting and the radical overcoming of the problem of transcendental psychologism.[1]

This epigraph from *Formal and Transcendental Logic* echoes Husserl's complaint in the foreword to the second part of volume two of the *Logical Investigations* about the "often heard, but to my mind grotesque reproach, that I may have rejected psychologism sharply in the first volume of my work, but that I fell back into psychologism in the second."[2] The epigraph, however, also suggests that the *Investigations* do not go far enough in overcoming psychologism. Only a transcendental phenomenology, it is said, suffices to overcome psychologistic prejudices. On this view, then, the "phenomenological" investigations found in the second volume of the *Investigations* have merely "paved the way" to the transcendental critique of all cognition found in Husserl's mature phenomenology. This paper poses two questions: (1) Why, given the rejection of psychologism, is there need for a phenomenology? and (2) Why is there a need for a *transcendental* phenomenology?

---

[1] E. HUSSERL, *Formal and Transcendental Logic*, trans. D. Cairns, The Hague: Martinus Nijhoff, 1969, 152 [*Formale und transzendentale Logik: Versuch einer Kritik der logischen Vernunft*, ed. P. Janssen, Hua XVII, The Hague: Martinus Nijhoff, 1974, 160–61]

[2] E. HUSSERL, *Logical Investigations*, trans. J. N. Findlay, 2 vol., London: Routledge and Kegan Paul, 1970, 662 [*Logische Untersuchungen. Zweiter Band. Zweiter Teil: Untersuchungen zur Phänomenologie und Theorie der Erkenntnis*, ed. U. Panzer, Husserliana XIX/2, The Hague: Martinus Nijhoff Publishers, 1984, 535]

I. THE NEED FOR A PHENOMENOLOGY

Characteristic of the psychologistic views against which Husserl argues are the claims that (1) the objects of logical knowledge (e.g., meanings, concepts, judgments, and logical laws insofar as they are known) are thought by the mind and, hence, immanent thereto, and (2) the laws that govern the relations among these logical objectivities are identical to the laws that govern acts of thinking. The second claim depends upon a certain understanding of the first claim. The second claim identifies logical laws and psychological laws; it reduces the ideality and universality of logical laws to the empirical generality of the psychological laws governing real acts of thinking and their real contents. It requires, therefore, that we understand the first claim to mean that insofar as logical objectivities are thought by the mind, they are immanent to and depend thereon. If this psychologistic understanding of the first claim were defeated, the second claim would fall with it. So, concentrating on the first claim that logical objectivities are immanent to mind or mind-dependent, we can express the psychologistic position as follows: let L signify "...is a logical objectivity," M signify "...is a mind," T signify "...thinks...," and R signify "...really inheres in...;" Then,

(1) $\Box \, (\forall x) \, \{Lx \rightarrow (\exists y) \, [(My \,\&\, Tyx) \,\&\, Rxy]\}$.

The denial of this psychologistic position can arise in different ways.[3] One way of denying psychologism would be to stress the mind-*independence* of logical objectivities, i.e., to deny that the existence of a mind thinking it is a necessary condition for something's being a logical objectivity. In other words, one might claim that it is necessarily the case for all logical objectivities that they need not be thought. Hence, a logical objectivity is what it is apart from any relation to mind, and any actual relation to mind would be purely contingent. On this view, of course, logical objectivities could not be really inherent in consciousness nor could the laws governing their combinations be psychological laws. This form of denial can be represented as

(2) $\Box \, (\forall x) \sim \{Lx \rightarrow (\exists y) \, [(My \,\&\, Tyx) \,\&\, Rxy]\}$.

This, apparently, is the path taken by Frege who is so concerned to separate meaning from presentations (*Vorstellungen*) that it is difficult—even for him!—to understand how they might in actuality be thought.[4]

---

[3] In what follows I am greatly indebted to R. HANNA'S very interesting discussions of the "Prolegomena" in his "Logical Cognition: Husserl's *Prolegomena* and the Truth in Psychologism," *Philosophy and Phenomenological Research* 53 (1993): 251–75, although I have changed his formulations to the point where he would probably not recognize them.

[4] Cf. G. FREGE, "Logic," in *Gottlob Frege: Posthumous Writings*, ed. H. Hermes *et al.*, Chicago:: University of Chicago Press, 1979, 145, where Frege speaks of the "most mysterious" character of how something non-mental, viz., a thought, comes into view in a mental act, but he insists that "we do not need to concern ourselves with it in logic." Cf. also J. N. MOHANTY, *Husserl and Frege*, Indianapolis: Indiana

(2) is not, however, the form Husserl's denial of psychologism takes. Husserl does not stress the mind-independence of meaning. Whereas Frege was concerned to sever the conditional relationship between logical objectivities and mind, Husserl is concerned not to sever that relation but to reject the identification of the logical with the empirical, of the ideal with the real, of the *a priori* with the *a posteriori*. Husserl, therefore, instead denies the *universal necessity* of the relation of logical objectivities to actual minds in order to leave open the discussion of how logical objectivities in general might be related to mind. Hence, Husserl's denial of psychologism might be symbolized as

(3) $\sim \Box \, (\forall x) \, \{Lx \to (\exists y) \, [(My \,\&\, Tyx) \,\&\, Rxy]\}$, or

(4) $\Diamond \, (\exists x) \, \{Lx \,\&\, \sim(\exists y) \, [(My \,\&\, Tyx) \,\&\, Rxy]\}$.

Given that Husserl's denial of logical psychologism is aimed primarily at the identification of the ideal and the real, of the logical and the empirical, of the *a priori* and the *a posteriori*, we can attempt to reformulate the sense of his denial as

(5) $\Diamond \, (\exists x) \, \{Lx \,\&\, (\exists y) \, [(My \,\&\, Tyx) \,\&\, \sim Rxy]\}$,

or, more simply and in a purely affirmative formulation, as

(6) $\Diamond \, (\exists x) \, [Lx \,\&\, (\exists y) \, (My \,\&\, Tyx)]$.

But (6), although true, falls short of capturing Husserl's position. Restoring the relation of logical objectivities to mind—at least as stated by (6)—continues to leave open the inference that logical objectivities are related to actual minds actually thinking them. Husserl, however, explicitly recognizes that logical objectivities exist as ideal objectivities even when no actual mind in fact thinks them: "But it is also...inwardly evident that truths are what they are, and that, in particular, laws, grounds, principles are what they are, whether we have insight into them or not."[5] Indeed, he insists that there need not even exist an actual mind capable of thinking them. In rejecting Sigwart's psychologistic anthropologism, Husserl says:

> If there are no intelligent beings, if the natural order excludes them, or if they are, in a *real* sense, impossible—or if there are no beings capable of knowing certain classes of truths—then such *ideal* possibilities [as truths] remain without fulfilling actuality. The

---

University Press, 1982, 37, and R. HANNA, "Logical Cognition," 252–53.

[5] E. HUSSERL, *Logical Investigations*, trans. J. N. Findlay, 2 vols., [London: Routledge and Kegan Paul, 1970], 233 [*Logische Untersuchungen. Erster Band: Prolegomena zur reinen Logik*, ed., E. Holenstein, Hua XVIII, The Hague: Martinus Nijhoff, 1975, 240].

> apprehension, knowledge, bringing to consciousness of truth (or of
> certain classes of truths), is nowhere ever realized. Each truth,
> however, remains in itself what it is, it retains its ideal being. (LI, 149
> [Hua XVIII, 135–36])

Nevertheless, as we see in the just quoted text, Husserl continues to insist on the point that part of the meaning of truth—in the full sense—is that it be capable of being grasped in rational insight. And immediately prior to the passage just quoted, Husserl asserts, "The statements 'It is the truth that [p]' and 'There could have been thinking beings having insight into judgments to the effect that [p]' are equivalent". (LI, 149 [Hua XVIII, 135]). Husserl would insist, in other words, that logical objectivities be related not to actual minds but to possible minds. Hence, Husserl's version of the antipsychologistic thesis is best formulated as

(7) $\Box\,(\forall x)\,[Lx \to \Diamond(\exists y)\,(My\,\&\,Tyx)]$, i.e.,

it is necessarily the case for all x that x is a logical objectivity only if it is possible that there exists some y such that y is a mind and y thinks x.

A major part of Husserl's problematic in the *Investigations*, then, is to account for the relation between meaning and possible mind while preserving the objectivity and ideality of meaning. He typically poses this problem as a problem in epistemology. In both the "Foreword" to the first edition (LI, 42 [Hua XVIII, 7]) and in the "Introduction" to the second volume (LI, 254 [Hua XIX/1, 12–13]), he speaks of the need to reflect on the question concerning the relationship between the subjectivity of knowing and the objectivity of the content known. It is descriptive psychology or, better, phenomenology that responds to this question. Phenomenology explores the relation of logical objectivities to mind by exploring the ideal, noetic conditions for the possibility of logical knowledge. "It is evident *a priori*," Husserl tells us,

> that thinking subjects must be in general able to perform, e.g., all the
> sorts of acts in which theoretical knowledge is made real. We must,
> in particular, as thinking beings, be able to see propositions as truths,
> and to see truths as consequences of other truths, and again to see
> laws as such, to see laws as explanatory grounds, and to see them as
> ultimate principles, etc. (LI, 233 [Hua XVIII, 240])

Without such abilities, logic could not serve as a normative discipline governing our actual judgments, arguments, and theories, and without a examination of these abilities and a clarification of what they achieve, we do not yet have a fully grounded logic. Pure logic, therefore, requires a founding theoretical science in which the nature of (possible) mind as thinking logical objectivities is explored such that norms for the formation and combination of such objectivities and for truthful thinking can be grounded and clarified. Descriptive psychology as an empirical science of actual minds is inadequate for this task; hence, the need for a phenomenology—an essential science—of mind, both actual and possible. This is the science Husserl has in mind when, at the conclusion of the "Prolegomena," he identifies three tasks for a pure logic, the first of which is the phenomenological clarification of primitive, logical concepts such as 'meaning,' 'concept,' 'proposition,' and 'truth' (LI, 244-45 [Hua XVIII, 236–37]), and it is to this task that Husserl turns in the second volume of the *Investigations*. These phenomenological investigations, far from a relapse into psychologism, are required by and clarify the sense of Husserl's nuanced version of anti-psychologism.

II. THE NEED FOR A TRANSCENDENTAL PHENOMENOLOGY

So much, then, regarding the need for a phenomenology to supplement Husserl's anti-psychologism. But why the need for a *transcendental* phenomenology? I shall argue that the turn toward an explicitly transcendental phenomenology both (a) solves a difficulty in the Husserlian accounts of meaning and intentionality as found in the first edition of the *Investigations* and (b) exploits an unrealized possibility in the theory of wholes and parts presented in the Third Investigation.

a) A "naïve" theory of meaning

Husserl's anti-psychologism maintains that logical objectivities are objective and ideal and that they can be brought into a relation to possible mind without reducing them to really inherent or immanent contents of consciousness. It is precisely at this point that the problematic character of Husserl's early notion of descriptive psychology comes to the fore. Husserl's use of this notion results in a misconception of the proper object of philosophical reflection. In the first edition of the *Investigations* Husserl enunciates "an important distinction ..., namely the distinction between the real or phenomenological (descriptive-psychological) content of an act and its intentional content". (LI, 576 [Hua XIX/1, 411]). The force of this distinction is to identify real, psychological contents with phenomenological contents and thereby to restrict the proper object of phenomenological description to what is really contained within the act. Intentional contents, on the other hand, are not included within the scope of a phenomenological description. Any differences in the object's significance for us, i.e., in the object as intended—one of the senses of "intentional content" (LI, 578 [Hua XIX/1, 414])—must be clarified by noting the changes in the real contents of the act, its quality or its matter or its presenting or representing contents.

Now this sounds suspiciously close to the psychologistic view that changes in the object's significance are changes in the phenomenological, i.e., the real, contents of the act. Husserl avoids psychologism, however, by making some real contents of the act, viz., its quality and matter, the instantiation of an essence, a meaning-species (cf. LI, 330 [Hua XIX/1, 105–6]). The meaning itself, through which the object is intended, remains objective and ideal, and the particular act's relation to meaning is one of instantiation. The identity of meaning among many acts intending the same object in the same way is the identity of a species (LI, 330 [Hua XIX/1, 105]).

But there is some sleight of hand here, for the notion of intentional essence is one of the senses disclosed in Husserl's discussion of *intentional* contents. Once we distinguish phenomenological from intentional contents and restrict phenomenological description to what is phenomenologically contained, the claim that the instantiation of an essence is part of the real, phenomenological content of an act does not solve our problem of accounting *phenomenologically* for the origin of ideal meanings. To avoid psychologism, the so-called *phenomenological* description must appeal to the (not descriptively contained) intentional essence precisely because the essence has a priority over its instantiation, but this appeal is, by hypothesis, barred. Such an appeal—necessary to avoid psychologism—carries us beyond the phenomenological contents of the act and cannot be included in a phenomenological description. The meaning-species appears as a *deus ex machina*.

Moreover, the view of meaning as an ideal species is, I think, in tension with the account of meaning-intending and meaning-fulfilling acts by virtue of the fact that it tends to shift the center of intentionality from the correlation of the act with its object to the ideal species itself. There are two aspects to this point. First, in the case of meaning-intending acts, the fact of being directed to a particular object in a determinate manner with a particular "how" of presentation is first and foremost a property of individual, concrete acts. Conscious experience is essentially intentional in its own right. However, the priority of the meaning-species to its instantiation risks dislocating the intentionality of experience from the act itself to the meaning or sense that it instantiates. It threatens to reduce what is fundamental to what is not fundamental; it threatens, in other words, to reduce the intentionality of consciousness to the intensionality of sense, to a semantic category. This view would make the act intentional by virtue of an intensional entity whose referential direction to an objectivity is apparently achieved independently of and prior to the intentionality of the acts instantiating the intensional entity. Such a view would make the intentional directedness of the act a function of the intensional referentiality of the meaning, rather than making the expression's meaningful reference to an object a function of the act's intentional character. It would leave us with a domain of pre-constituted meanings whose relation to acts once again becomes mysterious.

Second, the account of meaning as species raises a problem for understanding fulfillment. A meaning-fulfilling act involves the actual presence of the object to a subject, and the object is present in a manner that confirms the intended meaning, i.e., such that there is a coincidence or congruence (*Deckung*), an identity, between the object as signitively intended and the object as actually encountered. However, since the object as intended belongs to the intentional content of the act, the identity between the object as signitively intended and as actually encountered must be explained by an identity in the real contents of the acts. What appears in our experience as the identity of a concrete, individual objectivity to which different acts are directed is, then, explained instead as the specific identity of two instantiations of the same intentional essence. The meaning-species dislocates the identical, intended object just as intended from its proper role in fulfilling acts just as it dislocated the act from its proper role in the meaning-intending experience.

In brief, then, my claim is that Husserl, even though he recognized differences in the ideality belonging to normative essences and meaning-species (LI, 331 [Hua XIX/1, 107]), never adequately questioned in the *Investigations* whether the ideal must always be understood after the model of a species and whether the relation between the ideal and the real must always be understood after the model of instantiation. Husserl takes for granted the *nature* of meaning's ideality without ever subjecting it to an epistemological critique or to a clarifying analysis beyond saying that we become aware of it in a reflective act (LI, 332 [Hua XIX/1, 108]). But it is precisely this analysis, we have been told, that is the first task of a pure logic. Husserl must ask not only about the essential structures of meaningful acts but about the nature of meaning itself—in what its ideality consists—and how it is that we come to our awareness of it.

b) An unrealized possibility

Husserl's analyses of essential structures, including those of conscious acts, proceed by identifying what in the Third Investigation's discussion of parts and wholes he calls "non-independent parts" or "moments." Husserl commences this discussion with a very broad notion of 'part,' by which he means anything that is either a real component or constituent of the object in which it is found or a relational part by which an object finds itself really associated with other objects (LI, 437 [Hua XIX/1, 231]). Husserl then draws the distinction between independent and non-independent parts in presentational terms: "we have independent contents wherever the elements of a presentational complex (complex of contents) by their very nature *permit their separate presentation*, and we have dependent (non-independent) contents wherever this is not the case" (LI, 439 [Hua XIX/1, 233]).

Non-independent contents or parts, in other words, must be incorporated into and presented as part of a larger whole; they require supplementation by other parts. In recognizing a part as a moment, we grasp an essential necessity, viz., the necessary connection between this moment and the other moments necessarily supplementing it in the formation of a whole. This essential necessity rests on an objective, ideal law (LI, 446 [Hua XIX/1, 243]). We recognize, in other words, that it is universally and necessarily the case according to the very sense of the objects involved that a moment *of this type* be presented with moments of *other specific types* in the formation of wholes of certain species.

What is of interest in Husserl's discussion of wholes and parts is that he limits his notion of parts to *real* components and *real* relations. I want to suggest, however, that in the second edition of the *Investigations* Husserl manifests a more complete understanding of the import of his own discussion of parts and wholes, although he manifests this not in the Third Investigation but in the Fifth. It is not until the Fifth Investigation of the second edition that Husserl fully exploits the possibility of establishing wholes via intentional as well as real relations. To put the matter another way, I want to isolate what I take to be a shift in Husserl's understanding of the whole that is the object of phenomenological reflection.

By the time of the second edition of the *Investigations* and the publication of *Ideas I*, the distinction between phenomenological and intentional contents has been reformulated. Husserl now says, "[W]e introduce an important phenomenological distinction ..., namely the distinction between the real contents of an act and its intentional contents". (LI, 576 [Hua XIX/1, 411], translation modified). This is a radical change in the characterization of the proper object of philosophical reflection. Whereas Husserl in the first edition draws a distinction *between* phenomenological and intentional contents, he now draws a distinction *within* the phenomenological contents of the act between its real and intentional contents.

Husserl himself points to the significance of this change in a footnote in the Fifth Investigation of the second edition:

> In the first edition I wrote "real or phenomenological content." In fact the word "phenomenological," like the word "descriptive," was used in the first edition of this book exclusively in relation to the real (*reelle*) components of experience, and also in the present edition it has up to now been employed predominantly in that sense. This corresponds to the natural starting point of the psychological attitude.... [B]ut it became more and more noticeable that the description of the intentional objectivity as such, taken just as it is known in the concrete act-experience itself, presents another direction for purely intuitive descriptions to be carried out, a direction opposed to that of real (*reellen*) act-components and which must also be termed phenomenological. (LI, 576 [Hua XIX/1, 411], my translation)

Both kinds of contents—real and intentional—are now moments within the whole that is the intentional correlation, the act along with its object. The intentional relation of consciousness to the world is now recognized as a whole comprising non-independent parts, some of which are real and some of which are intentional. This richer understanding of the whole that is the proper object of philosophical reflection leads to fundamental changes in Husserl's account of intentionality and of meaning, for it allows for a new understanding of the ideality of meaning or sense. The intentional content of the act, its intentional object, its intended object just as intended—what Husserl comes to call the "noema"—is now considered an "ir-real" moment of the act, and by the time of *Formal and Transcendental Logic* Husserl explicitly acknowledges, first, the difference between the ir-reality belonging to meaning and that belonging to an essence or species and, second, his failure to distinguish them in the "Prolegomena". (cf. LI, 155 [Hua XVII, 163]). The ideality that Husserl calls "ir-reality" enables Husserl to dispense with the duplication of meaning (as ideal species and as instantiated) that we find in the first edition, to locate meaning directly in the act-object correlation, and to preserve the relation of meaning to mind all the while preserving the non-psychologistic character of his theory. Husserl now conceives meaning as the identical, ir-real, intentional correlate of multiple (possible) acts rather than as an ideal species-object instantiated in acts. Multiple acts are directed to the same object in the same determinate manner with the same "how" of presentation. They "mean" the same thing; the "meant object precisely as meant" is identical. Having distinguished the ir-reality of meaning from the ideality of a species, Husserl can distinguish the identity of meaning from the identity of a species. The relation of the one to the many in meaning, i.e., the relation of the identical, intended objectivity as meant—more precisely, the relation of the identical noematic sense—to the manifold of acts intending that identical objectivity in just that way, is different from the relation of instantiation, just as—analogously—the relation of an individual, identical physical object to a manifold of perceiving acts of different individuals is different from the relation of instantiation. Meanings are individuals capable of being grasped by many subjects; there is a manifold appropriate to them, although not the manifold of instantiation whereby the many acts would become characterized as themselves meanings.

We clearly see this new account of meaning in Husserl's discussion of judgment in *Formal and Transcendental Logic*. Acts of judging are directed in the first place to those objects about which we judge and their determinations. To be directed to the object and its determinations is, in general, to be directed to a categorially formed complex. The categorial forms are not simply available to perception but become available in continued inspections of the object and the thoughtful articulations and judging activity based thereon. In judging, our attention naturally remains turned to the identical, objective state of affairs and we are not aware of any logical reality that we might call the judgmental content or the proposition. However, we can reflectively direct our attention to the judged as such, to the judged state of affairs precisely as supposed; we might do so, for example, in those cases where someone reports his or her judgment to us and we doubt the correctness of it, neutralize our acceptance of it, and critically reflect upon it. In such a case, the state of affairs as supposed is not something we posit for ourselves; we simply consider it for confirmation or disconfirmation as the state of affairs supposed and affirmed by our interlocutor. At this point, the judgment takes on for us a double character, that of the categorially formed, judged state of affairs and that of the judgment merely as such, the supposition as supposed, the proposition, the judgment in the logical sense (cf. Hua XVII, §48).

The intended state of affairs and the proposition are properly distinguished, therefore, by means of a difference in the way we *focus* the meant objectivity. In the straightforward focus on objects, we apprehend the categorial objectivity or state of affairs as such; in the critical focus on the state of affairs as supposed, i.e., on the supposition itself, we apprehend the judgment or proposition (Hua XVII, §50), more precisely, the noematic sense of the intended state of affairs. The intentional ir-reality belonging to the judged state of affairs is the same ir-reality that belongs to the judgment; the identity of a particular state of affairs apprehensible in multiple acts is the same identity that belongs to the meaning multiply intended as an identical meaning. It is an individual and not a specific identity grounded in the real moments of acts.[6]

In understanding meaning in this way, Husserl no longer naively accepts a univocal notion of ideality as that belonging to a species or essence. But the overcoming of this naïveté is possible only when we examine the kinds of acts in which states of affairs are articulated and the kinds of acts in which the proposition is brought to awareness, i.e., the kinds of acts in which we direct our attention to meanings themselves, rather than meant objects. Moreover, insofar as logic is concerned not only with well-formed propositions but with consistency and truth as well, we must also examine the kinds of acts in which propositions are joined into well-formed arguments and theories as well as the kinds of acts in which truth is insightfully grasped. Our consideration of these ideal objectivities of meaning, proposition, argument, theory, and truth are, in other words, fully realized only when we examine them as correlates of and in correlation with those acts which disclose or constitute them. But this is precisely to undertake the project of a transcendental phenomenology in general and of a transcendental logic in particular, i.e., a transcendental phenomenology in relation to the categories of meaning and truth.

All of this, I am claiming, is foreshadowed in the *Logical Investigations* where we see a clear indication of the necessity—as a part of Husserl's anti-psychologism—for a phenomenology of logic and where we find motives—both negative and positive—for a transition to an explicitly transcendental clarification of the primitive categories of logic. It is in this manner that the phenomenology of the second volume of the *Investigations* has paved the way for a transcendental clarification of logic and for a final routing of psychologism in all its forms.

---

[6] This does not preclude, of course, the possibility that there are intended species of empirical objects or that there are intended species of acts, e.g., perception as such, memory as such, and so forth. I am arguing only that meaning is no longer considered a ideal species apprehended by means of an ideational abstraction of the real moments (specifically the matter and quality) of acts expressing that meaning.

JOCELYN BENOIST
University of Paris-I Panthéon-Sorbonne

NON-OBJECTIFYING ACTS

As Frege remarked before Austin, and Aristotle before Frege: language is not made of descriptive sentences only. A task traditionally assigned to logicians is to explain how to distinguish those sentences from others.

My purpose here is to determine what Husserl has to say about this boundary in his *Logical Investigations*.[1] The *Investigations* close with considerations about this problem, and, insofar as the work is described as "logical" and deals explicitly with logic, such a question is not to be avoided. Which sentences can have a truth-value? This question stands necessarily at the core of any "logical investigation". And it is the question involved in the question of the "descriptiveness" of our sentences in general.

According to Aristotle's *De Interpretatione*, 4, not every sentence (*logos*) is declarative (*apophantikos*). A sentence is declarative if and only if it has a truth-value (either the True or the False). All sentences do not have this property. For instance, a prayer does not have it, being neither true nor false. The treatise *De Interpretatione* explicitly puts aside utterances such as prayers, questions, etc. Aristotle says they are matters for Rhetoric or Poetics. In other terms, which are not Aristotle's, those are not *logical* topics. Logic is only concerned with apophantic sentences—what some modern authors name "propositions".

This distinction between apophantic and non-apophantic sentences has determined the whole logical tradition. It has unfortunately often restricted logical research proper in regard to non-apophantic sentences, which therefore have been entrusted to other disciplines. Non-apophantic sentences, however, have remained an important question for logic, as a question of preliminary delimitation, and of the *bounds* of "logic". As such, those sentences have appeared regularly in logical textbooks, precisely in the role of sentences "that can't be true or false".

Bolzano challenged this Aristotelian analysis. In his *Theory of Science*, he famously introduced the concept of "the proposition in itself" (*Satz an sich*), which designates the meaning (*Sinn*) of a string of meaningful elements (Bolzano speaks of "representations") which, taken as a whole, has the property of being true or false. In that sense, a *Satz an sich* is simply a meaning with the property of being endowed with a truth-value. A simple meaning can't be endowed in such a way; a determined compound of meanings is required to produce such a result. But not all compound meanings are propositions. To be a proposition, a sentence must have a given level of composition which makes the truth-value possible.

---

[1] E. HUSSERL, *Logische Untersuchungen I*, Hua XVIII, Den Haag: Martinus Nijhoff, 1975, *Logische Untersuchungen II*, Hua XIX/1-2, Den Haag: Martinus Nijhoff, 1984.

Bolzano recognizes in the Aristotelian concept of the *logos apophantikos* a concept that is akin to the "*Satz an sich*".[2] A *logos apophantikos* has a *Satz an sich* for its meaning. There is, however, a very deep difference between Bolzano and Aristotle: Bolzano hardly takes into account sentences which are not apophantic. It seems that, according to him, all sentences in the grammatical sense of the word are also propositions, *Sätze* in the logical sense of the word, or at least that they express propositions. One can not disregard the fact that for Bolzano, the word *Satz* means a semantical entity independent from language and from sentences. Sentences (i.e., *Sätze* in the grammatical sense of the word) express propositions (i.e., *Sätze* in the logical sense, *Sätze an sich*). Thus Bolzano's claim is: *all well-formed sentences express propositions, that is to say, a semantical content that is objectively true or false.* "All sentences" means not just descriptions but also questions, prayers, wishes, orders and exclamations.

Such is Bolzano's argument: for instance, a question really is a proposition, but not about what it asks. Its proposition expresses the desire to know what is being asked. In that sense, it is as descriptive as any other proposition. It can therefore be true or false—I may or may not really want to know about what I am asking.[3]

Bolzano thus reduces interrogative sentences and all other non-apophantic sentences to apophantic ones. He understands all sentences in an *informational* sense. The only question is one of the scope of the *informational* content. More precisely, we should remember that Bolzano includes the act (e.g., of asking) in the informational content. What are we to understand here by "act"? I will come back to this later on.

The Fregean position is radically different. Certainly, it is using a concept of the propositional content that could actually seem very close to Bolzano's. But, in spite of this remarkably close relation which has often been emphasized, sometimes with some misleading simplifications,[4] Frege's treatment of the question of non-apophantic sentences shows a dramatic break between both conceptions of the logical truth-bearer. According to Bolzano, propositional content (*Satz*) is in all cases informational and always has a descriptive sense—and in a certain sense the complete sentence achieves nothing but the propositional content it expresses. According to Frege now, propositional content, which may be true or false (he calls it "thought") is subject to enunciative variations and not descriptive "in itself", independently from the sentence in which it appears. And a sentence is not to be reduced to merely expressing "propositional content". In the effective sentence, something is added to propositional content, which contributes to making it "descriptive" or something else.

---

[2] B. BOLZANO, *Wissenschaftslehre*, Aalen: Scientia, 1837/1981, §21, Bd.I, p.83.

[3] B.BOLZANO, *Wissenschaftslehre* §22, Bd.I, p.88. Bolzano mentions DESTUTT DE TRACY (*Eléments d'Idéologie*, IIe Partie, *Grammaire*, ch.2) as agreeing with this theory.

[4] See for instance FR. NEF, *L'objet quelconque*, Paris: Vrin, 1998, 175. For a more accurate account, see W. KÜNNE, "Propositions in Bolzano and Frege", in W. KÜNNE, M. SIEBEL, M. TEXTOR (eds.): *Bolzano and Analytic Philosophy*, Grazer Philosophische Studien 53, Amsterdam/Atlanta: Rodopi, 1997..

Frege's views on this question are developed in a late essay of his, published in 1918 ("The Thought") which Husserl could not have read as he was writing his *Logical Investigations*. Apart from the fact that Frege's essay is subtitled "First Logical Investigation" (but by Frege!), we believe that accounting for Frege's position in that paper can be helpful in interpreting Husserl's own position in his *Logical Investigations*.

Frege's interest in thought (i.e., the part of the sense that can be true or false) moves him to exclude orders, wishes, and prayers. Those sentences do not clearly give a sense that can be true or false, even if they are meaningful. But it is quite a different matter with questions. Some questions, the ones which are completely determined by themselves, have a content of sense that can also be the content of a correlative affirmative (and so descriptive) sentence. This content can be intrinsically true, or false. It is indeed true or false, even if the question does not show it as true, or false—its truth or falseness is what the question is about. What is the difference between such a question and the correlative descriptive sentence? In any case, the difference is not one in *sense*—the only level of analysis considered by Bolzano. It concerns the way propositional content is presented and, in a certain sense, *used*. Interrogative sentences and assertive sentences contain the same "thought" but something more is to be found in an assertive sentence: assertion. Frege names it "a force". The point is that such a "force" is something alien to the semantical content of the sentence.

Propositional content is not assertive nor interrogative by itself. It needs to be asserted and its assertion—and here we come closer to the problem—is a kind of "act". Formulating a proposition in the sense of traditional logic is *doing* something.

There is no need to emphasize here the well-known fact that it is in this point of Frege's doctrine that the origin of Austin's views on language is to be found.

*

What about Husserl?

The point I am interested in is that for Husserl too, speaking of something is a kind of "act". Of course, one should be careful here. "Act" really is a very ambiguous term. When I say that according to Husserl speaking is an "act", this must naturally be interpreted in the sense that the word "act" has in *Logical Investigations*, namely, an *intentional* one. It is the first teaching of the First Investigation that speaking is a modality of intentionality, and as such is an "act" in the sense defined by the Fifth Investigation.

This raises several difficulties.

The most important and significant one is that if in a certain sense speaking is an act according to Frege, it is obviously not so in an intentional sense. There is a distinction between an intentional and a non-intentional conception of language. However, I take it that this very real problem has no bearing on the very question addressed here, if asked in these general terms: is there in a sentence a moment of "act" to be distinguished from a moment of "content"? and if there is, how are they to be distinguished? The question does not have the same form in both traditions, but it is the same question, at least from a logical point of view.

A less important question from my point of view is that of the so-called mentalistic way of intentional analysis.[5] This point makes Husserl's Brentanian philosophy apparently irrelevant to Fregean questions. Is Husserl a philosopher of language? One can have doubts about it. In the First Investigation, Husserl seems to be explaining the work of sentences by means of mental acts, the so-called "acts of meaning" (*Bedeuten*). Are these acts mental or not, and are they to be grasped, as is still often said, "in an introspective way"? I am not going to decide this question here. I just wish to point out that the acts we are dealing with are specifically acts of meaning. Meaning is an original modality of intentionality and, if Husserl doesn't have a philosophy of language—but then does Frege have one?—he clearly has at least a philosophy of significative modality of intentionality.[6] From a logical point of view, this can be enough for the matter presently at hand. Whether acts are effective acts of utterance or acts of "meaning", our problem is now only of the distinction between "meaning" and "content".

The main point in the philosophy of language, or at all events, of meaning presented in the First Investigation may be summarized under the following two heads:

1) meanings (as significations) are indissociable from a certain kind of acts: the very acts of meaning. It is a necessary consequence of the intentionalist point of view on meaning, one that favors a *verbal* sense of the word "meaning".

2) meanings as *contents* are ideal, and as such independent of the act of meaning, in spite of the fact that the latter is the foundation of the former and the only place where both are "real".

Both claims are quite contradictory and account for the extreme tension in the First Investigation: namely, a tension between Brentano and Bolzano.

This tension grows to a climax in chapter III of the First Investigation, where Husserl deals with the so-called problem of indexicality—what he himself calls the problem of the "essentially occasional expressions". How is the ideality of "content" to be preserved, where content implies a seemingly essential reference to the act itself, defined as an effective act, performed under certain circumstances?

Husserl's answer, coming at the end of that same chapter, is purely Bolzanian. Husserl presents it as the claim of "the limitlessness of objective reason". (Hua XIX, 95). Inasmuch as sentences in language are meant to express something of reality, their content has an objectivity, in spite of, and indeed *through*, variations in enunciation. In each enunciative situation, indexicals, which have to be included in the content of a proposition, determine a definite truth-value for the whole statement.

---

[5] For a study of this question, see B. SMITH, "Husserl, Language, and the Ontology of the Act", in D. BUZZETTI and M. FERRIANI (eds.), *Speculative Grammar, Universal Grammar, and Philosophical Analysis of Language*, Amsterdam: John Benjamins, 1987, 205-227.

[6] See J. BENOIST, *Phénoménologie, sémantique, ontologie: Husserl et la tradition logique autrichienne*, Paris: PUF, 1997, chap. 1.

What conclusions does Husserl draw from this? First, it should be considered that his analysis is ruled by the aim of a philosophy of logic concerned with the idea of *theory* as a deductive system of propositions, which are naturally supposed to be descriptive statements. But the question is precisely of the possibility, of the autonomy and limits of such a point of view. In any case, if such a point of view is at all possible, as suggested at the end of the *Prolegomena*, it is clear that "it is meaning and not the act of meaning (*Bedeutung und nicht Bedeuten*), concept and proposition, and not presentation and judgement, that are the standard in science". (LI, 325 [Hua XIX, 100], my translation); so that the final goal of Husserl's *Logical Investigations*, i.e., a theory of science (*Wissenschaftslehre*), would shift interest from the act of meaning (*Bedeuten*) to objectified meaning as constituting the substance of "theory"—and by the same token, the truth-bearer.

This shift in the point of view certainly constitutes a difficult problem for an intentionalist conception, evidently focused on the "act" of meaning. When one realizes that the great discovery at the opening of the First Investigation was that meaning itself is an "act", and an act of a specific sort, such a withdrawal of the act of meaning at the end of the same Investigation obviously raises a question. It is possible to understand which anti-psychological motives led Husserl to such a step. But is the "act" just an opportunity for meaning? Or rather, isn't the "act" *the very place* for meaning? And can meaning construed as propositional ever cancel the act in which it constitutes itself?

The same problem is to be found in the question of dividing sentences between apophantic and non-apophantic ones. What can Husserl do with the "act"-determination of the meaning?

The problem is one of the determination of the "act" as intentionality. It may be the case, according to Husserl, that meaning is essentially an "act", but act signifies as much as intentionality. Indeed, "intentionality" involves a relation to an object. It is not clear that this is enough to define it, but it is at least a necessary feature, and certainly the essential one.

If, then, intentionality is essentially defined by the relation to an object it involves, and so from a logical point of view by its "sense" as determining the relation to reference, it is not clear it allows for the act as opposed to "the content", defined as we did, following Frege's analysis.

To put it in other terms, the problem is one of Husserl's defining intentionality in *semantical* terms, thus emphasizing the *content* of intentionality.

Some distinctions are to be made, however. The Fifth Investigation develops the structure of the "act" in the following way: every "act" has a semantical content, called the "intentional matter". It determines how the object is intended, and in this sense the "meaning" of intentionality. But there are yet other components in a complete intentional act. Besides its matter, an intentional act has a quality. This difference may be of interest to us, because it is related to the "way" of the act itself. For instance, one may just present an object, or on the contrary assert its existence. From Husserl's point of view, this difference (i.e., the one between presentation and judgment) is one in "quality" of the act. In a certain sense, we are not *doing* the same thing with the act when presenting or when judging.

Now, isn't there a possibility to recover the Fregean distinction in other (i.e., intentionalist) terms? One could think so, since Husserl himself deals with the problem of questions from such a point of view. The following judgment: *There are intelligent beings on Mars*, has the same matter as the question: *Are there intelligent beings on Mars?* But the difference is one of quality. There is a question quality, as a wish quality, etc. (5. Inv., §20). This is an intentionalist answer to the Fregean problem which is apparently quite close to Frege's own answer. We have to distinguish semantical matter and way of the "act".

Thus the intentionalist character of Husserl's analysis would bring it closer to Frege's than to Bolzano's.

Unfortunately, the problem is slightly more complex. In the fifth chapter of his Fifth Investigation, Husserl goes over the conception (still Brentano's at this point) of the qualitative opposition between presentations and judgments he had developed earlier in the same Investigation. He denies there exists a real qualitative difference between presentations and judgments. It is rather one in categorial form and therefore in matter. This is an important claim in the construction of the *Logical Investigations*. In the Sixth Investigation, it entails the possibility for simple ("nominal") acts to have a fulfilment and thus the possibility for names to have a truth-value.

But from the point of view I am interested in, there is yet another conclusion to draw. According to this new view of the qualitative identity of presentations with judgments, Husserl suggests a new terminology expressing this identity beyond the ordinary concept of presentation: presentations and judgments, as respectively nominal acts and propositions are now both called "objectifying acts".

The great qualitative difference (§38) remains thus the one between acts (whether simple or not) bearing "belief" and acts that do not, i.e., between positional and non-positional acts. A qualitative alteration is possible in positional acts, to turn them into non-positional acts—in the sense of a "simple" presentation of what was intended in presentation or judgment.

Then, the question of course is: are there real non-objectifying acts, i.e., acts which are neither objectifying in a positional sense nor modifications of acts which are objectifying in a positional sense?

The answer, certainly, is yes. But how are objectifying and non-objectifying acts to be distinguished?[7] The former are characterized exactly by the possibility of a qualitative variation such as has been mentioned. It is only for objectifying acts that those qualitative variations just referred to may happen.

It will be said that a "simple" presentation of, for instance, a wish can be achieved. In this case, however, the presentation is a presentation exactly of the *act* of

---

[7] For this question, see U. MELLE, "Objektivierende und nicht-objektivierende Akte", in S. IJSSELING (ed.): *Husserl-Ausgabe und Husserl-Forschung,* Phaenomenologica 115, Dordrecht: Kluwer, 1990, 35-49.

wishing, and not of the thing wished. On the contrary, a modification of an objectifying act enables us to obtain not the act itself as an object but *what is intended* by the act. This is the distinctive feature of objectifying acts (§39).

This brings us to my main point. Objectifying acts are distinguished by the possibility to isolate—and present—something as their objective "contents", something as the objects they mean, *just as* they mean it. That is the sense of their "objectifying" character.

This is not the case of "non-objectifying" acts. But then how should we construct them?

In his *Logical Investigations*, Husserl's claim is that they are necessarily complex. At the basis lies necessarily some objectifying act. It is in this sense you can speak of *the thing wished* or *the thing ordered*: at the basis of the wish or the order, there lies an act of presentation giving the wish or the order their object. An act is built on another act (5. Inv., §§42-43). This possibility exists as well in the case of objectifying acts that can be constructed on top of one another. But in the case of non-objectifying acts, the secondary act (i.e., the non-objectifying one) does supply something specific: something that cannot be objectified. The act itself can be objectified, but *not what the act does*.

This sense of non-objectifying acts, tending towards a kind of dualism among acts, definitely brings Husserl very close to Frege. In the case of passing from objectifying (say, the presentation of a cake) to non-objectifying act (say, wishing for that same cake), the qualitative variation acquires a quite different sense from the qualitative variation of an objectifying act as such (from a presentation of the cake as given to the "simple" presentation of the cake, by the withdrawal of any position). In Frege's terms, it is not the same thing to isolate a thought asserted in a proposition and to apply to this thought some other force than the assertive force, e.g., to ask a question.

There is of course a great difference. Frege does not say that an interrogative use of thought requires and presupposes an assertive use—and to him thought itself is not an act, whether non-psychological or otherwise. According to Husserl, apparently, it does require it, since one kind of act has another kind for its basis. Therefore, Frege is not saying an interrogation is based on an assertion. Those are just two uses of thought. Husserl, on the other hand, maintains the priority of assertion (or at least of "position" and the variations it depends on) and after this, a certain kind of *complexity* of interrogation, and of all non-objectifying acts, a complexity objectifying acts do not necessarily have.

It remains that this strong qualitative difference introduced between those two kinds of acts, and precisely as acts, seems to validate the Austinian-Fregean analysis, against Bolzano's.

However, it is not the least astonishing feature in Husserl's *Logical Investigations* that a book reaching its conclusion with this very question should eventually recognize Bolzano to be right.

The paradox is that *it is in the kind of dualism allowed by his act-analysis that Husserl finds the possibility of the unification of language which is the condition for Bolzano's views.*

Actually, the Sixth Investigation concludes with the impossibility for other than objectifying acts to be sense-conferring. In other words, if it is to be assumed that speech has sense only by virtue of an "act" that "confers sense" (*Sinn verleiht*), i.e., the "meaning"-act, then such an act is necessarily an objectifying act. The act constituting speech as speech, since the definition of speech is to have sense, is an objectifying, and to put it briefly a descriptive, act. It is of course possible to base a non-objectifying act on that act. But in the exact sense in which to express means to express a sense, the grounded act, as it is non-objectifying, cannot be *expressed*.

The point here is that Husserl's analysis follows Bolzano's on a certain level: all sentences *as expressions* are descriptive.

Then on another level Husserl does not follow Bolzano's analysis. In fact, for Husserl, there are sentences in real language which are not descriptive, and their analysis as descriptive (in Bolzano's fashion) is missing something in them. Husserl's analysis is determined by a dualism which is foreign to Bolzano's. He actually rebukes Aristotle for the univocity of his analysis (6. Inv., §70). This may seem paradoxical. The argument goes as follows: Aristotle does indeed distinguish two forms of expression (*logos apophantikos vs. non-apophantikos*), but he is mistaken when he believes those are still forms of expression, with the word "expression" preserving a constant sense. One should recognize a disparity between those two kinds of expression, so that it is only the former—apophantic speech—which is expression properly speaking. It is only what is objectified that is expressed, which implies that the limits of expression as such are determined by the limits of objectification, as performed by objectifying acts.

After this, there may be other things in a sentence than what is expressed. The qualitative dimensions introduced by non-objectifying acts can modify the concrete expression and perception of what is expressed by the utterance, in the narrow sense of the word "expressed". Such modifications, however, remain extrinsical to content and to what is *said* in the essential signification of the word, unless incorporated into content, as in Bolzano. In such a case, however, they become *objects* and as such they are caught in an objectifying act. They cannot be expressed *as such* in the strong sense of the term. According to Husserl, their function is merely pragmatic—i.e., communicative and not expressive.

*

To conclude: Husserl was prevented at the time by the semantic character of intentionality from making the discovery of a real thought of the speech-"act", although the very "act-ness" he had himself assigned to intentionality had brought him very close to such a discovery.[8] This failure is in itself interesting, because it shows the ambiguity and the extreme tension of the first phenomenological theory of meaning, between sense and act. If this ambiguity raises logical problems which cannot be solved within the framework of the *Logical Investigations*, it seems to me that it contributes, however, to the descriptive richness of this work that did not want to leave anything aside. Perhaps such richness may be not completely useless today for philosophers of language.

---

[8] As to the legacy of the problem through Reinach's work, see H. PARRET, *Prolégomènes à la théorie de l'énonciation: de Husserl à la pragmatique*, Bern-Paris: Peter Lang, 1987, and B. SMITH, "Towards a history of speech act theory", in A. BURKHARDT (ed.), *Speech Acts, Meaning and Intentions. Critical Approaches to the Philosophy of John R. Searle*, Berlin-New York: Walter de Gruyter, 1990, 29-61.

DAVID WOODRUF SMITH
University of California, Irvine

WHAT IS "LOGICAL" IN HUSSERL'S *LOGICAL INVESTIGATIONS*? THE COPENHAGEN INTERPRETATION

In Wim Wenders's 1987 film *Himmel Über Berlin* (*Wings of Desire* in the English subtitle version), an angel moves silently among mortals, listening to their thoughts as they read in the Berlin public library. In this spirit, assume that Husserl is listening to our readings today of his *Logical Investigations* (1900-01).[1]

What would, or should, Husserl say today about the overall flow of ideas in *Logical Investigations*? How do the *Prolegomena* and the six Investigations hang together? Specifically, what does the *Logical Investigations* as a whole have to do with *logic* as we know it today, a century after the work appeared?

I shall argue that Husserl's *Logical Investigations* unfolds a systematic philosophy in which logic is integrated with ontology and phenomenology (and epistemology). For Husserl, logic is not only a calculus of valid inference codified in language. In Husserl's scheme, logic appraises forms of language, thought, meaning, and object, and the intentional relation of representation among them. In this way logic—what we today would call logical or formal semantics—is fundamentally tied into the theory of intentionality, which relates mind and language to world through ideal meanings. What unites the whole of *Logical Investigations*, then, is the formal structure of intentionality, with different parts of the structure analyzed in different parts of the *Logical Investigations*. My point is not to reduce the ontology and phenomenology of intentionality to logic, in the Husserlian system, but to outline the ways in which they are integrated. It is difficult to see this integration as we read piecemeal through the several Investigations. Yet hindsight, armed with the paradigm of 20th century formal semantics, reveals the unity of which I speak.

I call what follows: the Copenhagen interpretation of the *Logical Investigations*. In this interpretation, *Logical Investigations* is a "superposition" of seven interdependent theories which tends to collapse into one of seven discrete and seemingly independent "eigen" theories as each is observed separately. And as the Copenhagen interpretation of quantum mechanics seemed to press observation into the ultimate structure of physical reality, so the Copenhagen interpretation of the *Logical Investigations* will press intentionality into the fundamental structure of the world according to the *Logical Investigations*.

---

[1] I shall quote from J. N. Findlay's 1970 English translation, *Logical Investigations* (Volumes One and Two), of the German edition which combines the first edition of 1900-01 with revisions in the second edition of 1913 and revisions of the Sixth Investigation in the edition of 1920.

I. WHAT IS LOGICAL?

Logic is about good reasoning: valid inference, either deduction (preserving truth) or induction (proffering probability). Today's first-order predicate logic (following Frege, Whitehead and Russell, *et al.*) is a well-defined system of logic, specifying exactly what forms of inference are sanctioned in a well-defined symbolic language.

What role then does *logic* play—what is *logical*—in Husserl's *Logical Investigations*? These Investigations are about many things: the objectivity of logic, the objectivity of science or knowledge, meaning in speech acts, universals, parts/wholes, grammatical dependence, intentionality, intentional content, perception and intuition. Apart from the arguments that logic is objective, what has all the rest to do with *logic*?

Three answers arise: (1) All of the results of *Logical Investigations* are part of logic, widely conceived: a 19th century perspective. (2) Only a small part of *Logical Investigations* concerns logic, more narrowly conceived: a 20th century perspective. (3) In the philosophical system of *Logical Investigations*, logic as conceived today is integrated with speech-act theory, ontology, phenomenology, and epistemology: here is a 21st century perspective, unfolded below.

Others have traced Husserl's objective conception of logic and mathematics in reaction against 19th century philosophies of logic, especially psychologistic, normative, formalist, and "calculus" views of logic.[2] I propose instead to explore Husserl's positive conception of logic in a virtual response to 20th century philosophy of logic.

Assume the results of Frege, Whitehead-and-Russell, Gödel, Tarski, Carnap, Quine, Hintikka,[3] Kripke, Kaplan, *et al.*, accrued over the course of more than a century. What should we make of logical theory today if we also assume the results in Husserl's *Logical Investigations*? The key issues below are not of central concern to recent logicians looking to the foundations of logic, mathematics, and science. But they shall be our issues as Husserl joins us in spirit.

II. HUSSERL'S INTENTIONALIST VIEW OF LOGIC

The 19th century psychologism Husserl opposed was a naturalism limited to contingent psychological processes in human beings. In today's naturalism, those mental processes

---

[2] See in particular D. WILLARD, *Logic and the Objectivity of Knowledge: A Study of Husserl's Early Philosophy*, Athens, Ohio: Ohio University Press, 1984; J.N. MOHANTY, "The development of Husserl's thought." (In B. Smith and D. W. Smith (eds.), *The Cambridge Companion to Husserl*, Cambridge and New York: Cambridge University Press, 1995); and C. O. Hill and G. E Rosado Haddock (eds.), *Husserl or Frege? Meaning, Objectivity, and Mathematics*, Chicago and La Salle: Open Court, Carus Publishing Company, 2000.

[3] J. HINTIKKA, *Knowledge and Belief*, Ithaca: Cornell University Press, 1962; *Models and Modalities*, Dordrecht and Boston: D. Reidel Publishing Company, 1969.

are reduced to physical processes or functions in the brain.[4] Husserl today would still insist that logic is not about contingent processes: in minds or brains or societies. For Husserl, logic is about more than the behavior of sentences in natural systems of psychological or neural or social activity: it is about *ideal* structures of meaning, which happen to be realized in consciousness and expressed in language.

Husserl's model was Bolzano's *Wissenschaftslehre*, or *Theory of Science* (1837).[5] Bolzano defined logic as the theory of science, organizing systems of knowledge or objective ideas about objects (§6). However, by 1900 Husserl had developed the theory of intentionality, structured by a scheme of distinctions that had not been fully articulated before: the distinctions among subject, act, content or sense, and object of consciousness. Accordingly, in Husserl's system in the *Logical Investigations*, logic is tied into ontology, theory of language, and the theory of intentionality central to his phenomenology.

The concept of intentionality is indicated but not salient in the *Prolegomena*, where formal logic is defined. Then in the Fifth and Sixth of the *Logical Investigations*, intentionality is analyzed in detail and recursively folded back into the conception of logic.

Husserl would expand the philosophy of logic as we know it today to address the intentionality of judgments whose expression is codified in first-order logic. However, Husserl sharply contrasted the subjective and objective aspects of intentionality. Whereas acts of consciousness are "subjective" events, their contents are wholly "objective" ideal meanings, and their intentionality is defined in terms of these meanings. As we are about to see, these meanings are themselves part of the subject-matter of logic.

III. PURE OR FORMAL LOGIC

In the *Prolegomena to Pure Logic*, the first volume of the *Logical Investigations* (in the German edition), Husserl details his wide conception of "pure" or "formal" logic.[6] In

---

[4] However, see the line of argument in D. W. SMITH, "Intentionality Naturalized?" (In J. Petitot, F. J. Varela, B. Pachoud, and J.-M. Roy (eds.), *Naturalizing Phenomenology: Issues in Contemporary Phenomenology and Cognitive Science*, Stanford: Stanford University Press, 1999) and other essays in the same volume.

[5] B. BOLZANO, *Theory of Science: Attempt at a Detailed and in the main Novel Exposition of Logic With Constant Attention to Earlier Authors*. Edited and translated (selections) by R. George, Berkeley: University of California Press, 1972. German original, 1837. See also P. SIMONS, "Bolzano, Tarski, and the limits of logic", In P. Simons, *Philosophy and Logic in Central Europe from Bolzano to Tarski: Selected Essays*. Dordrecht and Boston: Kluwer Academic Publishers, 1992.

[6] B. SMITH, "Logic and Formal Ontology", in J. N. Mohanty and W. McKenna (eds.), *Husserl's Phenomenology: A Textbook*, Lanham: University Press of America, 1989, 29-67, aptly discusses many of the issues to follow. However, I want to stress how three distinct disciplines are related: formal logic, formal ontology, and (if you will, formal) phenomenology.

Chapter 11, titled "The Idea of Pure Logic", he writes, "We are ... interested in what makes science science, which is certainly not its psychology, nor any real [spatiotemporal or naturalistic] context into which acts of thought are fitted, but a certain objective or ideal interconnection which gives these acts ... an ideal validity."(§62) Following Bolzano's *Wissenschaftslehre*, Husserl conceives pure logic as focussed on "the Idea of Theory"(§66, LI, 235): the theory of theory. A particular theory has a systematic unity concerning its subject-matter, a unity defined by deduction from "basic laws" or axioms, forming "the *unity of a systematically complete theory*"(§63). This ideal is basically the same as that of later logicians, including Gödel, Tarski, and Quine. Technical results on completeness and incompleteness were of course Gödel's crowning achievement 30 years hence, constraining the ideal voiced by Husserl.

When Husserl uses the term 'Idea' with a capital 'I', he means "Idea" in the Kantian sense of a regulative ideal. Also he talks of the "conditions of the possibility" of knowledge and of theory (§§65-66). In this respect Husserl assumes a weakly Kantian conception of "transcendental" philosophy, that is, a philosophy of the conditions of the possibility of knowledge.[7] Nonetheless, Husserl's conception of pure logic is his own baby and not of Kant's time.

Husserl divides the task of pure logic into three parts: the theory of logical categories or forms, the theory of inference, and the theory of possible forms of theories (§§67-69). These three ranges of logical theory resemble what today's logicians call syntax, proof theory, and model theory. Yet Husserl's conception of these areas was unusually rich: here is where his conception of logic diverges from that of subsequent philosophers of logic, not least Quine, who famously rejected meanings, universals, essentialism, intentionality, and any forms of intuition thereof.[8]

Husserl assumes three levels of what we might call logically relevant entities: expression, meaning, and object. The correlations among these levels define what today we call semantics. For Husserl, we shall see, logic begins with the analysis of *categories* or *forms* on all three levels. Thus, logic analyzes not only forms of *sentences* (*pace* Quine), but more importantly forms of *meanings* including propositions (*pace* Frege), and furthermore—surprisingly—forms of the *objects* represented by sentences and the propositions they express. In the *Prolegomena* Husserl did not yet focus on expressions: they were to be treated in the First Investigation, where a speech act produces a sentence that expresses a meaning. Husserl's focus in the *Prolegomena* was rather on meanings themselves, which include propositions and their constituent concepts. Husserl took it that logic concerns objective contents of judgment or knowledge, and these contents are

---

[7] I. KANT, *Critique of Pure Reason*. Transl. and edited by P. Guyer and A. W. Wood, Cambridge and New York: Cambridge University Press, 1997, 1998. German original, 1781, revised 1787.

[8] See W. V. O. QUINE, *Methods of Logic*, New York: Holt, Rinehart and Winston, 1950, 1959; *Philosophy of Logic*, Englewood Cliffs, N. J.: Prentice-Hall, Inc., 1970; *Pursuit of Truth*, Cambridge, Massachusetts: Harvard University Press, 1992, 1990; *From Stimulus to Science*, Cambridge, Massachusetts: Harvard University Press, 1995.

meanings (*Sinne*), including propositions (*Sätze*), the latter expressed by complete declarative sentences. Bolzano and Frege would have agreed. But Husserl held that logic also addresses the *forms of objects* posited in judgments and represented by propositions and other forms of meanings. The categorial forms of objects include, notably, the forms of states of affairs.

Husserl details the tasks of logic in the climactic Chapter 11 of the *Prolegomena*. The title of §67 reads:

> The tasks of pure logic. First: the fixing of the pure categories of meaning, the pure categories of objects and their law-governed combinations.

So logic must begin by fixing the *categories* or *forms* of *meaning*:

> A given theory is a certain deductive combination of given propositions which are themselves certain sorts of combinations of given concepts. The Idea of the pertinent 'form' of the theory arises if we substitute variables for these given elements, whereby concepts of concepts and of other Ideas, replace straightforward concepts. Here belong the concepts: Concept, Proposition, Truth, etc.
>
> The concepts of the elementary connective forms naturally play a constitutive role here, those connective forms ... which are ... constitutive of the deductive unity of propositions, e.g. the conjunctive, disjunctive, hypothetical linkage of propositions ... (§67, LI, 237)

Every meaning is a certain form of concept or combination of concepts, such as a proposition, where the basic forms or categories of meanings are: Concept, Proposition, Truth, etc., plus the forms of propositional connective: And, Or, If-Then (and Not). These forms or types are specified by what we today would call the basic semantical concepts of Concept, Proposition, Truth, Connective, etc. Why is Truth in this list? Perhaps Husserl has in mind propositions that are true by virtue of their form alone. (See below on §68.)

IV. FORMAL LOGIC AND FORMAL ONTOLOGY

Surprisingly, Husserl also includes in the "first task" of logic laying down corresponding *categories* or *forms* of *object* represented by meanings in the above categories:

> In close connection with the concepts so far mentioned, i.e. the categories of meaning, and married to them by ideal laws, are other

> correlative concepts such as Object, State of Affairs, Unity, Plurality, Number, Relation, Connection etc. These are the pure, the formal *objective categories*. These too must be taken into account. In both cases we are dealing with nothing but concepts, whose notion makes clear that they are independent of the particularity of any material of knowledge, and under which all the concepts, propositions and states of affairs that specially appear in thought, must be ordered. (§67, LI, 237)

So logic lays down, in the first place, not only categories or forms of *meaning*, but also related categories or forms of *object*: "formal objective categories". Moreover, there are "ideal laws" "marrying" categories of meaning and categories of object. Such laws define what we today would call formal semantics. As we consider below, a Husserlian formal semantics would correlate forms of propositions with forms of states of affairs.

The forms of object are specified in what Husserl later called *formal ontology* (in *Ideas* I, §10[9]). Although this is a discipline distinct from logic, in the *Prolegomena* Husserl places formal ontology within the bounds of formal logic. To be more precise, we ought to say that formal logic depends on, or presupposes, formal ontology in that meanings of certain forms are said to represent objects of certain forms.

The formal categories of object listed by Husserl are: Object, State of Affairs, Unity, Plurality, Number, Relation, Connection, etc. (Husserl's systematic lists always end in 'etc.'.) Some of these are among Aristotle's original list of ten categories, understood as categories of things in the world (not in language). But State of Affairs appears on Husserl's list: a state of affairs combines objects with relations, qualities, or species. The categories of Unity and Plurality are of a different order. All these categories are *formal* because they apply to anything in any "material" domain of entities, posited in any substantive theory: here is Husserl's distinction between the formal and the material—in effect, the distinction between form and content projected from language or thought into the world.

The second task of logic, Husserl writes, is to find "the *laws* grounded in the two above classes of categorial concepts", and these laws concern

> the *objective validity* of the formal structures which thus arise: on the one hand, the truth or falsity of *meanings*, as such, purely on the basis of their categorial formal structure, on the other hand (in relation to their *objective* correlates), the being and not being of objects as such, of states of affairs as such, again on the basis of their pure, categorial form. (§68, LI, 238)

---

[9] E. HUSSERL, *Ideas pertaining to a Pure Phenomenology and a Phenomenological Philosophy, First Book: General Introduction to Pure Phenomenology*, translated by W. R. Boyce Gibson, London: George Allen & Unwin Ltd., and New York: Humanities Press, Inc., 1969. First English edition, 1931; German original, first published in 1913. Called *Ideas I*.

That is, we seek *logical truths*: propositions whose truth is based on their *form* alone. But, *nota bena*, corresponding to these propositions are *states of affairs* whose being is determined by their form alone. States of affairs are not propositions; they are the objective correlates of propositions, the "facts" represented by propositions.

Husserl continues:

> We have, on the *one* side, on the side of meaning, theories of inference, e.g. syllogistics, which is however only one such theory. On the other side, the side of the correlates [objects correlated with meanings], we have the pure theory of pluralities, which has its roots in the concepts of a plurality, [and] the pure theory of numbers, which has its roots in the concept of a number—each an independently rounded-off theory. (LI, 239)

So logic seeks, in its second task, formal *laws* that govern both meanings and objects. The formal laws of meanings include theories of inference, concerning which propositions entail which by virtue of their form: Frege's logic was well known to Husserl and was displacing Aristotle's syllogistic. Formal laws of correlative *objects* include, for Husserl, the "pure theory of pluralities" and the "pure theory of numbers": early set theory and early number theory were well known to Husserl, not least from his collaboration with Georg Cantor in Halle.[10] However, Husserl's formal ontology for this level of logic would not be limited to sets as we know them in today's set theory. For as the Third Investigation unfolds, we learn that the theory of parts/wholes and dependence also specifies formal aspects of objects, but this ontology does not reduce to set theory.[11] And remember that Husserl's list of formal objective categories includes State of Affairs.

The third task of logic, according to Husserl, is to develop "the theory of the possible forms of theories or the pure theory of manifolds"(§69, LI, 239ff). Husserl is not explicit enough here, so we must do some explication. Again we distinguish the levels of meaning and object. The theory of possible forms of theories concerns *meanings*, while the pure theory of manifolds concerns *objects*.

A *theory* is a system of propositions, concerning certain kinds of objects and their properties and relations. Accordingly, the theory of possible *forms of theories*

---

[10] See E. HUSSERL, *Early Writings in the Philosophy of Logic and Mathematics*. Translated by D. Willard, Dordrecht and Boston: Kluwer Academic Publishers, 1994. Original German texts here gathered, from 1890-1901; and the essays in C. O. Hill and G. E. Rosado Haddock, *Husserl or Frege?*, on the connections and differences between Husserl, Cantor, Frege, and others in late 19th century foundations of mathematics.

[11] Extending Husserlian part/whole theory, P. SIMONS, *Parts*, Oxford: Oxford University Press, 1987, pursues nonextensional mereology, which contrasts with set theory and with extensional mereology (where wholes are treated extensionally, rather like sets without braces). See also K. FINE, "Part-whole", in B. Smith and D. W. Smith (eds.), *The Cambridge Companion to Husserl*. Cambridge and New York: Cambridge University Press, 1995, reflecting on Husserl's part-whole theory.

concerns what unifies a group of propositions into a proper *theory*. Deductive closure unifies: a theory includes axiomatic propositions and all propositions deducible from them. However, unity is determined not only by deduction from axiomatic propositions, but furthermore by what Husserl in *Ideas* I called "horizons" of meaning. Husserl's focus in *Logical Investigations* is elsewhere, but the *Prolegomena* closes with a section (§72) concerned with "broadening the Idea of pure logic" to include "the pure theory of probability as a pure theory of empirical knowledge".[12] So propositions about an empirical domain of objects may be unified not only by deductive ties, but also by probabilistic ties.

The *objective structure* corresponding to a particular theory is a structure of objects unified in their essence, especially in regard to their identity. Husserl foresees the development of this structure in terms of "the Idea of a pure theory of manifolds [*Mannigfaltigkeiten*]" (§70).[13] The term '*Mannigfaltigkeit*' translates as 'multiplicity' or 'manifold'. Cantor used the term along with 'Menge' and 'Inbegriffe' for what we now call "sets". But Husserl took over the term '*Mannigfaltigkeit*' for his own purposes.

Husserl's ideal of a mathematical theory of "manifolds" drew on Leibniz's dream of a "*mathesis universalis*" (§60, LI, 219) understood as a universal formal theory of objects of any kind.[14] A *manifold*, or formal structure of objects, corresponding to the form of a theory would be a complex form of states of affairs projected by the theory.

Logical theory subsequently developed *model theory* to do something like this task.[15] But model theory remains extensional in its ontology: an algebraic model is defined within set theory as an ordered tuple of a form like <D, R> where D is a set of objects and R is a set of n-tuples among objects in D (approximating an *n*-place relation among objects in D). By contrast, Husserl's formal ontology posited ideal species (universals or essences), nonextensional wholes (not sets),[16] and states of affairs, which are "syntactically" structured combinations of objects and universals. The Second Investigation studies ideal species; the Third studies wholes and dependence; states of affairs recur in several places. So the formal objective structures Husserl aligns with

---

[12] See D. W. SMITH and R. MCINTYRE, *Husserl and Intentionality: A Study of Mind, Meaning, and Language*, Dordrect: D. Reidel Publishing Company, 1982. Now from Kluwer Academic Publishers, Dordrecht and Boston, Chapter V on horizon. The horizon of an experience includes only "motivated" possibilities, those with appropriate probability given what is prescribed by the content or noema of the experience.

[13] For an illuminating assessment of Husserl's ideal of a theory of manifolds, see C. O. HILL, "Husserl's *Mannigfaltigkeitslehre*", in C. O. Hill and G.E. Rosado Haddock, *Husserl or Frege?*

[14] Husserl later used '*Mannigfaltigkeit*' for a more special purpose when launching his notion of "horizon". See D. W. SMITH and R. MCINTYRE, *Husserl and Intentionality*, Chapter V.

[15] R. Tieszen and P. Martin-Löf have both made this observation to me in discussion.

[16] See P. SIMONS, *Parts*, distinguishing Husserlian part theory from extensional mereology, the latter akin to extensional set theory.

structures of meaning are richer than the set-theoretic structures used in model-theoretic semantics today, and of course richer than anything assumed in Quine's view of logic.

Husserl proposed a "division of labour" in logic between the work of "the mathematician" as "ingenious technician" and that of "the philosopher" as "pure theoretician". (§71, LI, 244-245). Husserl thus pressed the *philosophical* foundations of logic as theory of theory. In order to understand the very essence of *theory*, logic must look beyond its ingenious symbol systems to the essence of knowledge, intentionality, meaning and indeed universals or essences. Accordingly, in the lengthy course of the *Logical Investigations*, Husserl addressed the ontology of ideal species, parts/wholes, dependence, ideal content or meaning, and, entering into phenomenology, the role of meaning in intentionality. Here, in Husserl's ideal, the philosopher's results would join the mathematician's results on logic "for the first time to perfect pure, genuine, theoretical knowledge". (§71, LI, 245).

What we should see emerging in Husserl's conception of pure or formal logic are the outlines of a system of *formal semantics*, as we would call it today. A semantics grounded in Husserlian ontology and phenomenology would feature the *correlation* among sentences, judgements, propositions, and objective states of affairs. At the heart of this correlation lies intentionality, the explication of which was arguably Husserl's most original and significant contribution to philosophy.

V. FORM IN LANGUAGE, THOUGHT, MEANING, AND WORLD

In the *Prolegomena* and First Investigation, Husserl distinguishes between an expression (*Ausdrückung*) and the meaning (*Bedeutung*) or sense (*Sinn*) it expresses: thus, between a sentence (a type of expression) and the proposition (*Satz*, a type of meaning or sense) it expresses. (Husserl uses '*Satz*' for the meaning or proposition, with no specific term other than '*Ausdrückung*' for the sentence.) Expressions are physical signs (*Zeichen*), spoken or written words in a language. Meanings, by contrast, are ideal entities: ideal intentional contents brought to expression in language. And logic, for Husserl, is centrally concerned with structures of ideal meanings and what they represent—and thus, as logicians today stress, with truth and truth-conditions.

The First Investigation is Husserl's explication of the broadly Aristotelian view that language expresses thought. Specifically, on Husserl's analysis, in an act of speech one utters a sentence that expresses a meaning (*Bedeutung*), a proposition (*Satz*), which is the sense (*Sinn*) of one's underlying act of judgment, so the judgment "lends" its content to the expression produced in the speech act. The Fifth Investigation analyzes the general structure of intentionality: an act of consciousness is intentionally directed toward an appropriate object by way of its ideal content or sense. A special case is an act of judgment, whose content is a proposition and whose object is a state of affairs. Husserl is not always clear and explicit about the status of states of affairs, but his citing State of Affairs as an objective category entails that states of affairs are a special type of object distinct from the meanings that may represent them. In the first edition of

Logical Investigations (1900-01) Husserl takes the ideal content of an act to be an ideal species of the act, its type of intentionality; in the second edition of *Logical Investigations* (1913, 1920), he takes it to be an ideal particular of the sort he called noema or noematic sense in *Ideas* I (1913). In either case he takes intentional content to be a structured meaning, recognizing Concept and Proposition as categories of meaning.[17]

Husserl assumes, with other logicians like Bolzano and Frege, that *form*—"logical" form—applies not only to *sentences* (expressions, types and tokens) in a syntactically well-defined language, but also to *propositions* (ideal meanings) expressed by such sentences. But unlike most logicians, Husserl assumes that form applies also to *objects*, notably to *states of affairs*. For Husserl, the state of affairs that Bolzano is Austrian would be a complex object formed "syntactically" from the concrete individual Bolzano and the ideal species of being-Austrian. It is difficult to appreciate this claim in the *Prolegomena* because Husserl glosses over details of form, yet he indicates all the relevant points. (Compare *Logical Investigations*, *Prolegomena*, §67, LI, 237, quoted above, and the list of categories including State of Affairs, *Sachverhalt*.)

What should we make, then, of Husserl's claim that *form* applies to objective states of affairs as well as propositions and sentences? The best way to appreciate the claim is to see what it would look like when developed with an eye to the details of predicate logic, which Husserl well knew. That in effect is what Ludwig Wittgenstein did in his *Logisch-philosophisch Abhandlungen* (1921), known in English by the Latinate title *Tractatus Logico-Philosophicus*. We proceed with the *Tractatus* partly in mind.

Assume first-order predicate logic, and focus on the case of an atomic sentence. Take a sentence '**Rab**', formed from a two-place predicate or relation-term '**R**' and names '**a**' and '**b**'.

Given the detailed theory of expression Husserl unfolded in the First Investigation: a person's utterance of a sentence '**Rab**' "intimates" (*kundgibt*) his or her act of judging that "**Rab**", and this act "lends" its content or sense, the proposition <**Rab**>, to the sentence uttered, which thereby "expresses" the proposition <**Rab**>, which represents or intends the state of affairs [**Rab**].[18] Here we let single quotation marks cite a sentence, angle-brackets indicate the proposition it expresses, and square brackets indicate the possible state of affairs it represents; while double quotation marks cite the type or ideal species of an act of judging that "...".

---

[17] Husserl's account of the relations among language, meaning, and thought is detailed in D. W. SMITH and R. MCINTYRE, *Husserl and Intentionality*, Chapter IV. Consonant results are found in P. SIMONS, "Meaning and language", in B. Smith and D. W. Smith (eds.), *The Cambridge Companion to Husserl*, Cambridge and New York: Cambridge University Press, 1995.

[18] See D.W. SMITH and R. MCINTYRE, *Husserl and Intentionality*, Chapter IV.

Accordingly, we may reconstruct Husserl's model of the correlation among sentence, judgement-type, proposition, and state of affairs as follows:

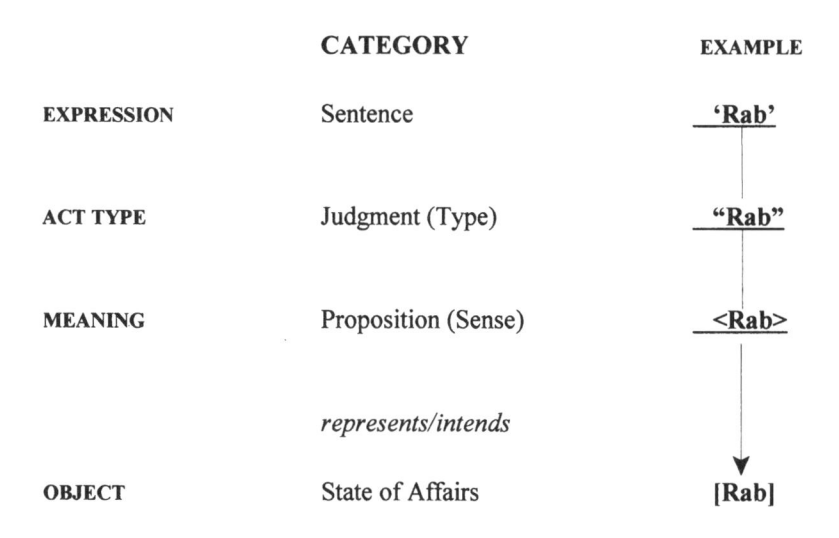

	CATEGORY	EXAMPLE
EXPRESSION	Sentence	**'Rab'**
ACT TYPE	Judgment (Type)	**"Rab"**
MEANING	Proposition (Sense)	**<Rab>**
	represents/intends	
OBJECT	State of Affairs	**[Rab]**

Note the formal ontology here assumed: the state of affairs [**Rab**] is formed "syntactically" from the relation **R** and the objects **a** and **b**. For Husserl, the formal objective categories Object, Relation, and State of Affairs belong to formal ontology, which has no business specifying what "material" kinds of objects or relations there are. Indeed, as we saw above, it is part of Husserl's conception of "pure logic" that logic fixes (or assumes) formal categories of *objects*. Material ontology is a further matter, specifying, for Husserl, kinds of objects in the regions of Nature, Culture, and Consciousness—these are the highest "material" essences or *summum genera*, and the formal categories apply to objects having these essences.[19]

In the light of 20th century logic, framed by Tarski's conception of truth,[20] we should see the above model as part of a *formal semantics* applied to an atomic sentence in predicate logic. Husserl (with us in spirit today) would certainly see the model in this way. Indeed, the sentence '**Rab**' represents the state of affairs [**Rab**] if and only if the component terms '**R**', '**a**', and '**b**' represent the relation **R** and objects **a** and **b**: these

---

[19] For details see my reconstruction of Husserl's ontology in D. W. SMITH, "Mind and body", in B. Smith and D. W. Smith (eds.), *The Cambridge Companion to Husserl*, Cambridge and New York: Cambridge University Press, 1995; and D.W. SMITH, "'Pure' Logic, Ontology, and Phenomenology", in *Revue internationale de philosophie*, 2001, issue edited by D. Føllesdal.

[20] See A. TARSKI, "The Concept of Truth in Formalized Languages", in A. TARSKI, *Logic, Semantics, Metamathematics*, Oxford: Clarendon Press, 1956. Second edition. Indianapolis: Hacket, 1983. Essay originally published in Polish, 1933; in German translation, 1936; and "The Semantic Conception of Truth", in L. Linsky (ed.), *Semantics and the Philosophy of Language*. Urbana: The University of Illinois Press, 1952, 1964. Original, 1944, in *Philosophy and Phenomenological Research* 4.

are the *truth-conditions* for an atomic sentence, assuming the ontology of states of affairs (which Tarski avoided). For a fully Husserlian semantics, however, a token of the sentence type '**Rab**' derives its logical force from the *intentional content* of the speaker's underlying judgment that (or of the judgment-type) "**Rab**".

In this Husserlian semantics, then, the sentence '**Rab**' uttered by a speaker represents the possible state of affairs [**Rab**] intended by the proposition <**Rab**> expressed by the sentence and borrowed from the speaker's underlying judgment that "**Rab**". Further, we assume, the name '**a**' represents the object **a** intended by the concept <**a**>, the name '**b**' represents the object **b** intended by the concept <**b**>, and the predicate '**R**' represents the relation **R** intended by the concept <**R**>. The judgment that "**Rab**" is a predicative act which rests on pre-predicative intentions of **R**, **a**, and **b**, with contents <**R**>, <**a**>, and <**b**> that represent **R**, **a**, and **b** respectively. These intentions of **R**, **a**, and **b** are parts of the judgment that "**Rab**" (where Husserl's ontology of parts is applied to acts), and their contents <**R**>, <**a**>, and <**b**> are parts of the proposition <**Rab**> (where the doctrine of part is applied to meanings).

For Husserl, I take it, *formal* structure is a special kind of part-whole structure. In the Third Investigation, Husserl analyzes the formal ontological structures of part-whole and dependence. Then in the Fourth Investigation, surprisingly, Husserl applies the *ontological forms* of part-whole and dependence to linguistic expressions, thus defining *grammatical form*. Thus, where Frege offered the metaphor that a name is "saturated" and a predicate "unsaturated", Husserl offered a *bona fide* ontology: a name is an independent part of a sentence, and a predicate '**R**_ _' is a dependent part of a sentence, thus a predicate requires—cannot exist as such without—names or terms to fill the blanks.

Husserl assumed, like Wittgenstein, that *form* applies on different levels (as above). But Husserl did not hold a "picture theory" like that of Wittgenstein's *Tractatus*, where form alone determines representation. Wittgenstein held that the form of the sentence '**Rab**' is *identical* with the form of the state of affairs [**Rab**] it represents. And according to Wittgenstein, that isomorphism is what makes that sentence represent or "picture" that state of affairs. Indeed, for Wittgenstein, the sentence '**Rab**' is itself a "fact", an existing state of affairs. For Husserl, however, given the intentionality of the judgment underlying the sentence, there is much more than form involved in what makes an expression represent an object. The full account unfolds in the rich story of intentionality in Husserl's phenomenology.

VI. ENTER INTENTIONALITY

The representational structure modelled in the diagram above is essentially the structure of intentionality. Language and thought are allied in this Husserlian model. Also, linguistic meaning and intentional sense or "content" are allied. The model covers only the special case of a propositional act or attitude expressed by uttering an atomic declarative sentence regimented in predicate logic. But the structure modelled is a salient type of intentionality.

Husserl conceived intentionality as the direction of an act of consciousness (or dispositional attitude such as belief) through a meaning toward an appropriate object in the world: thus does mind represent things in the world. In a speech act, on Husserl's analysis, language gives voice to the intentionality of an underlying act of consciousness, or an implicit attitude such as belief. The expression uttered thereby expresses the underlying act's meaning and is directed through the meaning toward an appropriate object in the world: thus does language represent things in the world. The details of this configuration of thought and expression are mapped out in the First and Fifth of the *Logical Investigations* and ramified in his *Ideas* I.[21]

Contrary to the rhetoric of Husserl's account of expression, language does not only borrow meaning from an autonomous substrate of thought. Twentieth century philosophy of language has stressed in many ways how our language also shapes, even facilitates, our thinking, especially discursive thought about culturally formed things in the world around us. In the Husserlian model above, these dual dependencies take their places. Then intentionality is the structure wherein thought *cum* language is directed via meaning toward appropriate objects in the world, where the relevant meaning may itself be shaped by both phenomenological forms of consciousness and social forms of language. Recent analyses of reference for names, kind terms, and indexicals unfold such dependencies among thought and language in causal, historical, and social linkages. Such analyses show clearly that form alone does not make mind or language represent.[22]

First-order predicate logic abstracts from these phenomenological and social conditions of language use, and from a good deal of the relevant ontology. Assuming Husserl's richer philosophy of logic, however, we may begin to frame an Husserlian semantics for the language of first-order predicate logic along the lines of the Husserlian model above.

VII. THE UNITY OF THE *LOGICAL INVESTIGATIONS*

What, then, is "logical" in the *Logical Investigations*? The short Husserlian answer should be: "The formal structure of intentionality, in thought and language." The familiar contemporary issues of logic ensue: inference, reference, predication, meaning, truth conditions. But Husserlian logical theory depends on Husserlian doctrines of ideal

---

[21] The details are reconstructed in D.W. SMITH and R. MCINTYRE, *Husserl and Intentionality*. What is new here is the way in which that analysis fits into the overall system of Husserl's *Logical Investigations*.

[22] This is especially clear in the case of indexical forms of awareness. See D.W. SMITH, *The Circle of Acquaintance: Perception, Consciousness, and Empathy*, Boston and Dordrecht: Kluwer Academic Publishers, 1989.

meaning, ideal species or essence, states of affairs, the relations between language and thought or judgment, and the intentional connection between meanings and objects including states of affairs. In Husserl's philosophical system, that is, logic is interdependent with ontology and phenomenology, in ways we have been charting.

The details of Husserl's system unfold over the long course of the *Prolegomena* and six Investigations. In highlight:

Pro. Logic is the theory of theories. A theory is a unified system of propositions. A proposition (*Satz*) is an objective ideal meaning (expressible by a declarative sentence).

I. Language consists in expressive acts of speech (or writing). A speech act intimates an underlying act of judgment and expresses the objective ideal content or sense (*Sinn*) of that act. That sense serves as the meaning (*Bedeutung*) of the expression uttered.

II. Concrete spatiotemporal objects (particulars) share ideal species (universals). Ideal species are not spatiotemporal but are objective. Meanings are a type of ideal species.

III. An object that is a whole or unity has parts. An independent part or "piece" can exist apart from the whole, but a dependent part or "moment" cannot. An instance of an ideal species is a moment in an object that is a member of that species.

IV. Part-whole relations apply to meanings. Propositions contain concepts as parts, some as dependent parts.

V. An act of consciousness has a subject or ego, a content or sense, and an object. An act is intentional insofar as it is directed toward its object (if such object exists). It is directed through its content or sense, a meaning, which represents the object.

VI. An act of perception or intuition depends on the occasion of its occurrence, in which its object is "present" to its subject. Even its ideal sense or meaning is occasional, depending on which object is "present" to the subject on that occasion.

Clearly, there are dependencies of content binding all these studies together. Moreover, the theory of intentionality depends on components of analyses in all these studies.

There is thus a unity of content in the overall theory of the *Logical Investigations*. And such unity is precisely what the *Prolegomena* itself prescribes for a theory, where logic is defined as the "theory of theory".

VIII. LOGIC, ONTOLOGY, AND PHENOMENOLOGY

If logic is defined—in an Husserlian spirit—as the theory of the structure of propositions and combinations thereof in theories (including deductions within theories), then logic does not subsume as *parts* the ontology and phenomenology unfolded in the six Investigations. Rather, logic is interdependent with certain theories in ontology and phenomenology. Specifically, Husserlian logical semantics presupposes (depends on) the ontology of ideal species, ideal meanings, part/whole and dependence, and the phenomenology of conscious experience, which propounds the structure of intentionality presupposed in Husserlian logical semantics.

We must distinguish, however, the intentional *character* of an act of consciousness from the intentional *relation* between the act and its object via its meaning. (These are my terms, Husserlian in spirit but not Husserl's.[23]) Phenomenology analyzes intentional character, which includes having an ideal content or meaning—but brackets intentional relations. Ontology analyzes the intentional relation that relates act, meaning, and object *cum* species. Then logical semantics, in the above model, abstracts the *form* of the intentional relation that connects forms of sentence, judgment-type, proposition, and state of affairs.

From today's perspective, that form determines the unity in Husserl's more than logical investigations.[24]

---

[23] See the Introduction to D. W. SMITH, *The Circle of Acquaintance*.

[24] Many of the issues here discussed come together in the logic, ontology, and phenomenology of self-awareness. See two complementary recent studies: D. W. SMITH, *The Circle of Acquaintance*, and D. ZAHAVI, *Self-Awareness and Alterity: A Phenomenological Investigation*, Evanston: Northwestern University Press, 1999. Where the former analyzes the formal structure of self-awareness (and other types of acquaintance, or "intuition"), the latter analyzes the material structures of the same intentional phenomena.

II

Realism and Idealism

DALLAS WILLARD
University of Southern California

THE WORLD WELL WON: HUSSERL'S EPISTEMIC REALISM ONE HUNDRED YEARS LATER

By "epistemic realism" I understand the view that the objects of veridical thought and perception both exist and have the characteristics they are therein discovered to have without regard to whether or not they are in any way actually present to any mind of any type.

The possibility of realism in this sense is, for Husserl, the same as the possibility of knowledge. As he indicates at the end of the first lecture in *The Idea of Phenomenology*, as well as at various places in the *Logical Investigations*, in the course of Modern thought,

> the ability of knowledge to make contact with an object has become enigmatic ... What becomes questionable is the possibility of knowledge, more precisely, the possibility of knowledge making contact with an objectivity that is, after all, what it is in itself. At bottom, what knowledge accomplishes, the sense of its claim to validity or justification ..., is in question; as is, on the other side, the sense of objectivity, which is and is what it is whether it is known or not, and yet as an objectivity is an objectivity of a possible knowledge, in principle knowable even if it has as a matter of fact never been known or will be known ...[1]

Epistemic realism in this sense is entirely consistent with Husserl's statement elsewhere that "... now as ever I hold every form of current philosophical realism to be absurd, as no less every idealism to which in its own arguments that realism stands contrasted, and which in fact it refutes."[2]

In my view, Husserl had resolved in principle all of the issues about the possibility of knowledge in the sense of epistemic realism by the time he finished the *Logical Investigations,* and he never later retracted the basic position which he there worked out. I realize, of course, that many disagree with this interpretation of his so-called "development," but here there is no possibility of taking up the many subtle issues involved in our disagreement.

---

[1] E. HUSSERL, *The Idea of Phenomenology*, trans. L. Hardy, Boston: Kluwer Academic Publishers, 1999, 20-21. All page references to the *Logical Investigations* are to the English translation: E. HUSSERL, *Logical Investigations*, trans. J. N. Findlay, New York: Humanities Press, 1970, abbreviated as LI.

[2] E. HUSSERL, *Ideas I*, trans. W. R. Boyce Gibson, London: George Allen & Unwin LTD, 1931, 19.

A few years after its appearance, Wilhelm Dilthey referred to Husserl's *Logical Investigations* as an "epoch making" book.[3] Questions could be raised as to what makes an epoch, and in one sense of "epoch" I suppose that the *Logical Investigations* did not make one. So far as the outward historical form of philosophy as a social reality is concerned, perhaps the *Logical Investigations* has created (so far) something more than a major stir, but also something less than an "epoch," in the manner of Descartes and Kant, for example.

In terms of philosophical illumination of the major surface problem of modern philosophy since Descartes, however—the mind's grasp of its world—I believe the *Logical Investigations* was and is epoch making. What it did, for those who thought it through, was to restore the rich manifold of the objectivities of human existence (from the objects of the most spontaneous experiences of nature and social relations to the highest levels of scientific abstraction, as well as the texture of human experience itself) to the status of true being. These no longer had to be things which in one way or another were explained away. To the juggernaut of reduction or nothing-but-ism, arising from thinkers such as Galileo and Hobbes, Husserl replied (and showed) that by far the most of what *they* wished to deny or to neglect as not truly being--or else to falsify in its essence by shoving it into the mind: all of that had its own right to existence, which could be fully demonstrated or observed in the proper circumstances.

Husserl was, of course, not the only great thinker of his day who was troubled about the reductionist outcome of Modern thought. Bergson and Whitehead were two of his contemporaries who were primarily committed to overcoming reductionism, and who, at least to their own minds, had overcome it. But they (and others who shared their concern) failed to provide anything like Husserl's exquisite analysis of thought, perception and knowledge, and hence their case is almost totally one built upon the supposedly absurd consequences of reductionism and analysis of some of the misunderstandings that lead to them. They have little to say about the precise structure of acts of consciousness in relation to their various kinds of objects.

Thus, in discussing how Galileo, Descartes and Locke dealt with "secondary" qualities, Whitehead remarks that, on their views,

> ... the mind in apprehending also experiences sensations which, properly speaking, are qualities of the mind alone. These sensations are projected by the mind so as to clothe appropriate bodies in external nature. Thus the bodies are perceived as with qualities which in reality do not belong to them .... Thus nature gets credit which should in truth be reserved for ourselves: the rose for its scent, the nightingale for his song, the sun for his radiance. The poets are

---

[3] H. SPIEGELBERG, *The Phenomenological Movement*, 2nd edition, two volumes, The Hague: Martinus Nijhoff, 1969, I/123.

entirely mistaken. They should address their lyrics to themselves, and should turn them into odes of self-congratulation on the excellency of the human mind. Nature is a dull affair, soundless, scentless, colorless; merely the hurrying of material, endlessly, meaninglessly.[4]

In fact it might be said that a major lesson of Modern thought is that, if you can't salvage "secondary" qualities, all will soon be lost. The reasons which lead to treating them as "mental" will soon force everything into the mind. As Sartre sharply pointed out in a little essay of 1939, the illusion of Modern philosophy is: "to know is to eat." "We have all believed," he says,

> that the spidery mind trapped things in its web, covered them with a white spit and slowly swallowed them, reducing them to its own substance ... The simplest and plainest among us vainly looked for something solid, something not just mental, but would encounter everywhere only a soft and very genteel mist: themselves.[5]

Sartre understood that "Against the digestive philosophy of empirico-criticism, of neo-Kantianism, against all 'psychologism', Husserl persistently affirmed that one cannot dissolve things in consciousness." "... Consciousness is an irreducible fact which no physical image can account for, except perhaps the quick, obscure image of a burst. To know is to 'burst toward', to tear oneself out of the moist gastric intimacy, veering out there beyond oneself, ...".[6]

*

Hume, it will be recalled, had taken up the question of "Why we attribute a *continued* existence to objects, even when they are not present to the senses; and why we suppose them to have an existence *distinct* from the mind and perception."[7] He concluded, as is well known, that it is neither sense nor reason, but only imagination "that produces the opinion of a *continued* or of a *distinct* existence,"[8] and that we have no evidence of the existence of anything apart from "the mind and perception."

This view of Hume, though supported by him upon assumptions and descriptions not generally shared by other great Modern philosophers, can, not unfairly,

---

[4] A. N. WHITEHEAD, *Science and the Modern World*, New York: Mentor Books, 1956, 55-56.

[5] J.-P. SARTRE, "Intentionality: a Fundamental Idea of Husserl's Phenomenology," trans. J. Fell, *The Journal of the British Society for Phenomenology* 1, 1970, 4-5.

[6] J.-P. SARTRE, "Intentionality," 4.

[7] D. HUME, *A Treatise of Human Nature*, ed. L. A. Selby-Bigge, London: Oxford University Press, 1955, Bk. I, Part iv, Sect. 11, p. 188.

[8] D. HUME, *A Treatise*, 188 and 193.

be regarded as an outcome of the Modern period of Western philosophy, and as one which, though formulated in significantly different ways, still dominates contemporary thought as we enter the 21st Century. This is true even though "mind and perception" is not usually now conceived of in the highly individualistic sense of Hume and other Modern philosophers prior to Kant. The "genteel mist" encountered is no longer the individual mind, but transcendental forms, history, language and culture, which are thought of as somehow fundamental to the individual (not it to them) and which perhaps even "construct" the individual.

Donald Davidson characteristically comments: "Yet if the mind can grapple without distortion with the real, the mind itself must be without categories and concepts. This featureless self is familiar from theories in quite different parts of the philosophical landscape.... In each case, the mind is divorced from the traits that constitute it."

Now of course, as Davidson himself insists, the mind simply cannot be divorced from the traits that constitute it. Nothing can. But the point to be taken from his statement quoted is that, *if* the mind has "categories and concepts," it *must* distort "the real" when it comes to "grapple" with it. But on the other hand it must have them so to "grapple." Hence the mind must distort its objects and therefore never has access to undistorted objects, i.e., to things as they are *apart from* the distorting caused by the grappling with or toward things "in themselves."[9]

Richard Rorty takes an even stronger position than Davidson, rejecting the idea that different "conceptual schemes" grapple with the same "matter." "The suggestion that our concepts shape neutral material no longer makes sense once there is nothing to serve as this material."[10] The whole idea of alternative conceptual frameworks and corresponding worlds loses its sense. Rorty simply rejects the idea of a world and, taking a page from Nietzsche's book, replaces that idea with some constraint placed on beliefs, and especially new beliefs, by the "vast body of platitudes, unquestioned perceptual reports, and the like," which are already in place. This "vast body" of course has no contactable "outside" any more than does Hume's "mind and perceptions." Hume admitted that belief in independent and continued existence can never be eradicated, "nor will any strained metaphysical conviction of the dependence of our perceptions be sufficient for that purpose."[11] I think Rorty would agree. But still the basic Humean view carries over to most of philosophy after the "linguistic turn," as it is sometimes called, and in some form to much of continental philosophy after Husserl.

Indeed, I often hear from people who are experts on Husserl's thought that he adopts a version of the same view: that he too holds to some very elaborate version of the epistemically encapsulated mind. Perhaps I am mistaken, but I think this view of the

---

[9] D. DAVIDSON, *Inquiries into Truth and Interpretation*, London: Oxford University Press, 1984, 185. Similarly Putnam and his rejection of the very idea of a quality "in itself." H. PUTNAM, *The Many Faces of Realism*, La Salle, IL.: Open Court, 1987, 8.

[10] R. RORTY, "The World Well Lost," in his *The Consequences of Pragmatism*, Minneapolis: University of Minnesota Press, 1982, 4.

[11] D. HUME, *A Treatise*, 214.

encapsulated mind is precisely the one Husserl successfully overturned in the *Logical Investigations* and presumes to be refuted in all his later works. A good way to appreciate Husserl's contribution is to emphasize that he believed Hume could be shown wrong, given the analysis of the act of consciousness which Husserl himself provides. A distinct and continued existence apart from consciousness is indeed possible for objects of consciousness of various types, especially the physical, since they owe nothing to the mind that contemplates them.

*

The possibility of recovering authentic knowledge of the amazing richness of manifold fields of being, including the human self, and especially the inexhaustible ideal realms of essence, resulted in a powerful surge of philosophical interest and activity among Husserl's younger associates. Indeed, the possibility of knowledge is tied very directly to the possibility of philosophy itself--which of course has been seriously in question among philosophers themselves for a century or so. If Husserl was right, there was hope. Something of significance could be done. Accomplishments, results, were possible. This hopeful outlook may have been what Jean Hering had in mind by speaking of a "phenomenological springtime."[12] In the Preface to the English translation of *Ideas* I Husserl speaks of the discovery of a new Atlantis, and, mixing his metaphors, of his having "actually wandered in the trackless wilds of a new continent and undertaken bits of virgin cultivation."[13] And, further mixing his metaphors, he speaks of "the infinite open country of the true philosophy, the 'Promised Land', which he sees, but himself will never set foot in."[14]

*

There are two major points in Husserl's analysis of cognition that provide the basis for his epistemic realism and the corresponding hopefulness.
 1. His theory of concepts (and propositions).
 2. His understanding of the polythetic or many-rayed nature of some—indeed most—acts of consciousness.
 Concepts have usually been thought of in one of two ways: as *acts* of minds upon objects, or as objects that stand *before* the mind. The former is the way of Kant and of the second Wittgenstein and, obviously, Davidson, Putnam, Rorty and many (perhaps most) others.
 The latter is the way of Locke, Frege, Russell and Alonzo Church. On this latter view the concept may also be the result of an act, a creation of the mind, as in the

---

[12] H. SPIEGELBERG, *The Phenomenological Movement*, 168

[13] E. HUSSERL, *Ideas I*, 23.

[14] E. HUSSERL, *Ideas I*, 28-29.

case of Locke and similar Empiricists, or it may not be, as with Frege and Church. But whether or not it is created, it is essentially an object of the mind and the theory never explains how the concept, which is to bring other things before the mind, is itself before the mind without a further concept that makes it so, and so on *in infinitum*. It also has great difficulty in explaining how the concepts brings things other than itself before the mind. These are some of the difficulties that lead Husserl to reject the "object" view of concepts—though of course they can become objects in special acts directed upon them. As to the former view of concepts, Husserl early on rejected the idea that the act of thought or language or its components did things *to* objects or *made* things.

On his view, the concept (which may become the meaning of a linguistic expression but need not do so) is not an object of the (mental or linguistic) act within which it functions, but rather is a *property* or characteristic of that act. (Similarly for the proposition or the judgment-in-the-logical-sense.) Husserl explains his view on this point in several places, most notably in §34 of the 4th chapter of the First Investigation (LI, 332) and in his review of Palagyi, where he credits Lotze's interpretation of Plato's 'ideas' with enabling him to make sense of Bolzano's *Vorstellungen an sich,* or concepts, by taking them as species.

As a property—the intentional bearing or specific aboutness—of a mental or linguistic act, the concept does not *explain* how the act is of or about its object. Rather, it *is* the ofness or aboutness, the specific intentionality, of the act for its object, and as a property it is repeatable in instances and shareable between persons, as one would have to expect of a property. One can find certain necessary conditions of an act being about or of specific objects, such as totalities or physical objects or other persons. But specific intentionality or meaning, the bearing of an act on an object or objects, which is the relevant concept, is a descriptive ultimate that cannot be defined or explained (cf. LI, §31, p. 400). It is a "natural sign."

Since the concept is a property of the act, it does not intervene between the act and its object, and does not close the mind off from the very objects or world that it was supposed to make accessible. It does not encapsulate the mind or its contents, any more than the properties of other things or events encapsulate them.

But, for Husserl, the concept also is not an activity of "making," shaping or using something (a sensation, image, or symbol) in a certain way. The Locke/Kant/Davidson picture of the mind forming something to produce objects is out of place for Husserl. In the important footnote to §13 of the fifth Investigation (LI, 563n) Husserl echoes Paul Natorp's caution against taking seriously talk of "mental activities" or "activities of consciousness," and adds: "We too reject the 'mythology of activities': we define 'acts' as intentional experiences, not as mental activities." And in passages already cited he comments that concepts, like numbers, "neither spring forth nor vanish with the act," but "are an ideally closed set of general objects, to which being thought or being expressed are alike contingent."(LI, 333).[15] Of course if they were acts

---

[15] Cf. Ch. II of *Ideas I*.

of shaping, forming or creating, this would not be true. The concept would "spring forth and vanish" with the act, for it would be the act.

Much more needs to be said about Husserl's view of the nature of concepts, especially because it is so contrary to prevailing ideas. But these few remarks must suffice for now.

The second basic point in Husserl's realist analysis of cognition was his understanding of the polythetic or many-rayed nature of most acts of consciousness. This makes possible—given that concepts and propositions (or representations and judgments) do not close us off from realities as they are—the experience of the fulfillment of an act, eventually by its object, and hence makes possible *Evidenz*, the *Erlebnis* of truth, the grasp of the correspondence of a thought with its object.

That is, we are capable of finding, at least in some cases, an object to be precisely as we thought it to be—or not—and of finding for every case of thought that is veridical *some* significant degree of fulfillment or verification. And since our thought does not by being of an object change it from what it is apart from thought, we can know that the object apart from our verifying thought will be exactly what it is when we are not conscious of it—precisely what Hume said we could not know. Hume was, therefore, mistaken, and supported his view only through systematically misdescribing the objects of consciousness.

The capacity to find something to be as we thought it to be is the result of the polythetic character of acts of fulfillment and, based thereon, clarification. In one act we find the object to be as we thought it to be, which is fulfillment; and we may then also *clarify* our concept of the object by matching—in Hume's language, but not with his meaning—our "ideas" to their corresponding "impression."

And, indeed, a metaphysics now becomes possible for the first time. Husserl has his own version of a "prolegomena for any future metaphysics," and that was central to his project. For we can clarify what it is for the objectivities of various kinds to exist or be, and then develop appropriate methods for determining whether they do or do not in fact exist.

Now of course there is a view widely and strongly held that it is *impossible* to compare an object with a concept, representation or judgment (proposition), to see if the object is as it is represented or judged to be. This is always based, so far as I can tell, upon the theory that when we turn to the object we only get another representation or judgment about the object and not the object itself. The Kant/Davidson view would yield this result, for sure, and interesting variants of it are found in Quine ("Ontological Relativity") and Wilfrid Sellars (the famous "Myth of the Given," etc.).

But this theory of the impossibility of comparing concept and object is based upon views of the concept and "judgment" that Husserl rejects. Hence, for him, given an adequate complexity and interweaving of the mental act, it is possible under appropriate conditions to compare the concept (representation, judgment) with its object to see if the object is or is not as it is represented. Denial of this is entirely based upon the assumption that concepts change things or block them from view, so that we can never experience them as they are when we are not experiencing them. (Of *course* we can't experience them without experiencing.) That is precisely the view that Husserl rejected. The mind is not only open to what transcends it, but it can in certain cases establish that what it opens upon is really there and genuinely exists *as* it is conceptualized—since conceptualization in no way effects it. Critique of knowledge (in Husserl's manner) therefore even "puts us in the position of being able to give an accurate and definitive interpretation of the results of the positive sciences with respect to what exists."[16]

*

Does realism, in the sense I have been discussing it, really matter? In the United States, at least, Richard Rorty and his literary counterpart, Stanley Fish, are famous for maintaining a form of pragmatism which says to this issue, "Who cares?" And Fish pretty well captures Rorty's point of view by asserting that *anything goes* if and so long as it can be made to go: that is, so long as it successfully takes on all criticisms and is left standing in the arena of discussion. "The arts, the sciences, the sense of right and wrong, and the institutions of society," Rorty says, "are not attempts to embody or formulate truth or goodness or beauty. They are attempts to solve problems--to modify our beliefs and desires and activities in ways that will bring us greater happiness than we have now."[17]

But three points must be made in reply to this "neo-pragmatism." First, quite clearly Rorty *et. al.* tell us *how things really are*, specifically, with respect to language, mind and world. Second, many views that have successfully stood the test of contemporary discussions were later found to be false. No doubt they were also false while successfully standing. Third, views that successfully stand up are sometimes not only false, but humanly disastrous. That is arguably the case within the "Crisis" that concerned Husserl in his last years. The capacity of discourse borrowed from the physical sciences to "stand up" and to defeat claims of knowledge from all other sources has led to a situation in Western culture where there is no longer an accessible body of moral knowledge that can serve as a basis for our individual or corporate existence. That is, now, a fact. Surely a humanly disastrous fact. But scientism now "stands up."

The issue of realism, in the sense here explained, is therefore a live one today, and one of vital human significance. It was precisely through rejecting—like Rorty—the traditional theories of intuition and concept (receptivity and spontaneity) and replacing them—unlike Rorty—with a view of concepts, experience and objectivities that allows us to discover a world as it is without regard to our thinking, perception, etc., that Husserl opened the possibility of our dealing with reality (and realities) in its (their) own terms without losing life and self in the process. A World well-won indeed.

---

[16] E. HUSSERL, *The Idea of Phenomenology*, 19.

[17] R. RORTY, "The World Well Lost," 16.

*

I have not said much about the "Ideal" in this talk, but without Husserl's strongly realistic view of the ideal (of universals, *Ideen* in his special, non-Kantian and non-Empiricist sense) none of the points I have made about concepts and acts would amount to much for his purposes. As he states in the little "Introduction" to the Second Investigation, "meanings [which are species] make up the domain of pure logic, so that to misread the essence of the species [or the ideal or the universal or the general object] must...be to strike at the very essence of logic."

Therefore one must work out a theory of abstraction, the concern of the Second Investigation, "so as to assure the basic foundations of pure logic and epistemology by defending the intrinsic right of specific (or ideal) objects to be granted objective status alongside of individual or real objects. This is the point on which relativistic, empiricistic psychologism differs from idealism [*Platonic* idealism], which alone represents the possibility of a self-consistent theory of knowledge." To talk of "idealism," he continues to say, "is not to talk of a metaphysical doctrine [primarily, a theory about the nature of the physical world], but of a theory of knowledge which recognizes the 'ideal' as a condition for the possibility of objective knowledge in general...."(LI, 338).

"The laws of pure logic are truths rooted in the concept of truth," he had earlier said (LI, 192), "and in concepts essentially related to this concept." And "The idea of this agreement ["between meaning and what is itself present, meant, between the actual sense of an assertion and the self-given state of affairs"—his words] is truth, whose ideality [or status as a universal] is its objectivity. It is not a chance fact that a propositional thought, occurring here and now, agrees with a given state of affairs: the agreement rather holds between a self-identical propositional meaning and a self-identical state of affairs. 'Validity' or 'objectivity', and their opposites, do not pertain to an assertion as a particular temporal experience, but to the assertion *in species*, to the pure, self-identical assertion 2 X 2 = 4, etc." (LI, 195) In this same section he maintains that the distinction between the real and the ideal (with the distinctions subordinate to it) is "the most fundamental of epistemological distinctions." If it is not correctly discerned, nothing can go right in the theory of knowledge after that. Chapter two of *Ideas* I should be read for even more forceful statements along these lines, especially §21 and §22.

Many Husserl experts would pass the Ideal off as noematic. The reasons I do not think the noematic can handle the Ideal are, mainly, these two:

1. Husserl explicitly says of the noema that its *esse* is percipi (§98 of *Ideas* I). It exists in being perceived or thought. He explicitly denies this of the Ideal (see §22 of *Ideas* I and §32 and §35 of the First Investigation). Therefore the ideal or universal cannot be the noematic.

2. The noematic falls under Ideal laws, and is what it is because of the essences which it exemplifies and the Idea-law connections between them. Rather than Ideal

beings (universals) depending on or being derived from the noematic, the noematic depends on and is derived from them.[18]

---

[18] For further discussion of what it is to be, and how it applies to the Ideal as well as the real, I refer to my *Logic and the Objectivity of Knowledge,* Athens, OH.: Ohio University Press, 1984, 187-188, etc. For further discussion of many points only mentioned in this paper, see my "The Integrity of the Mental Act: Husserlian Reflections on a Fregean Problem," in *Mind, Meaning and Mathematics*, ed. L. Haaparanta, Boston: Kluwer Academic Publishers, 1994, 235-262; and my "Knowledge," in *The Cambridge Companion to Husserl*, eds. B. Smith and D. W. Smith, New York: Cambridge University Press, 1995, 138-167.

RICHARD COBB-STEVENS
Boston College

"ARISTOTELIAN" THEMES IN HUSSERL'S *LOGICAL INVESTIGATIONS*

In 1683, Nicolas Malebranche and Antoine Arnauld began an extended and sometimes acrimonious debate about the viability of Aristotle's claim in the *De Anima* that in its cognitive function "the soul is somehow all things." According to Malebranche, the principle of physics that there can be no action at a distance applies also to the domain of cognitive activity. It is therefore unreasonable to believe, he observes, that our minds are literally in the sky when we contemplate the stars: "It is not likely that the soul should leave the body to stroll about the heavens, as it were, in order to behold these objects."[1] Neither is it believable that our minds are capable of "walking about" even in more familiar spaces, for example, that they leave our bodies in order to see houses at a near distance. In defense of Aristotle, Arnauld responds that it is inappropriate to construe intentional presence in terms of spatial or local presence. Were God to allow our mind to leave our body and to travel to the sun in order to see it, our mind would have made, Arnauld says, "a great and very useless voyage." It makes no difference whether bodies are present or absent, nearby or distant: "... it is for the mind the same thing."[2] Malebranche then responds that Arnauld, lacking a sense of irony, had taken his criticism too literally. The critique of the "walking-mind" had been intended only as a "good-natured ridicule" whose target was really the notion that the mind can know better what is closer, i.e., things that its body touches, or even the body itself. His point, he adds, was that the objects of the mind are intelligible, not material. The mind is not extended; it operates only within the realm of rationality, a purely intelligible realm which excludes everything material. Arnauld retorts that an intelligible sun is nothing other than the material sun as known. The point of Aristotle's claim, he insists, was that the primary objects of our cognition are things and persons in the world around us, be they nearby or distant, present or absent.[3]

Arnauld's defense of Aristotle did not carry the day. Such was the success and momentum of the new sciences that his position seemed to many of his contemporaries

---

[1] N. MALEBRANCHE, *The Search After Truth*, trans. T. M. Lennon and P. J. Olscamp, Columbus: Ohio State University Press, 1980, Vol. I, p. 217; *Oeuvres complètes de Malebranche*, ed. A. Robinet Paris: J. Vrin, 1958-70, Vol. I, 413. See also J. W. YOLTON, *Perceptual Acquaintance from Descartes to Reid*, Minneapolis: University of Minnesota Press, 1984, 47-49.

[2] "Quand Dieu aurait permis à nostre ame de sortir de notre corps pour aller trouver le soleil afin de le voir, elle aurait fait un grande voyage fort inutilement ... puisque présent ou éloigné c'est pour elle la même chose ..." A. ARNAULD, *Des vraies et fausses idées contre ce qu'enseigne l'auteur de la recherche de la vérité*, ed. Christiane Frémont, Paris: Librairie Fayard, 1986, 70. See J.W.YOLTON, *Perceptual Acquaintance*, 64-65.

[3] A. ARNAULD, *Des vraies et fausses idées*, 89-99.

to be of only antiquarian interest. Hobbes had already asserted that the new sciences require that perception be explained in terms of the movements of elements within a formless nature. All of the forms that we seem to perceive in things are illusory impressions provoked by the body's reaction to the pressure on its organs by motions of matter.[4] It would not be long before the last vestiges of Aristotle's position would succumb to increasingly more literal and more reductive versions of Malebranche's critique of the "walking-mind" such as may be found in the many subsequent attempts to account for intentionality in terms of physical causality. Modern philosophy would thus be left with a thoroughly confused methodological approach to what would come to known as the "enigma" of cognition.

This intriguing debate between Malebranche and Arnauld remains, I think you will agree, remarkably contemporary. Consider, for example, how contemporary cognitive scientists often intermingle phenomenological and causal categories in a hopelessly confused manner. Consider also how philosophers, even philosophers within the phenomenological tradition, often feel obliged to posit something present to the mind as the immediate target of our signitive intentions of absent things. This preoccupation also betrays an underlying confusion between intentionality and physical presence.

Husserl was, I believe, the first philosopher within the modern tradition to deal effectively with the ambiguities of the modern account of cognition. During the period from 1894 to 1900, his reflections on the incoherence of psychologism led him to make a decisive break with the modern epistemological model for the mind. In the *Logical Investigations*, his adherence to rigorous phenomenological description eventually achieved a methodological clarity uncontaminated by the confusions typical of the modern era. There is no evidence that he was markedly influenced by a reading of the relevant texts of pre-modern philosophers. And he surely did not set out, in the manner of Arnauld, to comment directly on Aristotle's writings on the soul. Yet he was able, by reason of a disciplined return *zu den Sachen selbst*, to achieve what amounts to a reconstruction of a fundamentally Aristotelian understanding of our cognitive powers. Heidegger's early lecture courses call attention in several places to Aristotelian themes in Husserl's works.[5] More recently, Robert Sokolowski has developed the view that phenomenology succeeds in integrating what is best in modern thought within a revitalized appreciation of the ancient and particularly the Aristotelian understanding of human reason.[6] In the same spirit, I propose to focus on three themes from the *Logical Investigations* that strike me as particularly Aristotelian: 1) the unmediated character of intentional directedness, 2) the relationship between seeing and speaking

---

[4] T. HOBBES, *Leviathan, or the Matter, Form, and Power of a Commonwealth Ecclesiastical and Civil. The English Works of Thomas Hobbes*, Vol. III. ed. W. Molesworth, Aalen: Scientia Verlag, 1966, 2-3.

[5] See, for example, M. HEIDEGGER, *The Metaphysical Foundations of Logic*, trans. M. Heim, Bloomington, Indiana University Press, 1984, §9-10, pp. 123-59.

[6] R. SOKOLOWSKI, *Introduction to Phenomenology*, Cambridge: Cambridge University Press, 2000, 203.

in categorial intentionality, and 3) the interplay of predication and assertion in judgment. There are other Aristotelian themes (parts and wholes, the status of universals, the discernment of essences) that might also be developed but I shall confine my comments to the aforementioned topics.

I. INTENTIONALITY AND ARISTOTELIAN "REALISM"

Two hundred years after the debate between Malebranche and Arnauld, the confusions that had plagued post-Cartesian interpreters of Aristotle were still very much in evidence among the immediate predecessors of Husserl. Consider, for example, the writings of Franz Brentano who proposed once again to take Aristotle as a guide for the restoration of a more coherent account of cognition. Commenting on Aristotle's dictum that the soul in its cognitive functions is somehow all things, Brentano observes that Aristotle was no doubt referring to a "psychological inhabitation (*Einwohnung*)" of objects known within the soul of the knower. He recalls that the Scholastic philosophers had used the term 'intentional' (and more frequently the term 'objective') to refer to the mode of being had by things known, in so far as they are known.[7] Unfortunately, however, Brentano tends to read a modern interpretation of immanence into the medieval and later Scholastic theme of *esse intentionale*. It is true that many texts from the latter tradition describe the intentional object (inner word, formal concept, expressed species) as a unique sort of intermediary, i.e., as a transparent sign through which the mind is related to reality.[8] This emphasis on the mediating function of formal concepts may well have prepared the way for the modern thesis that to know is to have representation of something (its idea or concept) within the mind's interiority. But the great medieval thinkers and the later Scholastics generally maintained that the intentional object *is* the very thing itself, considered as known. As Aquinas puts it: " ... that which is understood can be said to be both the thing itself and the conception of the intellect."[9] Brentano, however, distinguishes more radically between the intentional object and the extra-mental physical thing. He asserts, that every intentional experience "contains something as its object within itself," and he refers to this "immanent objectivity" as the "intentional in-existence of an object."[10] These expressions evoke the modern notion that impressions and ideas function as mental substitutes for inaccessible real objects of reference. Brentano also subscribes wholeheartedly to the modern interpretation of perception. He claims that our perceptions yield merely subjective

---

[7] F. BRENTANO, *Psychology from an Empirical Standpoint*, trans. A. C. Rancurello, D. B. Terrell & L. L. McAlister, London: Routledge & Kegan Paul, 1973, 88-89.

[8] See R. SOKOLOWSKI, *Presence and Absence: A Philosophical Investigation of Language and Being*, Bloomington: Indiana University Press, 1978, 62, n. 3.

[9] AQUINAS, *De Veritate*, IV, 2 ad 3.

[10] F. BRENTANO, *Psychology from an Empirical Standpoint*, 88-89.

appearances, and he appeals to physical causality alone in order to account for the relationship between these appearances and real objects. Corresponding to perceived colors, he observes, there are only the "vibrations" which emanate from the interaction of atoms, molecules, and forces. A thing's true being, therefore, is its hidden quantifiable reality accessible only to the methods of the natural sciences. Perceived objects do not really exist outside of us; they are *mere* phenomena.[11] These comments read like passages right out of the opening pages of Hobbes' *Leviathan*.

Aristotle himself does not seem to have thought it necessary to postulate any intermediary, however special, between intellect and thing known. Indeed, he suggests that the intellect must itself be free of formal structure, and hence empty of content, so that it can become all things. Aristotle first observes that it is not possible for the soul's faculties to become literally identical with things, "... for the stone does not exist in the soul, but rather the form [of the stone]."[12] To the modern reader (such as Brentano), this comment suggests that what we know are not things themselves but merely the forms of things which appear within the soul's inner space. As if to counter this impression, however, Aristotle next compares knowledge with touch. The intellect, says Aristotle, possesses the same sort of adaptability as the human hand. It takes on the forms of things in the way that the human hand grasps tools. The latter metaphor suggests that the soul reaches out to grasp forms in the things themselves. Although the hand has its own form, its malleability is such that it can adjust to the form of whatever it grasps. Moreover, as Stanley Rosen observes, the hand cannot grasp its own form. In a sense, therefore, the hand in its functional operations is formless. In a similar sense, the soul has no discernible shape. Unrestricted with regard to the kinds of objects to which it relates, its mode of being is to be (potentially) everything.[13]

Husserl's principal contribution to philosophy was his restoration and revitalization of this Aristotelian realism. The term 'realism' is notoriously over-determined and therefore highly ambiguous. As a result of the debates generated by the modern epistemological problem of how a self-enclosed consciousness can be related to an outside world, 'realism' is often taken to refer the view that philosophy is somehow capable of proving that we know things-in-themselves as they are apart from our knowing them. Neither Aristotle nor Husserl engaged in such a futile task. They both simply describe how things appear to us in an array of presentations. This descriptive realism is evident in Husserl's accounts of perception and categorial intuition but is even more forcefully manifested in his emphasis on our capacity to intend absent objects. According to Husserl, when we think or speak about things and facts in their absence, and when we perceive or register them, we deal with those things and facts and not with mental substitutes. Sokolowski points out that many readers of

---

[11] F. BRENTANO, *Psychology from an Empirical Standpoint*, 9-10.

[12] ARISTOTLE, *De Anima*, 431b30 - 432a1.

[13] ARISTOTLE, *De Anima*, 423a1-3. See S. ROSEN, "Thought and Touch: A Note on Aristotle's *De Anima,*" *Phronesis*, VI (1961), 127-37.

Husserl are at first skeptical of his claim that we truly intend what is absent. We are so accustomed to thinking of cognition in terms of the modern notion of mind as an enclosed theater of representations that we feel obliged to posit something within the mind as the immediate object of our signitive intentions of absent things. But Husserl insists on our capacity genuinely to intend what is absent. Indeed, this is what constitutes us as rational beings who can name things as identities across presence and absence and thus communicate through words rather than merely through signals. Husserl also developed the implications of this fundamental thesis. He repudiated Locke's interpretation of mind as an inner space ("the mind's cabinet"[14]) set off from the rest of nature and he rejected Kant's distinction between phenomena and things-in-themselves.[15]

It took some time, however, for Husserl to clarify the ambiguities generated by his dependence on the linguistic and conceptual framework of the empiricist tradition, which was the remote forerunner of late nineteenth-century psychologism. On the one hand, as early as 1894, in his essay "Psychological Studies in the Elements of Logic," he makes the unequivocal claim that our speech acts and cognitive intuitions truly target and present things in the world. Moreover, he distinguishes clearly between mental acts and their contents, a distinction that had been blurred by the empiricist notion of a mental "process," which in effect reduces cognitive acts to the mere having of associatively modified impressions. On the other hand, he uses the term 'contents' in an ambiguous fashion, sometimes to refer to ill-defined mental representations and sometimes to things in the world considered in so far as they are known.[16] This ambiguity testifies to the influence of Brentano on the early Husserl.

In the Fifth Investigation, however, Husserl objects to the above-mentioned expressions that Brentano had used to describe the status of intentional objects (immanent objectivity, intentional in-existence). He points out that these phrases suggest that the intentional object is located within the enclosure of the mind and that it functions as a substitute for the object of reference. He insists, on the contrary, that the intentional object and the object of reference are one and the same: "It need only be said to be acknowledged that the intentional object of a presentation is the same as its actual

---

[14] J. LOCKE, *An Essay Concerning Human Understanding*, ed. A. S. Pringle-Patterson, Oxford: Clarendon Press, 1928, Bk. I, ch. 2, §15; Bk. II, ch. 11, §17.

[15] See R. SOKOLOWSKI, *Introduction to Phenomenology*, 216: "The notion of a solitary, self-enclosed consciousness, aware only of itself and its own sensations and thoughts, was disposed of by Husserl's concept of intentionality ... We experience and perceive things, not just the appearances or impacts or impressions that things make on us. Things appear to us through a manifold of presentations. Husserl presented this realism not only by pointing out the self-contradictions of the Cartesian and Lockean position, of the way of ideas, but by working out detailed descriptive analyses of various forms of intentionality, analyses that proved themselves by virtue of their precision and convincingness. One does not prove realism; how could one do so. One displays it." See also 36-37.

[16] E. HUSSERL, "Psychological Studies in the Elements of Logic," in P. McCormick & F. Elliston (eds.) *Husserl: Shorter Works*, South Bend: Notre Dame University Press, 1981, 126-142. See D. WILLARD, *Logic and the Objectivity of Knowledge*, Athens, Ohio: Ohio University Press, 34-38.

object ... it is absurd to distinguish between them."[17] This is an unequivocal affirmation of realism (in the sense described above). Husserl also clarifies the relationship between intentional contents and intentional objects. He observes that the term 'intentional content' may legitimately be interpreted in the following ways: 1) as the intentional object (either the object *tout court*, or the object considered as it is intended); 2) as that feature (the act's matter) in virtue of which the act achieves determinate reference; 3) as the intentional essence of the act, i.e., the matter combined with its quality. The term 'quality' refers in this context to the type of intentional act, e.g., question, wish, statement, etc.[18]

These distinctions are consistent with Husserl's claim, in the First Investigation, that propositions are related to the acts in which they are expressed in a manner comparable to the way in which species are related to their instances. Considered as an intentional essence, the intentional content (matter and quality) is an ideal proposition that is independent of particular intentional acts. Taken as instantiated, the matter and quality are non-independent "moments" of a particular act.[19] John Drummond calls attention, however, to two passages which suggest that Husserl eventually modified this position. A note in the second edition (1913) strongly implies that his earlier description of intentional content as a particularized feature of the intentional act was a mistake that "corresponds to one's natural starting with the psychological point of view.")[20] In *Ideas I* (1913), he adds that what he had formerly taken to be a property of acts is really a property of the "meant as such".[21] In other words, Husserl finally identifies intentional matter and intentional object (in the sense of the "object considered as it is intended"). In conjunction with the above-mentioned strong claim that the intentional object of a presentation is the same as its actual object, these passages effectively eliminate any residue of the notion that we must postulate some sort of intermediary content between intentional acts and their objects.

Husserl thus makes it clear that the actual thing is given to us as the identity presented in a manifold of appearances. The impression that his later works succumbed to a traditional idealism is the result of misinterpretations of the reduction and of the transcendental attitude made possible by the reduction. We achieve the transcendental point of view by suspending our natural attitude of belief in the reality of things and the

---

[17] E. HUSSERL, *Logical Investigations*, trans. J. N. Findlay, London: Routledge & Kegan Paul, 1970, V, Appendix to §11 and 20, p. 595. See also V, §11, pp. 559-60.

[18] E. HUSSERL, *Logical Investigations*, V, §17, pp. 578-80, and §20, p. 589, §43, p. 657. See also J. DRUMMOND, *Husserlian Intentionality and Non-Foundational Realism: Noema and Object*, Dordrecht: Kluwer, 1990, 26-36.

[19] E. HUSSERL, *Logical Investigations*, I, §31, p. 330.

[20] E. HUSSERL, *Logical Investigations*, I, §576, n. 1.

[21] E. HUSSERL, *Ideas Pertaining to a Pure Phenomenology and to a Phenomenological Philosophy*, Book I, translated by F. Kersten, The Hague: Nijhoff, 1990, §128, p. 308. See J. DRUMMOND, *Husserlian Intentionality*, 26-36, 39-42.

world. Husserl emphasizes again and again that the purpose of this procedure is not to call natural convictions into doubt but rather simply to achieve a distance that will enable us to reflect on them in their full concreteness. For example, we step back from positing of things as real, but continue to maintain that positing as something upon which we reflect. We therefore maintain our contact with things in the world, but the change in focus initiated by the reduction now permits us to appreciate them precisely *as* intended objects.

Husserl's realism is not, however, simply a repetition of Aristotle's thesis that the soul is somehow all things. This is because Husserl's sense of realism had been forged by his radical break from the modern skepticism about the reality of the world based on the interpretation of mind as a subjective enclosure. His emphasis on empty intentionality, on our wondrous capacity to think and speak about absent objects, is the product of a post-critical sense of wonder not available to Aristotle. Aristotle had to deal with skeptical positions but not with the peculiarly modern skepticism that seemed to be a corollary of scientific progress itself. Husserl had to counter Hobbes's claim that the forms we seem to find in nature are merely illusory projections on a world that can in principle be reduced to elementary particles, forces, and laws. Husserl calls attention to the incoherence of this position noting that it would eventually culminate in Hume's skeptical conclusion that all the categories of objectivity, pre-scientific and scientific, are fictions.[22] Husserl's task, therefore, was not only to counter the modern reductive preference for the hidden over the manifest, but also to show that neither the manifest forms of things nor their hidden structures postulated by the new sciences are mere projections. To understand how he accomplished these tasks we may turn now to his analysis of categorial intentionality.

II. Categorial Intuition and the Aristotelian Theory of Substance

Let us consider for a moment what scientific knowledge meant for the ancients as opposed to the moderns. For Plato, theoretical knowledge meant contemplative insight into the forms manifested imperfectly in the natural order. For Aristotle, science was knowledge derived from sensuous and intellectual intuition of natural beings. The nature or form of a thing is revealed to us by its specific "look" (*eidos*). The species-look is "what" we know when we know some particular thing. This relationship between a particular and its form is the key to Aristotle's theory of substance. In a primary sense, substance is the individual (*tode ti*) which is both a "this" and a "what." In a secondary sense, substance is exclusively the "what" (*ti esti*).[23] Knowledge of a particular and its form always occurs as a unity and this prior unity is the condition for the subsequent

---

[22] E. Husserl, *The Crisis of European Sciences and Transcendental Phenomenology*, trans. D. Carr, Evanston: Northwestern Univ. Press, 1970, §23, p. 87.

[23] Aristotle, *Metaphysics*, 1028a10-15; *The Categories*, 1b11-18. See J. A. Smith, "*tode ti* in Aristotle," *Classical Review*, XXXV (1921), 19.

distinction between the particular and what it is.[24] For Aristotle, as Stanley Rosen puts it succinctly, nature is "neither produced nor modified (although it is "actualized") by the processes of cognition, whether intuitive or discursive."[25] Discursivity is a necessary supplement to the intuitive perception of form. Speech gives syntactical articulation and thus completion to the inarticulate insights of cognitive intuition. There is thus a continuity between intuitive and discursive *logos*. By contrast, the modern axiom first expressed by Vico and subtly espoused by Hobbes is that "we know only what we make." Theory is no longer founded on intellectual insight but rather on construction. There is only a small step from this position to Nietzsche's thesis that concepts are illusory cultural formations generated by the will to power. Like Hobbes, Nietzsche also defines science as the "... transformation of nature into concepts for the purposes of governing nature."[26]

Husserl developed his own theory of the interplay between perception and syntactical articulation in the process of criticizing the interpretation that British empiricism had given to the role of those components of a proposition that belong to its categorial form, e.g., prepositions, conjunctions, cases, and the copula. According to Locke and Hume, these syntactical components refer to intra-mental processes rather than to aspects of the world. Husserl dismisses this thesis on the grounds that we are directed towards things rather than towards inner processes when we use such expressions. Categorial forms are articulations in things that are brought about by our thinking about things. Simple perceptions achieve the presentation of objects as identities in a continuous flow of profiles of various features or properties. They may highlight this or that property but they do not present the unity of object and property as such. Predications present articulated ensembles. They present the "being together" of objects and properties.[27] Husserl stresses that the fulfilling intuition of any expression that names an object or ascribes a property to that object involves a surplus of sense that exceeds what is intuited in the simple perception of the particular object as having that property. He explicitly calls this surplus a "form," thereby associating its function with the work of presentation expressed by syntactical operators. Categorial intuitions thus effectively present the work of presentation expressed by syntactical terms and by the surplus senses of terms for objects and features. Husserl's account of categorial intuition

---

[24] ARISTOTLE, *Metaphysics*, 1041a7-27. See S. ROSEN, *The Limits of Analysis*, New York: Basic Books, 1980, 55-58. See also D. K. W. MODRAK, *Aristotle: The Power of Perception*, Chicago: Univ. of Chicago Press, 1987, 168.

[25] S. ROSEN, *Hermeneutics as Politics*, Oxford: Oxford University Press, 1987, 147-148.

[26] F. NIETZSCHE, *Werke*, ed. K. Schlechta, Munich, 1954-6, V, p. 440.

[27] E. HUSSERL, *Logical Investigations*, VI, §47-48, pp. 788-95. See also R. SOKOLOWSKI, "Husserl's Concept of Categorial Intuition," *Phenomenology and the Human Sciences* (formerly *Philosophical Topics*), XII (1981), 127-41, and J. TAMINIAUX, "Heidegger and Husserl's Logical Investigations: In Remembrance of Heidegger's Last Seminar (Zähringen, 1973)," in *Dialectic and Difference: Finitude in Modern Thought*, trans. R. Crease and J. Decker, Atlantic Highlands, NJ: Humanities Press, 1985, 91-114.

thus essentially restates Aristotle's account of the relationship between first and second substance. Predicative articulations are fulfilled by two interdependent modes of intuition: 1) the intuition of a particular through its specific look, and 2) the intuition of the look itself as instanced in the particular.

Once again, however, Husserl's account of categoriality is not simply a repetition of Aristotle's account of substance. Aristotle's discussion in the *Categories* takes for granted that perception and speech are presentations of things in the world. It would not have occurred to him that these presentations were in fact representations located within the mind's "glassy essence." Husserl had constantly to do battle with the modern notion that the primary object of perception and speech is something immediately present to the mind. This is why he devotes so much effort to a description of how empty and fulfilling intentionalities present things as identities across presence and absence. His discussion of these themes complements and enriches the more exclusively metaphysical discussion of the being and identity of things in Aristotle's works.

Husserl also discusses some uniquely modern modes of categoriality, algebraic equations and axiomatic systems. He points out that the discovery of algebra introduced a quite different sort of formality from that known by the Greeks. The algebraic mode of thought does not use symbols as substitutes for determinate objects. Rather, algebraic equations express indeterminate magnitudes and define the conditions for the possibility of their subsequent determinacy. Hence, the algebraic mode of thought is not immediately linked with an intuitive ontology of the physical world. Concepts like space, dimension and even number are understood in a purely mathematical sense, without direct reference to their ontological interpretations.[28] It would be inappropriate, therefore, to claim that the formal structure of such equations may be mapped directly onto the formal structures of the cosmic and subatomic realms. This would make for an altogether too facile restoration in modern terms of the Aristotelian notion of form. Moreover, the problem of correlating algebraic equations with structures of the world is further complicated by an additional nuance given to the modern sense of the formal by the incorporation of mathematical formulae within axiomatic systems. In the *Prolegomena*, Husserl briefly discusses the status of such systems and hints that the phenomenological method is well equipped to deal effectively with the "metaphysical fog" that had been generated by confused talk about the ontological status of spaces for which the axiom of parallels does not hold.[29] In *Formal and Transcendental Logic*, he disperses this metaphysical fog by distinguishing between apophantic systems and the application of such systems to the ontological domain. Mathematicians, he observes, may legitimately talk about the manifolds that are the objects of such apophantic systems without raising ontological questions about their actuality or even their

---

[28] See M. S. MAHONEY, "The Beginnings of Algebraic Thought in the Seventeenth Century," in *Descartes: Philosophy, Mathematics and Physics*, ed. S. Gaukroger, Sussex: Harvester, 1980, 142-143.

[29] E. HUSSERL, *Logical Investigations, Prolegomena*, §70, pp. 242-3.

possibility.[30] Although a manifold theory may sometimes have genuine applications within the ontological domain, as was the case for Riemann's geometry, the transition from apophantic to ontological domains does not occur by fiat. Ontological claims are always founded on the kind of evidence yielded by intuitions of things and their intelligible structures. Husserl remarks that if we focus upon the "intentional genesis" of such systems we find that they are rooted not only in syntactical forms but also in the "cores which seem to be functionless from a formal point of view." He adds that mathematicians and formal logicians easily overlook these cores because they are construed by their algebraic interpretation as "empty somethings" and thus taken as "theoretical irrelevancies."[31] For formal systems to have any meaning at all, they presuppose that judging is an already instituted intentional activity directed to objects of everyday experience that are then, in formalization, treated "as if" the objects in question were "irrelevant". This does not undermine the distinction between formal systems and their ontological interpretations. On the contrary, it specifies the reason why formal methods are relevant to knowledge and science. It follows that when mathematical systems pay off in eventual physical applications, this is not, as Descartes and Bacon thought, because our mathematical virtuosity gives us mastery over nature. The revelant mathematical systems are not projections of meaning upon a malleable nature but categorial achievements that disclose formal structures in the world.

III. JUDGMENT AS DISCLOSURE

"A statement," said Aristotle, "is a vocal-linguistic articulation which means something, which contains in itself a meaning-content in such a way that this or that part of a statement, when taken separately by itself, still has a meaning as a mere saying something, but not as an assertion or a denial."[32] Taken out of the context of sentences, simple nouns name individuals or classes, and verbs name activities or characteristics. Within the context of a sentence, however, a noun has the function of introducing a subject about which something is said, and a verb has the threefold function of signifying the subject's determination *as* something, of conveying by its tense a temporal reference, and of communicating the assertive character of the statement.[33] Note that by calling attention to the different functions of the verb, Aristotle suggests

---

[30] E. HUSSERL, *Formal and Transcendental Logic*, trans. D. Cairns, The Hague: Nijhoff, 1969, §40, pp. 108-110. See J. P. MILLER, *Numbers in Presence and Absence: A Study of Husserl's Philosophy of Mathematics*, The Hague: Nijhoff, 1982, 113-120.

[31] E. HUSSERL, *Formal and Transcendental Logic*, §89b, p. 218. I am grateful to James Dodd for calling this passage to my attention.

[32] ARISTOTLE, *On Interpretation*, I, iv, 16b 26-7. This translation is a modified version of the translation proposed by M. Heim in: M.. HEIDEGGER, *The Metaphysical Foundations of Logic*, trans. M. Heim, Bloomington: Indiana Univ. Press, 1978, 22-23.

[33] ARISTOTLE, *On Interpretation*, I, iii, 16b 6-25.

that assertion and predication are logically distinct though closely intertwined achievements. We know, moreover, from his analysis of the continuity between perception and predication in the *Categories* that, for Aristotle, to judge is first and foremost to articulate in an assertive manner the mode of "belonging" that obtains between things and their features. As he puts it, we can hardly conceive of judgmental synthesis "apart from the things thus combined."[34] Judging is therefore directed primarily upon things and their perceived features, not upon propositions as such.

Descartes was the first to claim explicitly that judgment is primarily the assumption of a stance with regard to a complex conceptual content. His methodical doubt required a modification of the traditional understanding of judgment, for it could no longer be assumed that a judgment's assertive articulations deal with things and their properties in the extra-mental world. Descartes therefore distinguished three types of mental acts (*cogitationes*): the entertaining of ideas or combinations of ideas, the assumption of voluntary or affective stances, and the making of judgments.[35] To order concepts into a predicative combination is one thing. To judge that what is thus said actually describes a state of affairs in the world is another.[36] Hume also distinguished between the ordering of ideas into a predicative content and judging that what is so ordered is the case in reality.

Brentano subscribed to this modern interpretation of the relationship between assertive character of judgment and its content. His reformulation of Descartes' tripartite division mentions presentations, emotions, and judgments. All three are described as acts of mental directedness upon something.[37] By "presentation" Brentano means an act in which something is consciously registered. By "emotion" he means an affective attitude taken in regard to some presentation. By "judgment" he means an act of "acceptance (as true) or rejection (as false)" directed upon some presentation. Brentano concludes that presentations have a founding priority with regard to emotions and judgments, inasmuch as the latter acts rely on presentations to provide the contents upon which they are directed.[38] Judgment is essentially the acceptance or rejection of what is presented in a neutral fashion to the mind. There is no reason, he adds, to presume that presentations must be complex (i.e., propositional). Indeed, he finally contends that

---

[34] ARISTOTLE, *On Interpretation*, I, iii, 16b 25-26. See M. HEIDEGGER, *The Metaphysical Foundations of Logic*, §1, p. 22-30.

[35] R. DESCARTES, *Medit. III, The Philosophical Writings*, trans. J. Cottingham. R. Stoothof, and D. Murdoch, Cambridge: Cambridge Univ. Press, 1984, II, p. 25-26; *Oeuvres de Descartes*, ed. Ch. Adam and P. Tannery, Paris, 1964-76, VII, p. 37. In the *Principles of Philosophy*, Descartes speaks only of perceptions and volitions, and counts acts of judgment as acts of volition. *The Philosophical Writings*, I, p. 216-218 (*Oeuvres*, I, pp. 32 and 35).

[36] R. DESCARTES, *Principles of Philosophy, The Philosophical Writings*, I, 204-207; *Oeuvres*, I, 18-21. See M. HEIDEGGER, *The Metaphysical Foundations of Logic*, §1, p. 35.

[37] F. BRENTANO, *Psychology from an Empirical Standpoint*, 79.

[38] F. BRENTANO, *Psychology from an Empirical Standpoint*, 198-199.

the presentations upon which judgments are directed are bereft of the syntactical articulations characteristic of our linguistic expressions. This position was apparently motivated by his resistance to the notion of admitting states of affairs into the ontological realm.

In the Fifth Investigation, Husserl makes a compelling critique of Brentano's thesis that judgment is the taking of a position with regard to a presented content. As we mentioned above, he first distinguishes two components which together comprise the intentional essence of an act: its quality and its matter. According to Husserl, Brentano's thesis leads to ambiguities, unless it is interpreted in the following manner. A neutral presentation must be considered as a complete intentional act, having both quality and matter. When I frame a proposition as a mere hypothesis, I engage in a complete act whose quality may be described as non-positional. When I subsequently assert the same claim, whose content may be affirmative or negative, I modify the quality from non-positional to positional. Thus, the act-qualities change while the act-matters remain constant.[39] Moreover, when I do entertain a proposition as such, I do not thereby collapse its content into a syntax-free whole. To claim that judgments have to do with simple objects rather than syntactically structured objects is to suggest that judgments necessarily nominalize their contents. Nominalization occurs when we name what had heretofore been asserted thus converting an originally articulated object into a compressed whole which may then serve as the subject of a another judgment.[40] But this is not what happens when we consider a proposition as such. In the latter situation, we maintain the articulated structure of the proposition while simply neutralizing our assent.

Husserl thus agrees with Brentano that we must distinguish between predication and judgmental assertion. However, he disagrees with Brentano's description of judgment as an acceptance or rejection of a neutralized presentation. In our straightforward dealings with the world, we are ordinarily preoccupied with things and their properties, rather than with what we are saying. Husserl makes it clear that even when we talk about present or absent facts we are talking about those facts and not about propositions: "... we judge about the thing it concerns, and not about the statement's meaning, about the judgment in the logical sense. This latter first becomes objective for us in a reflex act of thought in which we ... look back on the statement just made."[41] Husserl also points out that Brentano's account of judgment unfortunately suggests that the event of truth always requires a comparison between a thematized content and the fact which it articulates. The belief that such-and-such is the case arises out of what Husserl calls "the context of fulfillment."[42] Judgment is therefore an assertive attitude which pervades a statement and which is governed by anticipated (or

---

[39] E. HUSSERL, *Logical Investigations*, V, §22-31, pp. 597-619.

[40] E. HUSSERL, *Logical Investigations*, V, §37-8, pp. 636-41. See R. SOKOLOWSKI, *Presence and Absence*, 52

[41] E. HUSSERL, *Logical Investigations*, I, §34, p. 332.

[42] E. HUSSERL, *Logical Investigations*, V, §29, p. 615.

concomitantly experienced) intuitions of the forms of things, rather than by some sort of appraisal of the sense of the statement.

Formal and Transcendental Logic contributes some refinements to Husserl's theories of judgment and truth. In this later work, Husserl draws a crucial distinction between two types of truth: truth as correctness and truth as actual presence. The critical sense of truth, i.e., truth as correctness, occurs when a proposition is verified by matching it to the relevant intuited fact. This process involves a shift from an apophantic focus on the proposition as such (the fact taken as supposed) to an ontological focus on a remembered or reenacted registration of that fact in the fullness of its presence.[43] Truth as actual presence occurs in the manifestation of a fact in its fullness. The latter mode of truth is more fundamental, and often occurs without being preceded by any focus on a proposition as such. In the latter instance, the transition from empty to full articulation of facts takes place entirely within an ontological focus. Judgment is essentially an assertive articulation that brings a state of affairs to disclosure.

This refinement is the product of Husserl's struggle with the ambiguities generated by the modern interpretation of mind as an enclosure cut off from the world. The modern tendency to construe judgments as appraisals of propositional contents, and thus to acknowledge only the truth of correctness and to neglect the truth of disclosure is closely linked to the modern loss of a robust sense of Aristotelian realism. Husserl's reaffirmation of the Aristotelian notion of judgment is, therefore, more than a mere repetition. It brings out a sense of truth that is latent but not fully articulated in Aristotle's account of judgment.

IV. CONCLUSION

In his recent book, *The Last Word*, Thomas Nagel suggests that philosophy does not yet have, and indeed may never have, the linguistic or conceptual categories requisite for a fully coordinating phenomenological and objective viewpoints. Indeed, he suspects that the desire to have a complete and coherent account of the whole betrays a form of idealism that limits what there is and how things are to what we can in principle think about. Scientism, he says, is an example of such an idealism because it dictates that a single type of human knowledge exhausts our understanding of the universe and what can be said about it.[44] It seems to me that the greatest strength of Husserl's phenomenology is that its emphasis on the correlation between intentional acts and attitudes and the different ways in which things are manifested permits him to achieve methodological clarity about the kinds of intentionality operative in the experience of everyday life, in the exact sciences, in the physical sciences, and in philosophy itself. Phenomenology clarifies and dissipates the ambiguities that undergird debates such as

---

[43] E. HUSSERL, *Formal and Transcendental Logic*, §46, p. 127. See also R. SOKOLOWSKI, *Husserlian Meditations*, 233-234; 281-282.

[44] T. NAGEL, *The View From Nowhere*, Oxford: Oxford Univ. Press, 1986, 9.

the one between Malebranche and Arnauld. It does not provide us with an overarching linguistic and conceptual framework, but it does permit us to distinguish and coordinate in a non-reductive manner the multiple ways in which things manifest their truth.

DAN ZAHAVI
University of Copenhagen

METAPHYSICAL NEUTRALITY IN
LOGICAL INVESTIGATIONS

Metaphysische Fragen gehen uns hier nicht an. ...
Prolegomena

One of the striking features of *Logical Investigations* is its *metaphysical neutrality*. What are the implications of this neutrality? Should it be counted among the many virtues of the work, or rather mourned as a fateful shortcoming? In an article published in the beginning of the 1990s, I answered this question rather unequivocally.[1] At that time I considered the neutrality in question to be highly problematic. In the meantime, however, I have had the pleasure of reading Jocelyn Benoist's recent work *Phénoménologie, sémantique, ontologie,* where he argues for the opposite conclusion, criticizing my own interpretation in the process. In the light of this criticism, I would like to use this occasion to reconsider the question anew.

I. The Question of Metaphysical Neutrality

Let me start by examining the textual evidence that speaks in favor of interpreting *Logical Investigations* as being metaphysically neutral.

In the preface to the work, Husserl describes his overall project. He characterizes *Logical Investigations* as providing a new foundation for pure logic and epistemology (LI, 42 [Hua XVIII, 6]). It is in particular the status of logic and the conditions of possibility for scientific knowledge and theory which has his interest. However, the concept of epistemology used by Husserl in *Logical Investigations* is slightly different from the one currently in use. According to Husserl, the cardinal question for a theory of knowledge is to establish how objective knowledge is possible, i.e., to spell out the conditions of possibility for knowledge. The task is not to examine whether (and how) consciousness can attain knowledge of a mind-independent reality. These very types of question, as well as all questions as to whether or not there is at all an external reality, are rejected by Husserl as being *metaphysical questions*, which have to place in epistemology (LI, 264 [Hua XIX, 26]).

More generally, Husserl understands metaphysics as a narrow discipline which investigates and assesses the metaphysical presuppositions of those sciences which deal

---

[1] D. ZAHAVI, "Constitution and ontology. Some remarks on Husserl's ontological position in the *Logical Investigations.*" *Husserl Studies* 9, 1992, 111-124. Cf. D. ZAHAVI *Intentionalität und Konstitution. Eine Einführung in Husserls Logische Untersuchungen.* Copenhagen: Museum Tusculanum Press, 1992.

with *reality*. More specifically, its main task is to answer questions concerning the nature and existence of external reality. In contrast, the scope of a theory of science (*Wissenschaftslehre*) is much broader. It is concerned with the conditions of possibility for all types of sciences, including ideal sciences such as mathematics, which are completely disinterested in any questions concerning existence (LI, 59 [Hua XVIII, 27]). It is in light of this distinction that Husserl can claim that a theory of science constitutes the real foundational discipline, and that it has a clear priority over metaphysics (LI, 221 [Hua XVIII, 226]).

If we leaf through the book, we will find numerous passages affirming this rejection of metaphysics. In the introduction to the second part, Husserl describes phenomenology as a *neutral* investigation (LI, 249 [Hua XIX, 6), and claims that epistemological concerns precede every metaphysics (LI, 265 [Hua XIX, 27]). Husserl then goes on to emphasize that all of the six ensuing investigations are distinguished by their metaphysical presuppositionlessness, for, as he writes, the aim of phenomenology is exactly to *describe* and *understand* the ideal structures of knowledge, not to *explain* how knowledge comes about (LI, 265-66 [Hua XIX, 27-28]).

In the Second Investigation Husserl brusquely rejects the metaphysical definition of the being-in-itself as something which is transcendent to and independent of consciousness, and argues that all metaphysical definitions of reality (*Realität*) should be set aside (LI, 352 [Hua XIX, 129], cf. LI, 411 [Hua XIX, 201]).[2] Later, in the Fifth Investigation, he explicitly stresses the difference between the metaphysical and the phenomenological endeavor, and goes on to say that the descriptive difference between experience and object is valid regardless of one's take on the question concerning the nature of the being-in-itself. In fact, it is a difference which precedes every metaphysics (LI, 569 [Hua XIX, 401]). Finally, in the Sixth Investigation, Husserl criticizes Kant for not having managed to stay clear of a metaphysically contaminated epistemology, and then claims that metaphysical theories are uncalled for when it comes to an understanding of the relation between the laws of nature and the laws of reason. What is needed are not *explanations*, but phenomenological *clarifications* of meaning, thinking, and knowing (LI, 831, 833 [Hua XIX, 729, 732]).

In light of these statements it is not difficult to establish a solid link between the descriptive nature of phenomenology and its metaphysical neutrality. The task of phenomenology is to describe that which is given, exactly as it is given, rather than to get lost in metaphysical constructions. And as Benoist has pointed out, the line of thought is not that if we wish to do phenomenology we will have to be metaphysically neutral. It is the other way around. If we wish to establish a radical theory of science and epistemology we will have to be metaphysically neutral, and the only way to become so is by adopting a phenomenological methodology.[3]

---

[2] In his "Entwurf einer Vorrede zu den 'Logischen Untersuchungen (1913)'." *Tijdskrift voor Philosophie* 1, 1939, 325, Husserl accuses Lotze for having failed to do so and consequently for having fallen victim to a mythological metaphysics.

[3] J. BENOIST, *Phénoménologie, sémantique, ontologie,* Paris: PUF, 1997, 209.

II. REALISM - IDEALISM

By now it should have become clear that Husserl does in fact advocate a metaphysical neutrality in *Logical Investigations*. But what exactly does this imply? What kinds of questions or problems are suspended or overcome due to this neutrality? Given that Husserl regards the question concerning the existence of an external reality as a metaphysical question which is irrelevant to phenomenology, it is not so difficult to pinpoint the crucial issue, which is Husserl's stance towards metaphysical realism and idealism. Both positions are exactly metaphysical and consequently to be shunned.

Let me expand a bit on this assessment, since it is not completely uncontroversial. After all, it was not only Husserl's Göttingen students who read *Logical Investigations* as a realist manifesto. Prominent scholars like Lévinas and Findlay have defended a similar interpretation. Thus, in *Théorie de l'intuition dans la phénoménologie de Husserl* Lévinas argues that Husserl's early theory of intentionality must be taken in support of a realism, and in an article entitled "Phenomenology, Realism, and Logic" written 40 years later, Findlay has claimed that Husserl was originally a metaphysical realist, and that he only became a metaphysical idealist after his transcendental turn.[4]

Can this realistic interpretation of Husserl's early theory of intentionality hold up to closer scrutiny? In the Fifth Investigation Husserl is careful to point out that the intentional relationship between the act and the object is exactly intentional, and neither real nor causal. Moreover, he famously argues that intentionality is an intrinsic feature of consciousness, and not something which appears or disappears depending upon whether or not the intentional object exists:

> In real (*reell*) phenomenological treatment, objectivity counts as nothing: in general, it transcends the act. *It makes no difference what sort of being we give our object, or with what sense or justification we do so, whether this being is real* (real) *or ideal, genuine, possible or impossible, the act remains 'directed upon' its object.* If one now asks how something non-existent or transcendent can be the intentional object in an act in which it has no being, one can only give the answer we gave above, which is also a wholly sufficient one. The object is an intentional object: this means there is an act having a determinate intention, and determinate in a way which makes it an intention towards this object. This 'reference to an object' belongs peculiarly and intrinsically to an act-experience and the experiences manifesting it are by definition intentional experiences or acts. *All*

---

[4] J.N. FINDLAY, "Phenomenology, Realism and Logic." *Journal of the British Society for Phenomenology* 3/3, 1972, 235-244; E. LÉVINAS, *Théorie de l'intuition dans la phénoménologie de Husserl.* Paris: J. Vrin, 1978.

differences in mode of objective reference are descriptive differences in intentional experiences. (LI, 587 [Hua XIX, 427])

Given this unequivocal statement it seems mistaken to look for some kind of counterpart to Kant's refutation of idealism in Husserl's early theory of intentionality. Husserl is certainly not arguing that one on the basis of the object-directedness of consciousness can infer that if consciousness exists then there must necessarily also exist something mind-independent towards which it can be directed.

Occasionally, another aspect of Husserl's theory of intentionality has been taken in favor of a (direct) realism, namely his strong criticism of representationalism. The textual basis for this interpretation has been a passage in the Fifth Investigation, where Husserl ridicules the attempt to distinguish between the intentional object on the one hand and the real and transcendent object on the other:

> It need only be said to be acknowledged *that the intentional object of a presentation is the same as its actual object, and on occasion as its external object, and that it is absurd to distinguish between them.* The transcendent object would not be the object of *this* presentation, if it was not *its* intentional object. This is plainly a merely analytic proposition. The object of of the presentation, of the 'intention', *is* and *means* what is presented, the intentional object. (LI, 595-596 [Hua XIX, 439]. See also Hua III/1, 207-8)

The argument has been that since Husserl denies this distinction, the implication must be that he does in fact take us to have real, transcendent, mind-independent objects as our intentional objects, for which reason he must be a realist. However, this conclusion is premature. Husserl's identification of the intentional object and the real object must be read in a particular context, namely as a criticism of Twardowski's triadic theory of intentionality, and merely signifies that the intentional object is the real object of the intention, i.e., that there is no difference between the *intentional object* and the *intended object*. Twardowski claimed that our directedness towards the real intended object is mediated by an intra-mental intentional object which represents the real object.[5] In contrast, Husserl claims that the only object which we can be directed at is the object of our intention, i.e., the intentional object. This is not to say that all intentional objects are real, but only that if the intended object really exists, then it is this real object, and no other, which is our intentional object. In other words, the distinction to be made is not the one between the intentional object and the real object, but the one between the merely intentional object, and the real and intentional object. As Husserl writes:

---

[5] K. TWARDOWSKI, *Zur Lehre vom Inhalt und Gegenstand der Vorstellungen*. Wien: Philosophia Verlag, 1982.

'The object is merely intentional' does not, of course, mean that it exists, but only in an intention, of which it is a real (*reelles*) part, or that some shadow of it exists. It means rather that the intention, the reference to an object so qualified, exists, but not that the object does. If the intentional object exists, the intention, the reference, does not exist alone, but the thing referred to exists also. (LI, 596 [Hua XIX, 439])

As long as the object does not exist, it has no mode of existence at all, it is only intended (*vermeint*) (LI, 558 [Hua XIX, 386]). If the object exists, however, it is not only intended but also *given*. To put it differently: according to Husserl we do indeed intend real existing objects. But that our intentional objects are real and existing is a purely descriptive characterization. It does not carry any metaphysical connotations. Husserl's distinction between the really existing intentional object and the merely intentional object is based on descriptive variations in the mode of givenness of the object, i.e., all that is signified by the expression 'real object' is that the intended object *appears* as existent. It is *presented* in a perceptual mode of givenness. As the last sentence in *Logical Investigations* has it: "One must not forget, of course, that 'actual' [*wirklich*] does not here mean the same as 'external to consciousness', but the same as 'not merely putative'."(LI, 869 [Hua XIX, 775]).[6]

So much for a realistic interpretation of Husserl's theory of intentionality in *Logical Investigations*.[7] The attempt to read the work in an idealistic vein has been far less widespread. Perhaps because Husserl himself unequivocally condemns any kind of phenomenalism:

---

[6] Although Husserl's assertion is contextually related to a discussion of the sensations, it has a wider application. See for instance his parallel discussion in the Second Investigation (LI, 359 [Hua XIX, 139]).

[7] It has occasionally been claimed that even though Husserl is not a metaphysical realist when it comes to spatiotemporal objects, his Platonism in the *Prolegomena* does commit him to some kind of metaphysical realism about ideal objects. In reply, it might first of all be pointed out that Husserl himself subsequently emphasized that he was not trying to argue for the *existence* of ideal objects in a separate supernatural realm, but that he was simply engaged in a defense of the *validity* of ideality. In short, he was advocating a *logical* and not an *ontological* Platonism (Hua XXII, 156-157). Secondly, Husserl's 'Platonism' is mainly to be found in the *Prolegomena*, but the main part of this text dates back from 1896, and it has often been debated whether it truly forms an integrated whole with the rest of the *Logical Investigations*. In other words, it remains contested whether the *Prolegomena* is at all a phenomenological piece of work, or whether it does not rather remain pre-phenomenological. Thirdly, and most importantly, even if one concedes that it is possible to find assertions that seems to indicate a realism in regard to ideal objects, this does obviously not change the fact that Husserl quite explicitly speaks out against metaphysical realism and that he defines phenomenology in terms of a metaphysical neutrality. In short, even if Husserl's 'Platonism' does commit him to some form of metaphysical realism, this would not turn *Logical Investigations* into a piece of realist metaphysics, it would only confirm (cf. p. 101 below) that the work contains some serious internal tensions.

> It is the fundamental defect of phenomenalistic theories that they draw no distinction between appearance (*Erscheinung*) as intentional experience, and the apparent object (the subject of the objective predicates), and therefore identify the experienced complex of sensations with the complex of objective features. (LI, 546 [Hua XIX, 371])

> However we may decide the question of the existence or non-existence of phenomenal external things, we cannot doubt that the reality of each such perceived thing cannot be understood as the reality of a perceived complex of sensations in a perceiving consciousness. (LI, 862 [Hua XIX, 764–65])

On a purely descriptive level, there is a manifestational difference between the object and the experience. It is this descriptive difference which phenomenalism and subjective idealism ignores, and which therefore legitimizes a phenomenological refutation of these two metaphysical positions (cf. LI, 547 [Hua XIX, 371]).

To a certain extent, it might actually be said that Husserl's criticism of representationalism does support a kind of *direct* realism. We are 'zunächst und zumeist' directed at real existing objects, and this directedness is not mediated by any intra-mental objects. But if one wants to call this epistemological position realism, it has to be emphasized that it is a realism based on experience. It is an experiential or internal realism, and it has no affinities with a metaphysical, external, realism.

In the same breath, and perhaps even more appropriately, one might say that Husserl's criticism of representationalism can be seen as a criticism of both realism and idealism. If one defines the opposition between realism and idealism with the use of the doublet internal representation/external reality—whereas idealism claims that the only entity existing is the intra-mental representation, realism claims that the mental representation corresponds to an extra-mental and mind-independent object—it is obvious that Husserl must reject both.

Of course, this fact also illustrates that it would be a mistake to interpret Husserl's metaphysical neutrality as a mere expression of impotence. That Husserl is metaphysical neutral neither implies that he is incapable of criticizing certain metaphysical positions, nor that he has nothing whatsoever to say on the realism-idealism issue. It does entail, however, that whatever he has to say on the issue must be based on descriptive analyses of the structure of intentionality.

III. Liberation or Restriction

Finally to the central question: how should we appraise Husserl's metaphysical neutrality? Is it to be regarded as a weakness or a strength? Is Husserl's refusal to commit himself to either a metaphysical idealism or realism a fatal flaw, does it condemn phenomenology to remain within such narrow boundaries that an answer to the central metaphysical questions will forever remain outside its reach, or is it rather to be considered as a decisive advantage, as a refusal to choose between two equally unattractive positions, and therefore as a liberating move that opens up new vistas?

As already mentioned, Benoist opts for the second conclusion. To pinpoint his central claim: the decisive merit of *Logical Investigations* is its discovery of a new non-mentalistic notion of phenomenon and appearance. This discovery once and for all situates the phenomenological enterprise beyond not only every kind of representationalism and phenomenalism, but also beyond any dispute between idealism and realism:

> On ne peut être plus clair: le 'problème métaphysique' de la connaissance, à savoir précisément la question du choix entre le réalisme et l'idéalisme, est supprimé par la phénoménologie. S'il l'est, c'est que se placer dans une attitude purement descriptive, c'est déconstruire les conditions mêmes du problème, à savoir les interprétations objectivantes prédéterminées (et en elles-mêmes 'métaphysiques') qui modifient toujours déjà le donné et altèrent son caractère phénoménologiquement déterminé. C'est qui apparaît, en tant que pur apparaître, n'est ni dedans ni dehors, ni moi, ni non-moi. C'est pur 'phénomène', 'donné'.[8]

One should consequently avoid misinterpreting the phenomenon mentalistically or psychologically. Rather, we are dealing with a question of givenness: a givenness that is more fundamental than the fact that it is a givenness of something for somebody. Thus, Benoist takes givenness to be the central concept of phenomenology, and argues that it is only within this field or framework that it makes sense to discuss issues like reality, ideality, subjectivity, and objectivity.[9] This is exactly why Husserl sought to replace the notions of inner and outer (notions which he claimed had their origin in a naïve commonsensical metaphysics) with the phenomenological difference between adequate and inadequate givenness. To speak of something as inner or outer (psychical or physical) is to engage in a founded and highly misleading metaphysical interpretation, and for that reason descriptive phenomenology should stay clear of those categories (cf. LI, 786, 814 [Hua XIX, 673, 708]).

It is important not to conceive of this as implying a defense of some kind of *neutral monism*, since Husserl himself quite explicitly rejects such a program as being phenomenologically false:

---

[8] J. BENOIST, *Phénoménologie, sémantique, ontologie*, 228. Cf. 274.

[9] J. BENOIST, *Phénoménologie, sémantique, ontologie*, 285. It is not clear to me, however, how Benoist would reconcile this interpretation with the fact that Husserl in *Logical Investigations* advocates the existence of non-intentional experiences.

>These two, the colour-sensation and the object's objective colouring, are often confounded. In our time people have favoured a form of words according to which both are the same thing, only seen from a different standpoint, or with a different interest: psychologically or subjectively speaking, one has a sensation, physically or objectively speaking, one has a property of an external thing. [...] It is phenomenologically false to say that the difference between a conscious content in perception, and the external object perceived (or perceptually intended) in it, is a mere difference in mode of treatment [...]. (LI, 537-538 [Hua XIX, 359])

Although givenness is basic and therefore prior to an ontological distinction between inner and outer, psychical and physical, it is not undifferentiated. On the contrary, on the purely descriptive level there is a manifestational difference between the experience and the object. There are two sides to a phenomenon: It does not only comprise the experience *qua* access to the object, but also the object *qua* appearing. This difference is internal to the given, and is not the result of a subsequent metaphysical interpretation.

*

Let me initially say that I am sympathetic towards Benoist's appraisal of Husserl's metaphysical neutrality, since it—in contrast to my own former interpretation—makes *Logical Investigations* into a more interesting philosophical work. When this is said, I also have to add, however, that I am unable to follow him all the way. First of all, and this is even acknowledged by Benoist himself, not everything in *Logical Investigations* supports his interpretation. Secondly, I think there is an unresolved tension in Benoist's interpretation which I will try to spell out in a moment. And finally, I think that even if one does accept Benoist's reading, Husserl's metaphysical neutrality will still entail some highly problematic implications.

1. Back in 1919, Heidegger made the observation that Husserl's original self-interpretation of *Logical Investigations* was very inadequate, and that it was consequently necessary to distinguish between Husserl's meta-reflections and his actual analyses.[10] One of the reasons for this critical remark was Husserl's characterization of phenomenology as a descriptive psychology in the introduction to the second part of the work (LI, 262 [Hua XIX, 24]), a characterization which Husserl was to regret and reject already in 1903 and with good reasons since it failed to capture what was actually at stake (Hua XXII, 206-208).[11] Why then mention this initial blunder? Because it does

---

[10] M. HEIDEGGER, *Grundprobleme der Phänomenologie 1919/20*. Frankfurt a.M.: Vittorio Klostermann, 1993, 13-15. Cf. M. HEIDEGGER, *Prolegomena zur Geschichte des Zeitbegriffs*. Frankfurt a.M.: Vittorio Klostermann, 1979, 31.

[11] Cf. LI 47-48 [Hua XVIII, 12-13] and E. HUSSERL, "Entwurf einer Vorrede", 325.

not match very well with the interpretation of Husserl's metaphysical neutrality presented above. As Benoist himself admits: To interpret the phenomenological investigation of the structure of appearance and phenomena in psychological terms constitutes nothing but a mentalistic relapse back into metaphysics.[12]

This is not the only discrepancy and internal tension in *Logical Investigations*, however. In the introduction, Husserl also appears to identify phenomenology with the analysis of the immanent (*reell*) content of mental acts, and asserts that one has to turn the theoretical interest away from the objects and towards the acts (LI, 255, 265 [Hua XIX, 14, 28]). This methodological restriction is frequently repeated later in the work. In the Third and Fifth Investigation Husserl distinguishes between the immanent and phenomenological content on the one hand, and the intentional content on the other (LI, 442, 576 [Hua XIX, 237, 411]), and he also stresses the importance of discounting the intentional object in the description of the act, because of the act-transcendence of the object (LI, 256, 587 [Hua XIX, 16, 427]). In other words, if one looks at Husserl's programmatic statements he seems to exclude both the intentional *content* as well as the intentional *object* from the sphere of research (cf. LI, 415 [Hua XIX, 206]). All that is left to phenomenology seems to be noetic analyses.

A clear contrast to these utterances is, however, already to be found in the very same introduction. Thus, Husserl also declares that the act possesses both a proper (immanent) content and an ideal intentional content (LI, 259-60 [Hua XIX, 21]), and that the objective reference is a descriptive trait of the intentional experience itself (LI, 264 [Hua XIX, 25]). Husserl's last comment is confirmed in the Fifth Investigation, with its focus on intentionality. A careful study of this Investigation immediately reveals that Husserl constantly makes references to both the intentional object and the intentional content in his analysis. Not only does his investigation disclose that the act is *composed* of an immanent content, it also *instantiates* an intentional content, and *constitutes* an intentional object.

Nevertheless, the fact remains that a reading of Husserl's metaphysical neutrality which seeks to link it to the discovery of a notion of givenness that precedes a static opposition between subject and object clashes with quite a number of Husserl's own methodological reflections. That *Logical Investigations* had been far too noetically oriented was clear to Husserl by the time of the second edition of the work. As he adds in a long footnote in the Fifth Investigation:

> In the First Edition I wrote 'real *or* phenomenological' for 'real'. The word 'phenomenological' like the word 'descriptive' was used in the First Edition only in connection with *real* (*reelle*) elements of experience, and in the present edition it has so far been used predominantely in this sense. This corresponds to one's natural starting with the psychological point of view. It became plainer and plainer, however, as I reviewed the completed Investigations and

---

[12] J. BENOIST, *Phénoménologie, sémantique, ontologie*, 215.

pondered on their themes more deeply—particularly from this point onwards—that the description of intentional objectivity as such, as we are conscious of it in the concrete act-experience, represents a distinct descriptive dimension where purely intuitive description may be adequately practiced, a dimension opposed to that of real (*reellen*) act-constituents, but which also deserves to be called 'phenomenological'. These methodological extensions lead to important extensions of the field of problems now opening before us and considerable improvements due to a fully conscious separation of descriptive levels. Cf. my *Ideen zu einer reinen Phänomenologie*, Book I, and particularly what is said of *Noesis* and *Noema* in section III. (LI, 576 [Hua XIX, 411]. Cf. Hua XVIII, 13, Hua III/1, 296)

2. If I now turn to the second of my reservations, I think it is virtually impossible to appraise the phenomenological project in *Logical Investigations* without taking a stand on its relation to Husserl's later works.

- A classical interpretation of the relationship between Husserl's early descriptive phenomenology and his later transcendental phenomenology is that the latter represents a fatal turn from a metaphysical realism to a metaphysical idealism. As we have already seen, this interpretation fails for a very simple reason: Husserl did not advocate a metaphysical realism in *Logical Investigations*. Moreover, it is debatable whether Husserl ever advocated a metaphysical idealism.

- Another interpretation argues that Husserl's transcendental turn must be welcomed, since it represents an attempt to overcome some of the shortcomings of *Logical Investigations*. In other words, it was in order to solve problems inherent in his descriptive phenomenology that Husserl was forced to adopt a transcendental standpoint. Needless to say, this reading is in tune with Husserl's own account of the matter. If one looks at texts written in the years following *Logical Investigations*, one will find frequent remarks regretting its flaws. In a letter to Hans Cornelius from September 1906, for instance, Husserl writes that his reflections on the nature of phenomenology in the introduction contained a very inadequate expression of the actual method and sense of the Investigations (Hua Dok III/2, 29).[13] And in the lecture course *Einleitung in die Logik und Erkenntnistheorie* from 1906-7 Husserl argues that it is necessary to leave the project of a descriptive phenomenology behind in favor of a transcendental phenomenology if one wishes to truly clarify the relation between the act, the meaning, and the intended transcendent object. (Hua XXIV, 425-427)

---

[13] Cf. Hua IX, 29 and E. HUSSERL, "Entwurf einer Vorrede", 109, 124, 329.

If one favors the second interpretation, as I do, it would be natural to welcome an interpretation of *Logical Investigations* which reads it in a transcendental or proto-transcendental manner. For if such a reading were possible, it would make a case for downplaying the difference between Husserl's descriptive phenomenology and his transcendental phenomenology, and consequently give less reason to criticize the type of phenomenology that we find in *Logical Investigations*.

Husserl himself subsequently claimed that *Logical Investigations* did in fact contain transcendental elements (Hua XXIV, 425, cf. Hua II, 91), a claim the young Heidegger also seemed to share. Thus in the lecture course *Grundprobleme der Phänomenologie* from 1919/20 Heidegger criticizes 'die Lippschen Schule' for taking *Logical Investigations* as a work in descriptive psychology, thereby overlooking the 'eigentlich stimulierende transzendentale Motiv'.[14]

Does Benoist's interpretation of *Logical Investigations* proceed along the same line? Does it offer us a proto-transcendental reading of the work? The radicality of Benoist's interpretation might become clearer if one compares it to the one offered by De Boer. De Boer has argued that Husserl in *Logical Investigations* firmly believed in the existence of an objective reality (the world of physics) behind the world of the phenomena, but that Husserl regarded this belief as a metaphysical presupposition from which his *psychological* analysis of intentionality could be isolated.[15] This reading certainly represents a non-transcendental interpretation of *Logical Investigations*. Not only does De Boer interpret Husserl's metaphysical neutrality very differently from Benoist—Husserl is metaphysically neutral not because he questions the legitimacy of the metaphysical questions, but simply because he takes metaphysical issues to lie beyond the realm of phenomenology—but De Boer even takes Husserl to be engaged in descriptive psychology. In contrast, Benoist's claim that the major contribution of the *Logical Investigations* consists in its elaboration of a new notion of givenness, a givenness which is taken to be so fundamental that it constitutes the framework within which discussions about issues like reality, ideality, subjectivity and objectivity can take place, sounds distinctly transcendental. In fact, the idea that the notion of givenness precedes the distinction between subject and object is an idea ordinarily associated with the much later, transcendental, Husserl.[16] Thus, one way to interpret Husserl's notion

---

[14] M. HEIDEGGER, *Grundprobleme der Phänomenologie 1919/20*, 15. This statement is rather surprising since it flatly contradicts the later Heidegger's more well-known interpretation, according to which the descriptive project in *Logical Investigations* was preferable to Husserl's later work, exactly because it was not yet contaminated by any transcendental concerns. As Heidegger formulates it in *Zur Sache des Denkens*: "Husserl selbst, der in den 'Logischen Untersuchungen' - vor allem in der VI. - nahe an die eigentliche Seinsfrage kam, konnte es in der damaligen philosophischen Atmosphäre nicht durchhalten; er geriet unter den Einfluß Natorps und vollzog die Wendung zur transzendentalen Phänomenologie, die ihren ersten Höhepunkt in den 'Ideen' erreichte. Damit war aber das Prinzip der Phänomenologie preisgegeben."(M. HEIDEGGER, *Zur Sache des Denkens*, Tübingen: Max Niemeyer, 1988, 47).

[15] T. DE BOER, *The Development of Husserl's Thought*, The Hague: Martinus Nijhoff, 1978, 195-197.

[16] For a very early statement cf. Hua XXIV, 242.

of 'fungierende Intentionalität' is by saying that it precedes the separation between inside and outside, subject and object, ego and world, and that all of these derived and founded distinctions simply articulate its differentiated structure.[17] A similar transcendental orientation appears when Benoist emphasizes that Husserl's account of intentionality in *Logical Investigations* should not merely be understood as an investigation of consciousness, but also as a clarification of the phenomenological status of the object, that is, that an investigation of intentionality must necessarily span both sides of the correlation.[18] In short, it seems natural to take Benoist's reading of Husserl's metaphysical neutrality as a proto-transcendental re-interpretation of *Logical Investigations*.

However, this is not at all the way Benoist sees it. Although he concedes that Husserl himself tended to interpret his own transcendental turn as a more consequent rethinking of the project that was launched in *Logical Investigations*,[19] Benoist nevertheless insists that Husserl's early descriptive phenomenology remains untainted by any form of transcendentalism.[20]

I find this attempt to block a proto-transcendental interpretation of *Logical Investigations* somewhat odd, but I suspect that it is in part motivated by Benoist's classical and rather narrow Kantian definition of the concept 'transcendental', which he explicitly links to such issues as transcendental deduction and foundationalism.[21] I am, however, by no means sure that the Husserlian notion of transcendental philosophy coincides with the Kantian one, either methodologically or substantially. To put it differently, I fully concur with Benoist if the point he wishes to make is that the project defended by Husserl in *Logical Investigations* is different from the Kantian. However, I think something similar holds true even after Husserl's transcendental turn, and in that case there is no reason to emphasize *Logical Investigations* at the expense of his later works.[22] Or to be more precise, there might certainly be reasons to prefer *Logical*

---

[17] Cf. G. BRAND, *Welt, Ich und Zeit. Nach unveröffentlichten Manuskripten Edmund Husserls*, The Hague: Martinus Nijhoff, 1955, 28; J.G HART, *The Person and the Common Life*, Dordrecht: Kluwer Academic Publishers, 1992, 12; D. ZAHAVI, *Self-awareness and Alterity*, Evanston: Northwestern University Press, 1999, 121.

[18] J. BENOIST, *Phénoménologie, sémantique, ontologie*, 281.

[19] J. BENOIST, *Phénoménologie, sémantique, ontologie*, 208.

[20] J. BENOIST, *Phénoménologie, sémantique, ontologie*, 298.

[21] J. BENOIST, *Phénoménologie, sémantique, ontologie*, 298. Benoist also seems to welcome Husserl's non-egological position in *Logical Investigations* with its explicit criticism of any kind of I-metaphysics. I am more dubious about the merits of a non-egological position, but it would lead too far if I were to discuss this issue here. Cf. however D. ZAHAVI, "Self and Consciousness" in D. Zahavi (ed.): *Exploring the self. Philosophical and psychopathological perspectives on self-experience*, Amsterdam: John Benjamins, 2000, 55-74; D. ZAHAVI, "The Three Concepts of Consciousness in *Logische Untersuchungen*." *Husserl Studies* 18, 2002, 51-64.

[22] Ultimately, I think that Husserl's notion of the transcendental is so broad that it might even be used to capture what is at stake in the works of the later Wittgenstein or the early Merleau-Ponty.

Investigations to, say, *Ideas I,* but these reasons do not have to do with the fact that the first is descriptive and the other transcendental, but rather with the fact that *Logical Investigations* is not committed to the Cartesian approach to phenomenology that one finds in *Ideas I*. On the contrary, in some respects *Logical Investigations* seems to have more affinities with Husserl's ontological approach to phenomenology that we find, for instance, in *Crisis.*

One further detail concerns Benoist's claim that Husserl in *Logical Investigations* had moved beyond the alternative between realism and idealism. It is certainly true that Husserl did not commit himself to either a metaphysical realism or idealism, but the real question is whether he had also managed to transcend that very opposition. An answer to this question ultimately depends upon how one defines the terms 'realism' and 'idealism'. As we have already seen, it is possible to define them in a way that makes both of them unsuitable when it comes to a characterization of Husserl's early phenomenology. To provide another such definition: if one defines idealism as the position that claims that subjectivity can persist without the world, and realism as a position that claims that the world can persist without subjectivity, then it is obvious that a position that insists on a strict correlation between the two is beyond both realism and idealism. But, and that is the simple point I wish to make, given such a definition of realism it is also relatively easy to describe Husserl's position as a kind of idealism, or to be more exact, as a kind of *anti-realism,* namely, insofar as it is incompatible with the realism in question. (The lesson to learn is undoubtedly that the very notions of realism and idealism are so elastic that they are close to being useless.)[23]

3. Let me finally turn to my last and most important reservation. One way to test whether the conception of phenomenology that is expounded in *Logical Investigations* is liberating or restrictive is to ask whether there are any important philosophical issues that it rules out by definition. We have already seen that Husserl rejected the question as to the existence of an external reality as a metaphysical question which was irrelevant to phenomenology. One can react to this rejection of metaphysics in a number of different ways:

- One reaction is to say that the rejection of metaphysics and metaphysical issues is a liberating move, for the simple reason that these traditional questions are

---

[23] When it comes to Husserl's later position the opinions are also divided. Although many interpreters would argue that Husserl's avowed transcendental idealism is beyond both idealism and realism, there are many ways to interpret this claim. 1) One interpretation argues that transcendental idealism is beyond both realism and idealism in the sense that it strictly speaking is concerned with quite different matters altogether, that is, transcendental idealism simply lacks metaphysical impact. 2) Another possibility is to argue that transcendental idealism is beyond the traditional alternative between realism and idealism insofar as it actually seeks to combine elements from both positions. 3) Finally, it might also be argued that Husserl's transcendental idealism transcends the alternative insofar as it makes us realize that both metaphysical realism and subjective idealism (together with a lot of traditional metaphysical heritage) are strictly speaking nonsensical.

- pseudo-problems which have already spellbound philosophers for far too long.

- Another, rather different, response is to claim that it becomes phenomenology to finally acknowledge that it is merely a descriptive enterprise, and not the universal answer to all questions. In other words, there is a difference between phenomenology and metaphysics, and although the first might prepare the way for the latter, it does not in itself contain the resources to tackle metaphysical issues, and should therefore keep silent about that which it cannot speak.

- In contrast to these first two reactions which, for different reasons, welcome Husserl's metaphysical neutrality, the third option regrets it. It concedes that metaphysical problems are real problems, but since it also thinks that phenomenology has an important contribution to make in this area, it deplores Husserl's metaphysical neutrality as a self-imposed and unnecessary straitjacket.

Personally, I have a certain sympathy for all three reactions. (In fact I think they are less incompatible than one might assume at first glance. Thus, it could very well be argued that there is a variety of different metaphysical questions, and that some might fall in the first category, some in the second and some in the third, i.e., there are metaphysicals pseudoproblems which phenomenology is wise to abandon, metaphysical questions which are beyond its reach, and metaphysical questions which it is capable of addressing.) But even if one wholeheartedly embraces the first rather Wittgensteinian response, as I believe Benoist does, this will not solve the problem and remove all of the difficulties.

One of the striking features of Husserl's analysis of intentionality in *Logical Investigations* is his repeated claim that the difference between a veridical perception and a non-veridical perception (say, an illusion or a hallucination) is irrelevant to phenomenology. In fact, the *existence* of the intentional object is phenomenologically irrelevant, since the intrinsic nature of the act is supposed to remain the same regardless of whether or not the object exists (LI, 537, 539, 559, 565-66 [Hua XIX, 358, 360, 387, 396]). This attitude which seems to follow as a direct consequence of Husserl's metaphysical neutrality entails some highly problematic implications, one of them being that phenomenology is incapable of distinguishing between hallucinations and perceptions. In both cases we are dealing with a situation where the intentional object is *presented* in an intuitive mode of givenness. Whether or not this object also exists objectively is, however, a question which is methodologically suspended. But is this outcome philosophically satisfactory? Regardless of one's attitude towards metaphysics, if one wants to reserve a place for phenomenology in epistemology, the answer must be no. A theory of knowledge that is incapable of distinguishing between hallucinations and perceptions, between the merely intentional and the objective, is deficient. But in that case, there are good reasons to regret the metaphysical neutrality of Husserl's descriptive phenomenology. After Husserl's transcendental turn, however, these distinctions were no longer regarded as being irrelevant. On the contrary, Husserl's strong interest in the problem of intersubjectivity was exactly motivated by his wish to clarify the question of objectivity.[24] That Husserl's attitude towards metaphysics changed later is also clear from the following passages:

> Finally, I wish to point out—so as to avoid misunderstandings—that phenomenology excludes only that naive type of metaphysics which operates with absurd things in themselves, but it does not exclude metaphysics altogether. (Hua I, 38–39)

> Phenomenology is anti-metaphysical insofar as it rejects any metaphysics that moves in empty formal substructions. Like all genuine philosophical problems, however, everything metaphysical returns to a phenomenological basis, and it is here that it finds its transcendental form and method, genuinely drawn from intuition. (Hua IX, 253. Cf. Hua V, 141)[25]

To avoid misunderstandings, it must be emphasized that my criticism of Husserl's initial stance towards metaphysics should not be seen as an endorsement of every metaphysical endeavor. It is most definitely neither an attempt to deny the difference between the object-oriented nature of metaphysics and the reflective orientation of transcendental thought, nor an attempt to downplay the decisive difference between the natural and the phenomenological attitude. Ultimately, it is possible to define metaphysics in a variety of different ways, say 1) as a speculatively constructed philosophical system, 2) as a science of supersensible or transphenomenal entities, 3) as an objectivistic attempt to describe reality from a view from nowhere, i.e., as an attempt to provide an absolute non-perspectival account of reality, 4) as an answer to the old question of *why* there is something rather than nothing, 5) as a mode of thinking founded upon the 'logic' of binary oppositions, 6) as an attempt to answer the perennial questions concerning the meaning of factual human life, or 7) simply as a systematic reflection on the nature of existing reality. It is only if metaphysics is taken in the last 'minimal' sense that I consider metaphysical neutrality, and the attempt to distinguish sharply between meaning and being, as a questionable transcendental-phenomenological move, a move that threatens to reintroduce some kind of two-world theory: the world as it is for us, and the world as it is in itself. As Fink remarks in an article from 1939, only a complete misunderstanding of the aim of phenomenology leads to the mistaken but often repeated claim that Husserl's phenomenology is not interested in reality, not interested in the

---

[24] For an extensive discussion cf. D. ZAHAVI, *Husserl and Transcendental Intersubjectivity*, Athens: Ohio University Press, 2001.

[25] As L. LANDGREBE puts it, the reduction is Husserl's way to the metaphysical core-problems, *(Der Weg der Phänomenologie. Das Problem der ursprünglichen Erfahrung*, Gütersloh, Gerd Mohn, 1963, 26).

question of being, but only in subjective meaningformations in intentional consciousness.[26]

To conclude: I believe that Benoist has been successful in arguing that Husserl's metaphysical neutrality in *Logical Investigations* does indeed have its strong points. The work contains an important attempt to overcome the traditional separation between inner and outer, physical and psychical, subjectivity and world by focusing on givenness as the central category. Nevertheless, I still believe that there is a price to pay for this neutrality, and in the case in question, I believe the price to be too high.

---

[26] E. FINK, "Das Problem der Phänomenologie Edmund Husserls," *Revue Internationale de Philosophie I*, 1939, 257.

III

Categorial Intuition

ULLRICH MELLE
Husserl Archives—University of Leuven

HUSSERL'S REVISION OF THE SIXTH LOGICAL INVESTIGATION

I. THE HISTORY OF HUSSERL'S WORK ON THE REVISION OF THE SIXTH LOGICAL INVESTIGATION

Husserl was thinking of a revision of the *Logical Investigations* already in 1905 in connection with the failed plan for an English translation. In 1911 he began working on such a revision but because of his work on the first and second book of the *Ideas*, the work was delayed until after the publication of the *Ideas I* in April 1913. In the preface to the second edition of the *Prolegomena* and of the first five Investigations which appeared in the autumn of 1913 Husserl tells the reader that instead of republishing the *Logical Investigations* he originally planned to replace them by a series of systematic studies. When he realised, though, that this would take years to accomplish, he decided to write the *Ideas* first and to republish the *Logical Investigations* immediately afterwards. The *Logical Investigations* were to be revised so that they could be read and used as a complement to the *Ideas*, in that they would introduce the reader to concrete phenomenological work. The reader would first study the *Logical Investigations* and get acquainted with "attempts at genuinely executed fundamental work on the immediately envisaged and seized things themselves" and "with a group of fundamental questions in explicit investigation". Then, he would turn to the *Ideas* for the elucidation of the method from ultimate sources, the delineation of the main structures of pure consciousness and the systematic presentation of the fields of investigation (cf. LI, 44-45 [Hua XVIII, 9f]).

This conception of a complementary relationship between the *Ideas* and the new edition of the *Logical Investigations* gave rise to a dilemma. It was impossible to raise the *Logical Investigations* completely and as a whole to the level of the *Ideas*. This would have meant to postpone the publication of the second edition *ad calendas graecas*. A simple reprint, on the other hand, was insufficient for the intended use of the *Logical Investigations* as a complement to the *Ideas*. With a heavy heart Husserl chose a middle path between a total revision and a simple reprint. Husserl mentions three guidelines which he followed when revising the *Logical Investigations*. First, nothing would be retained of which he was not fully convinced that it was, even if not true, at least worthy of a careful study. Second, whatever could be improved without fundamentally changing the course and style of the work would be improved. Third, and most important regarding the Sixth Investigation, in the course of the *Logical Investigations* the reader should be gradually led to a higher level of insight so that in the final Investigation the level of the *Ideas* would be reached. According to this guideline only the revised sixth Investigation had to be wholly and fully at the level of the just published *Ideas I*. That meant, effectively, that what Husserl had regarded to be impossible regarding the whole of the *Logical Investigations* had to be achieved at least with regard to the Sixth Investigation: a radical and total revision.

Immediately after the publication of the *Ideas I* in April 1913, Husserl began to work on the revision of the *Logical Investigations*. In only two months he completed the revision of the *Prolegomena* and the first five Investigations. In approximately the middle of June Husserl turned towards the Sixth Investigation. On June 23 he wrote to Daubert: "I am in the middle of the revision of the sixth Investigation. Pity me! I have to finish the print (version) till the end of July."(Hua Dok. III/2, 65) Already in July the introduction and the first three chapters, as well as the first four paragraphs of the fourth chapter of the first part of the Sixth Investigation, were printed.

It is clear, from the proofs of the Introduction and of the first chapter, that Husserl started to revise the text of the Sixth Investigation in the same way as he had revised the previous five Investigations and the *Prolegomena*. He did not fundamentally alter the text of the first edition; the number, sequence and titles of the paragraphs are preserved, and he included even the same mistake in the numbering of the paragraphs in the first edition (it jumps from § 9 to § 11). Only at certain places was the text explicitly raised to the level of the *Ideas I*, by referring to the correlation between noesis and noema or to the difference between descriptive psychology and phenomenology. Just as in the revision of the *Prolegomena* and the first five Investigations, Husserl made ample use of the annotations in his author's copy of the *Logical Investigations*.

After he had received the prints of the Introduction and the first chapter, Husserl realised that a more radical revision was needed if he wanted to raise the Sixth Investigation to the level of the latest stage of his philosophical thinking. He started to rewrite the first chapter. Eventually he rewrote and enlarged the first five paragraphs of the first chapter using some of the pages from the proofs which were extensively revised. The proofs of the second, third and the first paragraphs of the fourth chapter and their detailed revision, together with the hand-written completion of the fourth chapter and the manuscript of the new fifth chapter show how much more radical and far-reaching the revision of the Sixth Investigation became.

On July 31 Husserl's wife wrote to Daubert that Husserl was working intensively on the Sixth Investigation: "It is hard work, the Sixth Investigation, the hardest that he has ever done." (Hua Dok. III/2, 68). In the middle of August the work came to a halt. Husserl went on vacation. At this point only the first part of the Sixth Investigation had been thoroughly revised and rewritten. The text of the chapters 2 – 4 had doubled in size compared to the first edition. During his vacation Husserl was visited by Daubert and it is very likely that they discussed Husserl's drafts for the revised Sixth Investigation. Unfortunately, we do not know anything about these discussions, including whether they had any influence on the decision Husserl made in the autumn of 1913 not to proceed with the revision of the Sixth Investigation.

When Husserl returned from vacation he tried to write a lengthy preface to the new edition of the *Logical Investigations*. But this work, too, he could not bring to a conclusion. The two fragmentary manuscripts were published after Husserl's death by Eugen Fink in the first issue of the *Tijdschrift voor Filosofie*. Finally, in October 1913 the new and revised edition of the *Logical Investigations* was published—without the Sixth Investigation. In the preface to this new edition Husserl gives the misleading impression that the new edition of the Sixth Investigation is completed and in print.

Notes about a new ordering of the drafts from the summer written on the back of an invitation to a conference which lasted from October 4–6, indicate that in October Husserl had not yet abandoned these drafts. However, in a letter to Gustav von Spett from December 29 (cf. Hua Dok. III/3, 531). Husserl writes that he has suffered from exhaustion during the previous months and that this has led to a further postponement of the publication of the Sixth Investigation "for a couple of months". As the letter makes clear further on, Husserl had in the meantime, i.e., since October, decided not to proceed with the revision from the summer of 1913, but to write a completely new Sixth Investigation. He mentions that he wants to do this on the basis of his extensive studies from the years 1902 to 1910. This refers to two extensive collections of older manuscripts Husserl put together as research material for his project of a new Sixth Investigation. It is probable that Husserl was busy for a while with collecting and studying this material.

In February 1914 Husserl writes to Aloys Fischer: "Right now I am in the middle of the new conception ("Neuausarbeitung") of the VI. Investigation." (Hua Dok III/2, 83), and in a letter from April 1914 he tells Rudolf Eisler that he is busy recomposing the final volume of his *Logical Investigations* (Hua Dok. III/6, 81). His work on the new Sixth Investigation in the winter, spring and early summer of 1914 consists of the writing of a new introduction and a new first chapter plus a number of research manuscripts which, thematically, are almost exclusively related to the newly conceived first chapter. The latest text from this radical effort to rewrite the Sixth Investigation is a "plan" for a "new presentation" from the summer of 1914. It shows that Husserl was still searching for a satisfying conception for the new Sixth Investigation. As he himself had predicted to try to rewrite the *Logical Investigations* meant to postpone its publication *ad calendas graecas*.

In 1917 Edith Stein used the revised proofs and manuscripts of the second, third and fourth chapter plus a few other manuscripts to compose two separate treatises entitled "The Emptiness Modification" and "Possibility and Consciousness of Possibility" for publication in the *Jahrbuch*. Since Husserl nowhere commented on Stein's work and since there are no corrections or remarks by Husserl nor any other traces of his reading in Stein's handwritten copies, it is possible that at the time he did not look at Stein's work.

In the spring of 1921 the second, only slightly revised, edition of the Sixth Investigation is finally published. In the preface to this edition Husserl expresses his regret that he was unable to publish the radically revised text of the Sixth Investigation as announced in the preface to the second edition of the *Prolegomena* and the first five Investigations from October 1913.

Probably in the early summer of 1924 Ludwig Landgrebe made typewritten copies of the new draft of the first chapter from 1914 plus a few short supplementary texts, from Stein's two treatises and from the stenographic manuscript of the fifth chapter from the summer of 1913. There are only a few amendments and remarks by Husserl, mostly in the typescript of the fifth chapter and in the typescript of the supplementary texts to the first chapter. It is not clear whether at that point Husserl was still thinking of a publication of the material.[1]

*

It is a great pity that Husserl, in the autumn of 1913 abandoned his work from the summer on the revision of the Sixth Investigation in order to write a completely new text. The drafts from the summer of 1913 are of an exceptional quality. They show that Husserl was well on his way to incorporate the most recent results of his vast research into the structures of intuitive, signitive and categorial acts, of perception, fantasy and judging, of modalities, modifications and intentional implications into a phenomenological theory of knowledge. The manuscripts he wrote for the new Sixth Investigation in 1914 are devoted to a new theory of signs and signification and, as such, are of great philosophical interest. But, with the exception of the new draft of the first chapter (possibly only of a part of the first chapter), they do not advance beyond the stage of research manuscripts. Of major importance in Husserl's analyses in these manuscripts is the difference between signitive and significative intention, the first intention being the tendency which issues from the sign and leads on to the meaning giving act, the second being the intention of the meaning-giving act itself. Intention in the form of a tendency, or a striving has to be distinguished here from intention in the sense of being consciously directed either emptily in an act of meaning or intuitively towards an object. In conjunction with the distinction between signitive and significative acts Husserl revises and simplifies his theory of fulfilment. In the state of fulfilment the empty intention has been supplanted by the intuitive intention, and the awareness of the verbal expression is directly related to the intuitive intention. Whereas in the old theory of the *Logical Investigations* the expression consists of the word-sign together with its meaning intention, in the new theory it is only the word-sign with its signitive intention which expresses either an empty meaning intention or an intuitive intention. What this amounts to is that, in this new theory, the verbal expression is reduced to its sign-function.[2]

*

---

[1] The whole body of Husserl's work on the revision of the Sixth Logical Investigation from the summer of 1913 and from the first half of 1914 is going to be published in two volumes in the *Husserliana* series.

[2] For a more detailed analysis of some of the texts from 1914 cf. my article "Signitive und signifikative Intentionen", *Husserl-Studies* 15/3, 1998/99, 167-181. Cf. further C. SINIGALIA, "Zeichen und Bedeutung. Zu einer Umarbeitung der Sechsten Logischen Untersuchung", *Husserl Studies* 14/3, 1997/98, 179-217 and R. BERNET, "Husserl's theory of signs revisited", in *Edmund Husserl and the Phenomenological Tradition. Essays in Phenomenology*, ed. by R. Sokolowski, Catholic University of America Press: Washington (DC), 1988, 1–24.

Returning to the work on the revision in the summer of 1913, the question arises why Husserl abandoned this work in the autumn of 1913. There are no indications that Husserl was dissatisfied with the overall quality of his work from the summer. His little "lie" in the preface of the second edition of the *Prolegomena* and the first five Investigations, that the Sixth Investigation was completed and in print, strongly suggests otherwise. There was certainly still much work to be done; in fact the whole second part of the Sixth Investigation still had to be worked through. But this would certainly not have been more work than writing a completely new text. A certain problem may have been that the revised text of the first part was already twice as long as the original text. A more serious problem existed regarding the original composition of the Sixth Investigation. It is one of the important new insights in the revised text that all meaning-giving acts are categorial acts which can only be fulfilled by categorial intuitions. According to this insight categorial acts have to be taken into account from the start whereas in the first edition they are only subsequently dealt with in the second part.

Judging from the manuscripts Husserl wrote for the new conception of the Sixth Investigation, there may be yet another reason for his abandonment of the revision from the summer of 1913. Husserl was particularly dissatisfied with the first Investigation. The new Sixth Investigation was to remedy the deficiencies of the first, particularly regarding the theory of signs. Finally there is an indication, in a letter to Hans Vaihinger from April 1914 (cf. Hua Dok. III/5, 212), that he turned away from the drafts from the summer because they did not originate in his current research activities and interests but only tried to integrate and summarise the results of his research from the previous years.

II. The New Draft of the First Chapter

The most important new insight in the new draft of the first chapter, or rather of the first five paragraphs of the first chapter is already intimated in his lecture-course on the theory of meaning from 1908. It consists in the statement that only acts of thought, i.e., categorial acts, can function as meaning-giving and meaning-fulfilling acts. According to the first edition, occasional expressions and proper names are acts of signification which refer directly and without categorial formation to an object and which are fulfilled by perception or by imagination. The new draft makes it clear that perception as such cannot fulfil a meaning intention, because all meaning intentions, even the nominal ones, are categorial and propositional acts, i.e., acts with a propositional function. Such acts can only be fulfilled by categorial intuitions, i.e., perceptions or imaginations which have been categorially formed.

If only categorial acts can be acts of meaning—be it as meaning giving or meaning fulfilling acts—then acts in order to be expressed, have to be transformed into categorial acts. The first edition opposes two possible answers to the question of which kinds of acts can function as meaning-giving acts. According to the first answer, all acts, of whatever kind, can be expressed, and by being expressed they function as meaning giving acts for these expressions. According to the second answer, to express is the function of particular expressive acts which create an intellectual expression of the act which is to be expressed. But does this not require a recognition, a classification of the act to be expressed "according to form and content"? In the first edition it is only in the final chapter, in § 67, that Husserl states that, as a result of his investigations into the relationship between meaning and corresponding intuition, we are immune to the mistaken view that the expression of an act requires the recognition of the act. In the new draft Husserl makes it clear from the start that to express an act does not mean that the expressed act is objectified, but that the signifying act and the expressed act form a unity of fulfilment.

In the first edition, however, only objectifying acts could be directly expressed without another mediating objectifying act. Non-objectifying acts became expressed like objects, that is only by way of the expression of an objectifying act directed at them. In the new draft, objectifying and non-objectifyting acts have to be categorially formed to be able to be expressed as acts which fulfil corresponding significative acts. This complete correspondence between categorial acts of meaning and categorial acts of fulfilment raises the question whether in the case of a fulfilled expression we can still distinguish a meaning giving act and a meaning fulfilling act. This question, which remains unanswered in the new draft, will be taken up again and will play an important role in the research manuscripts from 1914. Husserl will there argue that the intuitive act simply replaces the empty act when the expression is fulfilled.

III. THE REVISION OF THE SECOND AND THIRD CHAPTER

As to the proofs of the revised second and third chapter, they are of great interest because of the extensive treatment of empty intentions contained therein. Nowhere else has Husserl analysed empty intentions in such detail. This was recognised by Edith Stein when she read the texts in 1917. By deleting a number of paragraphs and adding material from two manuscripts on empty intentions, Stein formed a separate treatise out of the proofs of the revised second and third chapter to be published in the *Jahrbuch* under the title of "Emptiness Modification" ("Leermodifikation").

The fragmentary proofs of the revised second chapter—the proofs of §§ 14, 15 and of the beginning of § 15a are missing—contain three completely new paragraphs on empty intention. The revised text contains two important changes to the teachings of the first edition, in both of which empty intentions are involved. First, Husserl criticises his old account of wordless cognition. In the first edition Husserl maintained that wordless cognition consists of fulfilled meaning intentions which have detached themselves from the signitive contents which usually belong to them. In the new text Husserl claims that in wordless cognition, even where we cannot find the word, we are conscious of the word, albeit in a completely empty way. The word-sign has sunk into complete darkness but we are still conscious of it. Secondly, Husserl makes a distinction now between the signitive intentions on the one hand and the empty intentions in a perception on the other hand. A certain analogy between these intentions cannot be denied, but there is a clear essential difference between them. The analogy between these empty intentions in perception and the empty significative intentions consists in the fact that, in both cases, intuitive and empty intentions are connected by associative excitation and unification. But in the case of signitive intentions the acts involved relate two objects which are alien in their content ("sachfremd"), the sign and the object meant, to each other. In the case of perception we have the concrete unity of one real object which is constituted out of intentionally constituted elements which themselves are constituted in dependent and connected elementary intentions. The new paragraphs in the revised text are devoted to a description of the empty intention in perception.

Each perceptual intention of a thing is a unitary intention consisting of dependent elementary intentions. There are two fundamental kinds of elementary intentions in perception: intuitive intentions and empty intentions of contiguity. Husserl gives a concise description of the continuous unity of fulfilment of a perception. Two different series of coincidences ("Deckung") have to be distinguished: on the one hand the continuous coincidence connecting the continuous presentations of one and the same appearing moment of the object, on the other hand the continuous coincidence which connects that which comes to appearance for the first time with that which previously came to giveness. In accordance with these two different kinds of coincidence there are in perception two different kinds of indications which point beyond ("Fort- und Hinausweisungen"). First there are intuitive indications that point from that which appears in a certain orientation towards the same moment appearing in ever new orientations; secondly, connected with these intuitive intentions, there are empty intentions of contiguity which point beyond that which appears towards that which is contiguous with it but has not yet come to appearance. The first indications point inwards to an ever richer perception of one moment or side of the object, the second outwards to an ever more comprehensive perception of the object as a whole.

Husserl further pursues the analysis of perception and of empty representation in the revised text of chapter three, making use of his mature phenomenology of perception, fantasy and imagination, of his analysis of time-consciousness, and of his account of the constitution of the phantom and of the material thing. Whereas the first edition speaks of the aim of absolute knowledge in the ascending series of fulfilments and of a presentation from all sides, Husserl now points out that neither a thing as a whole nor any moment of a thing is ever given absolutely in a finite act of perception but only "in an endless play of intentions and fulfilments". It turns out that not only the perception of phantoms and things, but, equally, the perception of immanent objects includes empty intentions. The immanent object, too, is constituted necessarily in a continuous process of fulfilment of such empty intentions. It is the temporal character of the immanent object and its perception which necessarily makes this perception a mixture of already fulfilled, no longer fulfilled and not yet fulfilled intentions.

Husserl's analysis of the empty intention in the revised third chapter is connected to the overcoming of the residual sensualism in the first edition. There sense-data were conceived as a kind of stuff which filled an empty form, consisting of the matter and the quality of an act. This stuff was to be formed not only into the appearing of a particular object but also into the perceptual, imaginative or significative way of appearing. The apperceptive form ("Auffassungsform") determined whether the neutral stuff was to serve as intuitive or significative representatives ("Repräsentanten") and if as intuitive ones whether as sense-data or phantasms. Husserl liberated himself from this form of sensualism through his discovery that fantasy and imagination are intentional modifications of perception. In the revised text of the third chapter Husserl argues that the empty intention equally must be conceived of as an intentional modification.

In the first edition it was suggested that fulfilment and the increase of fulfilment are a matter of pouring an increasing amount of intuitive content into an empty form or that, in the opposite direction, an intuition can gradually be emptied of intuitive content until it turns into an empty representation. According to this view the filling would be a third, separate component besides matter and quality, a component which would simply be absent in an empty representation so that the empty intention would merely be qualified matter. This view Husserl now regards as unacceptable. A difference has to be made between an empty representation and an obscure intuition, i.e., an intuition emptied of intuitive content. Otherwise we are faced with an infinite regress regarding the empty intentions which belong to transcendent perceptions. If these were obscure intuitions, we would have to distinguish again between an intuitively given core and an emptily given fringe regarding their objects and the manners of givenness of these objects which would imply new empty intentions, and so on. Each transcendent perception would contain an actual infinity of representational components contained in ("ineinandergeschachtelt") each other. Empty representations are not intuitions emptied of intuitive content; they are peculiar intentional modifications of intuitions. They are not reproductive modifications like fantasy and remembering because, as such, they would contain reproductively modified moments of intuitive and empty givenness. This again would imply an actual infinity of representational components.

It is interesting to note that in one of the older manuscripts, parts of which Stein incorporated into her draft of a treatise, Husserl regards the concrete empty representation as a reproduction ("Vergegenwärtigung") which reproduces the perception with all its moments. By a concrete empty representation Husserl means a separate and independent act of representation. When perceiving the furniture in a lit room, if the light is suddenly switched off, the objects in the room are still given to us, albeit in an empty way in such a concrete empty representation. Another example Husserl gives for such a concrete empty representation is the interruption of a fantasy or memory ("Intermittieren der Phantasie"). The gap in our intuitive awareness does not mean that we lose consciousness, but instead of the previous intuitive intention we now have an empty intention, followed by the return of the intuitive awareness. If such concrete empty representations are reproductions of perceptions, then these concrete empty representations have to be distinguished from the empty intentions which are part of a perception in order to avoid the problem of the actual infinity of representational components. Descriptively, however, it is difficult to see a difference in the kind of emptiness of concrete empty representations and of non-independent empty intentions in perception. According to the new conception of the emptiness modification as a peculiar non-reproductive modification of intuition, we do not need to differentiate any longer between different kinds of emptiness.

Besides his analysis of the emptiness modification, Husserl, in his revision of the third chapter, gives a more elaborate account of the graduations of the filling. He now distinguishes a noematic from a noetic concept of the filling. The first refers to the extent to which an object comes to self-givenness, the latter to the pure intuitive content of a perception. This intuitive content is, as Husserl stresses again, even in immanent perception always mixed with empty intentional components.

As to the gradations of the filling, Husserl distinguishes between the range ("Umfang") and richness of the filling on the one hand and the liveliness and clarity of the objective presentation on the other. Closely related to the modifications of intuitive clarity are gradual differences between adumbrations: they either become more favourable or less favourable. These differences form an ascending series culminating in the optimal adumbrations, and they do so in accordance with a certain practical attitude. A further difference that belongs to the apprehension is the difference between determinateness and indeterminateness. In connection with this last difference Husserl deals with the motivating circumstances and the predelineation of a system of directions of fulfilment by the apperception. He here comes back to the difference between the indications which refer internally and those that refer beyond that which is intuitively given. There is a double relation between the core and the fringe involved in each outer perception, the one relating to the difference between appearing and non-appearing, but emptily co-presented, determinations of the object, the other to the difference between the various intuitive manners of givenness of one and the same determination. In accordance with this double relation there are two kinds of fulfilment: i) fulfilment by a total identification, in which the intending and the fulfilling act have the same matter; ii) fulfilment as closer determination, in which the matter changes.

Husserl has added nine paragraphs to the third chapter in which he gives a detailed analysis of transcendent perception which culminates in the view, presented in *Ideas I,* that absolute completeness is in principle an unrealisable idea in the realm of the transcendent intuition, an idea in the Kantian sense. Husserl remarks that the relationship between the representing contents and the represented moments of the object was misconstrued in the first edition as a representation by similarity. But the sensed colour ("Farbempfindung") and the colour of the thing are not really similar as if they belonged to the same kind. The sensation is a real immanent datum with its peculiar "quasi-extension" through which the colour of the thing as an objective moment of an extended thing is presented.

Husserl further points out that the concept of complete givenness or adequation regarding outer perception is in need of clarification. Already in the first edition, in § 29, Husserl had stated that an adequate representation in the form of a synthesis of representations is possible regarding the determinations of the surface of a material thing. Husserl refers here to what he later calls the phantom. In the revised text he explicates that a perception from all sides in a finite continuous synthesis in which the object is completely given is possible regarding a phantom but not regarding a thing. But even a phantom which is completely given, leaves open the possibility of a new givenness under new circumstances which would radically change its apprehension: it is always possible that the phantom turns out to be a material thing.

IV. THE REVISION OF THE FOURTH CHAPTER

The new draft of the fourth chapter is more than four times as long as the old text. The first half of it is devoted to an analysis of ideal and real possibility and the way they are given.

Whereas free acts of fantasy are sufficient for ideal possibilities to be given, real possibilities require like actualities and probabilities positing intuitions which are not freely at our command. Real possibilities are originally given in intuitions in which something suggests itself as possible; such possibilities have a certain weight, something speaks for them. In presuming we decide in favour of or against a certain real possibility.

For a better understanding of the difference between the cognition of reality and the grasping of possibilities, Husserl continues with his analysis of transcendent intuition. He distinguishes independent and conditioned possibilities. The unity of a transcendent thing can be explicated in causal and hypothetical syntheses. Any such explication leads always again to the positing of ground and consequence ("Grund- und Folgesetzung").

To each actual perception belongs a horizon of real possibilities of further experiences. They are all motivated through the actual thesis of experience. But through this whole horizon of real possibilities runs an important demarcation between those possibilities which are positively indicated by the content of the original experience and those which are not. The first, if realised, will be experienced as a fulfilment or closer determination of the previous perceptual intention and its object, the latter as disappointment, as a determination of the object as different from how it was previously intended or even as not being at all.

From each actual perception as a starting point an infinity of harmonious series of possibilities for further intuitions can be constructed. Each of these series is motivated by the initial perception, each would fulfil the perceptual intention harmoniously. They are all equally "good" possibilities. Each step in the progressing perception of the object implies an exclusion of certain possibilities of the previously motivated series. These excluded series of possibilities are now in conflict with the horizon of possibilities motivated by the latest stage of the perception. Each new experience can always open up new positively motivated horizons of possibilities of further experiences.

The investigation of the possibilities of experience involved in an actual experience leads to the determination of the reality of the thing as a Kantian idea. The reality of the thing is given exactly insofar as the real thing is given, that is, the progressing givenness of the real and the legitimisation of its reality are inseparably joined. This is different for the possible thing and the possibility of this thing. The possibility of a thing is guaranteed as soon as the possible thing as such is originally given. The progressive givenness of the possible thing does not at all increase the legitimisation for the possibility itself.

The investigation into the mode of possibility and of perceptual explication in the form of ground and consequence gives rise to a lengthy excursus about assumptions in relation to other act modalities and about the synthesis of motivation which underlies the hypothetical judgement. This excursus together with the final paragraph about "ideal impossibility, conflict, negation," forms the second half of the draft of the revised and enlarged chapter four. It is an important contribution to the phenomenological theory of judgement.

The act of assuming is an objectifying act but in contradistinction to, e.g,. probability, "assumability" is not something which either exists or does not exist and as such has to be justified. Assuming is an act of freedom. Whereas we cannot believe, conjecture, seriously doubt, or question whatever we like, we can assume each and everything, even that $2 \times 2 = 5$, as long as it makes sense in terms of pure grammar. Assuming is closely related to neutrality consciousness. Each positing consciousness can be transformed into an assuming by the mediation of its neutralisation.

An assuming can motivate another assuming. It then takes on the character of a presupposition for something which is posited as a consequence. Such a motivational synthesis of assumptions has to be distinguished from a causal synthesis and judgment which connects two propositional positings, as well as from a hypothetical judgment. The motivational synthesis of assumptions itself is not yet a judgment but only a hypothetical assumption. In each hypothetical synthesis of assumptions, however, a categorial judgment is implied. We can always form the categorial proposition: The presupposition A grounds the assumption B. This categorial positing synthesis is the true hypothetical judgment.

In the final paragraph Husserl first presents a detailed analysis of the preconceptual and pre-predicative consciousness of conflict in perception. These passages anticipate Husserl's later genetic investigations into the origin of the structure and forms of judgment in pre-predicative experience. Husserl then goes on to analyse the negative categorial judgment and how it is related to the positive judgment. The negative predication presupposes a positive predication, be it in the form of a thesis of certainty or only in the form of a conjecture or imputation which is then negated. The negation is directed against the proposed predicate. The negative predication is not reducible to a positive one with a negative predicate.

V. THE NEW DRAFT OF THE FIFTH CHAPTER

The new draft of the fifth chapter is almost a third longer than the text of the first edition. More than half of the draft is devoted to the argument for transcendental idealism. But Husserl first resumes the analysis of the modalities of being of the previous chapter, underlining the incompleteness of these investigations: "Everywhere huge problems open up". (Ms. A I 18, 57b).

The four concepts of truth are dealt with in a much shorter and more concise fashion than in the first edition. In the first edition Husserl makes use of his theory of categorial representation in connection with the first concept of truth: truth as the complete coincidence ("Deckung") of the meant and the given as such. According to this concept truth is the correlate of an identifying act. Evidence as the experience ("Erlebnis") of such a coincidence is nothing else than the actual performance of the adequate identification. But that evidence is the experience of truth does not yet mean that evidence is a thematic grasp of truth. It needs a specific act of objectifying apperception in order to transform the actual performance of the identifying act of coincidence into a thematic grasp of truth. In the first edition Husserl refers here to an addition to § 8 in the first chapter and to chapter seven in which he deals with categorial representation. In the addition to § 8 Husserl explicitly states that we do not have a fully constituted act of identification between a significative act and an intuitive act as long as "the moment of connecting unification [...] does not yet function as a representative for an objectivating apperception." (LI, 697 [Hua XIX/2, 569], my transl.). In the proofs of the revised first chapter Husserl eliminated the quoted sentence since it was not in agreement with the new noematic conception of the thematic grasp of categorial objects which he introduced in the revised text of the fifth chapter. Instead of identification, Husserl here speaks of the unity of agreement ("Einheit der Übereinstimmung") between what is meant and what is given. In the evident judgment this unity of agreement is experienced but not explicitly given as the relation of agreement. Such an explicit opposition between the correlate of the meaning-giving act and the correlate of the fulfilling act as well as their explicit identification, is possible only in a noematic reflection on these correlates. The coincidence which is unthematically experienced in an evident judgment can then be transformed into an explicit identification in which we grasp the agreement which is called truth.

After the presentation of the four concepts of truth, Husserl analyses the difference between empirical-occasional truths and ideal truths of essence. When comparing the adequacy of immanent perception with the adequacy of eidetic intuition, Husserl distinguishes two meanings of adequacy which correspond closely to his distinction between apodictic and adequate evidence from the *Cartesian Meditations*.

The account of occasional and ideal truths turns into an argument for a radical form of idealism regarding real being. This argument does not make any use of the epoché or the transcendental reduction. As in the *Ideas*, Husserl does not even use the term "idealism" in the text itself. It is only in the table of contents in Landgrebe's typescript from 1924 that Husserl added "phenomenological idealism" to the title of the fourth paragraph. Whereas truths about essences do not require the real existence, nor even the real possibility of a consciousness and of a judging related to them, empirical truths do require the real possibility of corresponding experiences and judgments, and that means the real possibility of conscious subjects. Such a real possibility in its turn is unthinkable without a really existing pure Ego. "The phenomenologically reduced pure consciousness not as a possible one, but as an actual one, is the bearer of the real world." (Ms. A I 18, 62b).

The argument for transcendental idealism is further supported by a comparison between the justification of ideal and real being. Whereas for ideal being the ideal possibility of knowing is equal to the actual knowing, for a real thing the ideal possibility of legitimisation is only equal to the ideal possibility and not the actuality of its being. Of course, there are things which are not actually experienced. Their actuality requires that real possibilities of experiencing them exist. But it is an actual consciousness by which certain ideal possibilities become real possibilities. Real possibilities are motivated by the actual experiences of an actual consciousness. Ultimately, Husserl concludes, "only actual consciousness in the form of actual experience can legitimate real being [...]". (Ms. A I 16, 66a). Each empirical being and truth is necessarily relative to an actual subjectivity.

Husserl's unfinished work on the revision of the Sixth Logical Investigation in the summer of 1913 ends with the argument for transcendental idealism. At this point the *Logical Investigations* have finally been transposed into the new key of the *Ideas I*.

DIETER LOHMAR
University of Wuppertal, University of Cologne

HUSSERL'S CONCEPT OF CATEGORIAL INTUITION

I. WHAT FULFILLS THE CATEGORIAL ELEMENTS OF THINKING?

The question Husserl tries to address with his theory of categorial intuition can easily be exemplified. Let us say I make the claim "The book is lying on the table" or "The table is green." In these expressions occur elements which can be easily fulfilled in sense perception, for example the book, the table, and the green color. But what gives fulfilment to the 'lying on the table' or the 'being green' of the book? For those intentions directed at 'states of affairs' (Sachverhalte), it seems impossible that they could be fulfilled by sense perception alone.

In sense perception I can see the 'green', but I cannot see the 'being green' in the same way. We might generalize this and claim that predicative being is not something perceivable. But not being fulfillable in sensibility alone does not include only predicative being but all categorial Forms, i.e., the forms 'one,' 'and,' 'all,' 'if,' 'then,' 'or,' 'all,' 'no,' 'not' and so on. But on the other hand, not only must there be acts which emptily intend these categorial forms, but also acts which fulfill such intentions.

Assume that we are in a room with a blue carpet. In our everyday attitude we know that in this situation there is a notable difference between the judgments 'The carpet is blue' and 'The carpet is red.' The first is intuitively fulfilled, whereas the second is not. Although we are very well aware of this difference it is not easy to determine exactly where it lies and on what it is based. Besides this it is obvious that we will not be able to make the difference clear without an analysis of the contribution of sense perception. But this will not solve the problem completely, as has already been pointed out. For this reason Husserl "extends" the concept of intuition, which is normally limited to sense perception, and formulates the concept of categorial intuition.

Intentions of real things are fulfillable by sense perception, whether inner or outer perception. Thus we might call ideal objects those objects which are only fulfilled in categorial intuition, as Husserl suggests (cf. LI, 787 [Hua XIX, 674]).[1] An object of simple perception ("schlichte Akte") is thus directly present, immediately given, present "in one blow"(Cf. LI, 787, 788 [Hua XIX, 674, 676] and EU, 301). Objects of sense perceptions are 'there' for us in one step of constitution in which they are intended and also given. By contrast, categorial objects can be intended and given only in a complex series of distinct founding acts which are grasped together by a comprehensive act which itself has a new, different intention. In this founded act there is a new object intended and also given which could not be intended or given in the founding acts. It is

---

[1] The German edition of the *Logische Untersuchungen* in the Husserliana series will be cited in the usual way (Hua Volume-Nr., page). E. Husserl's *Erfahrung und Urteil*, Hamburg 1964, will be cited as 'EU'. Some original terminology of Husserl's will be given in brackets within the text without further references to make the translation more lucid. I am grateful for the help of James Dodd with the English text.

obvious that simple perceptions can be extended over a given time. Continuous perceptions of the same object can be divided in time and rest on different sense data ("reelle Gegebenheiten"). But in such temporally extended perceptions of the same thing, in each phase of givenness the object is already intended and given, and thus no act of higher order needs to be performed.

A continuous perception is a combination of partial acts within one act, which is not the same thing as a founded act. This is also true for all objectifying acts which intend an object in identifying syntheses. This kind of givenness of identity can be understood as an unthematic performance of identifying syntheses which, though they have the same object, do not have identity as their object. In comparison to such acts, those in which identity is intended are of a higher order.

To understand the close relatedness and differences between these two kinds of identification requires a detailed analysis of the difference between thematic, categorial identification and simple, unthematic acts of identification, which Husserl proposes in § 47 of the Sixth Investigation. When we are directed to intentional objects, the simple form of identification is always already in place. When we see or walk around a house, we have a series of blended acts of perception. In each of these simple acts (schlichte Akte) is a primary object, the house, and along with or in these acts is a series of secondary objects, for example windows, walls, doors, etc., which are also noticed but, with respect to attention, remain 'in the background' (cf. LI, 579f, 584, 585-6 [Hua XIX, 415f, 423, 425]).[2] That means that even if I am now looking at a window on one side, it is nevertheless the house which is still the primary object of my perception. We might say that we usually see the house through seeing individual parts of it, we see it "in" seeing the window or "in" seeing the wall. Nevertheless, all of these individual parts of the house belong to the complete intentional sense of the house.

Most intentional objects have similar features as that of the house, that is, they consist not only in a single intention, but a combination of an explicit primary intention of the whole object and a 'set' of implicit secondary intentions, which Husserl names partial intentions ("Partialintentionen"). These partial intentions are themselves characterized by the fact that in intending the house I already have the conviction that I could make each of them the theme of an explicit intention. Thus the insight that intentionality has a horizon ("Horizontintentionalität") is being prepared already in the *Logical Investigations*.

In the continuous process of seeing an object we have a series of acts with the same primary object and which have the same partial intentions in common. But not all of the partial intentions are fulfilled at the same time. For example, we always have an opposite side which we cannot perceive but which we nevertheless intend. But this shows us that the fulfilled sense perception of each partial intention cannot be decisive for the identification of an object. But it is decisive for identification that the complete set of partial intentions (whether they are fulfilled or not) coincides in the flowing transition from one phase of the perception to another.

---

[2] The terminology of primary and secondary intentions is also found at LI, 648, 651 [Hua XIX, 515 and 519], but with a completely different use and context.

In this context the concept of 'coincidence' only names our ability to be aware that we still intend the same 'set' of partial intentions in an object in the flowing transition from one sensually given perspective of the object to another. We could write this as the set:

{this house: $Wi_1, Wi_2, \mathbf{Wi_3}, D_1, D_2, Wa_1, Wa_2, Wa_3, Wa_4, Ro_1, ...$}
{this house: $Wi_1, Wi_2, Wi_3, \mathbf{D_1}, D_2, Wa_1, Wa_2, Wa_3, Wa_4, Ro_1, ...$}
{this house: $Wi_1, Wi_2, Wi_3, D_1, \mathbf{D_2}, Wa_1, Wa_2, Wa_3, Wa_4, Ro_1, ...$}

All of the partial intentions listed belong to the primary object, the house, and differ in their respective fulfilments. The differences in fulfilment of intentions of windows, doors, walls, the roof etc. are indicated with bold print. If I am looking at the front of the house I cannot see the back. But it is important to stress that the performance of the identifying syntheses does not depend on the sense fulfilment of a partial intention of a particular part of the object. It only depends on the coincidence of the partial intentions as intentions and not on the grade of fulfilment of such intentions.[3]

In the flowing transition of a continuous perception this 'synthesis of coincidence' (of all partial intentions) is noticed, but the identity of the perceived object is not the theme of my intention. I am still directed primarily to 'this house there,' but this is also an identifying synthesis. We might say that identity is only 'experienced' in identifying synthesis but not thematized. If I so to speak 'take a step back' and thematize this experienced identity, and claim that 'all along it was the same object I perceived!', then I perform an act of an higher order which is founded in the continuous, simple perception and which has identity as its object.

We might be tempted to interpret this difference as a simple shift of interest or as a case of a change of apperception. But to make this very clear from the beginning: this interpretation is not appropriate for it ignores important characteristics of the categorical intuition. In the Fifth Investigation, Husserl points to the possibility of a change of apperception on the basis of the same identical contents of sense (reelle Inhalte) with the well-known example of the woman greeting visitors from a special arrangement of mirrors at a fair ("Panoptikum", "Spiegelkabinett"). This is a principal characteristic of the process of apperception. If we were to apply this model of apperception to the synthesis of coincidence between partial intentions, we might interpret this relation in the following way: in unthematic identifying syntheses, the syntheses of coincidence are only experienced but not interpreted as the presentation of the identity of the perceived object. In thematic identification the same syntheses of

---

[3] This does not imply that the fulfilment of the individual partial intentions has no function for the fulfilment of the categorial intention. But it is important to stress that the important 'syntheses of coincidence' can also function within a context of signitive intentions, for example in mathematics.

coincidence are not only experienced, but function as the basis of a new apperception. Now they function as a presentation of the thematic identity of the object.[4]

What is ignored to a large extent in this model is the special character of the fulfilling contents, i.e., the synthesis of coincidence, which we can only 'have' in actively performing the transition from one intentional act to another. We cannot have this synthesis of coincidence, so to speak, 'in a stock'. If we stress only the change of apperception as source of categorial intuition, the neccessary contribution of the categorial act as a whole is ignored. It will turn out that we must re-perform (wieder-vollziehen) the series of acts that have this synthesis of coincidence as result to reach intuitivity of the categorial intentions.[5]

Now we already have an overview about some general problems of the phenomenology of knowledge and Husserl's descriptive and conceptual tools to solve these problems. But we should keep in mind that Husserl's theory of categorial intuition is broadly regarded as difficult and thus problematic. Some critics also think it is opaque or even completely wrong. Some claim that there is simply no such thing as 'categorial intuition'.[6] Sometimes it is even suspected that later Husserl completely rejected his theory of categorial intuition. This suspicion is partly aroused by Husserl's critique of his own interpretation of categorial representatives (kategorialer Repräsentant). This critique is simply too short and too unprecise. In the preface to the second Edition of the Sixth Investigation, Husserl wrote that he no longer held his theory of categorial

---

[4] Husserl also tries to make this difference more precise by calling the first case a "not yet conceptualized experience of Identity" ("unbegriffenes Erlebnis", cf. LI, 696 [Hua XIX, 568]), suggesting that in thematic identity the synthesis of coincidence is apprehended (interpreted) with the use of the concept of identity.

[5] I have discussed these alternative models, i.e., the alternative between a model which requires a re-performing (Wieder-Vollzugs-Modell) or the other model, which requires only a 'simple' change of apperception of the same content (Umwandlungs-Modell) extensively in *Erfahrung und kategoriales Denken*, Dordrecht, 1998, 205-210 and 259-264.

[6] This opinion is mentioned by G. Soldati ("Das Problem ist, daß viele Philosophen bezweifeln, daß es so etwas gibt") in: G. SOLDATI, "Rezension von: Dieter Münch, Intention und Zeichen, Frankfurt 1993", *Philosophische Rundschau* 41, 1994, 273. The most important sources on the theme of categorial intuition in Husserl are: E. TUGENDHAT, *Der Wahrheitsbegriff bei Husserl und Heidegger*, Berlin, 1970, 111-136; R. SOKOLOWSKI, *The Formation of Husserl's Concept of Constitution*, Den Haag, 1970, 65-71; R. SOKOLOWSKI, *Husserlian Meditations. How words present things*, Evanston, 1974, §§ 10-17; E. STRÖKER, "Husserls Evidenzprinzip", *Zeitschrift für philosophische Forschung* 32, 1978, 3-30; R. SOKOLOWSKI, "Husserl's Concept of categorial intuition", *Phenomenology and the Human Sciences. Philosophical Topics* 12, 1981, Supplement, 127-141; D. WILLARD, *Logic and the Objectivity of Knowledge*, Athens, 1984, 232-241; G. E. ROSADO HADDOCK, "Husserl's epistemology and the foundation of platonism in mathematics",*Husserl-Studies* 4, 1987, 81-102; D. LOHMAR, *Phänomenologie der Mathematik*, Dordrecht 1989, 44-69; D. LOHMAR, "Wo lag der Fehler der kategorialen Repräsentanten?" *Husserl-Studies* 7, 1990, 179-197; TH. M. SEEBOHM, "Kategoriale Anschauung", *Phänomenologische Forschungen* 23, 1990, 9-47; R. COBB-STEVENS, "Being and Categorical Intuition", *Review of Metaphysics* 44, 1990, 43-66; K. BORT, "Kategoriale Anschauung", in: *Kategorie und Kategorialität*, edited by D. Koch and K. Bort, Würzburg, 1990, 303-319; and D. LOHMAR, *Erfahrung und kategoriales Denken*, Dordrecht, 1998, 178-273.

representation.[7] Therefore, an appropriate interpretation of Husserl's intentions must free itself from the misleading elements of his initial interpretation of categorial representation in the seventh Chapter of the Sixth Logical Investigation.[8] In this regard we must later return to the characteristics of syntheses of coincidence which play a central role in Husserl's theory of predicative cognition as well as in prepredicative experience.

II. SIMPLE AND CATEGORIAL ACTS

Husserl's distinction between simple and categorial intuition in the sixth Chapter of the Sixth Investigation is the basis for the phenomenological theory of knowledge. The contrast of simple and categorial acts is explained by means of act analysis. Simple intuition in the form of sense perception presents its object "directly," "immediately," in a "single step" ("in einer Aktstufe", LI, 787 [Hua XIX, 674]), "in one blow" ("mit einem Schlag", LI, 788 [Hua XIX, 676]), and its presenting function does not rest on founding acts.[9]

Categorial intuition is founded. In this case we do not use the concept of mutual founding but the concept of one-sided foundation.[10] Categorial intuition does not refer to its object in simple, one-rayed acts but always in jointed, higher order acts which rest on founding acts. The objects of founding acts are synthetically placed into a categorial relation within the founded categorial act. Thus in categorial acts new objects are intended, i.e., categorial objects which can only be intended (and given) in such founded acts. The intuitivity of categorial intuition is only due to acts which consist of stages of founding and founded.

We might interpret this complex founded structure as a kind of Egyptian pyramid. If one component of the foundation of the pyramid is missing, then one cannot completely construct the next floor. Another metaphor for complex founded categorial acts might be a race course. In the less complex cases of categorial intuition the founding acts are simple perceptions. The condition for the intuitivity of the categorial act is that of having passed through each of the founding particular intentions. As in the case of simple objects, in categorial acts there are also degrees of intuitivity, and thus

---

[7] Husserl writes that he no longer accepts the theory of categorical representation (daß er "die Lehre von der kategorialen Repräsentation nicht mehr billigt"), cf. LI, 668f [Hua XIX, 534 f].

[8] Cf. D. LOHMAR, "Wo lag der Fehler des kategorialen Repräsentanten?", 179-197.

[9] In contrast to categorial intention, which implies founding acts with different intentional objects, the continuous perception of a real object is a simple "blending" of intentions within one and the same intention.

[10] In the Third Investigation the concept of mutual foundation is predominant, but in the Sixth Investigation Husserl favors the concept of one-sided foundation. Cf. LI, 466f, 476-78, 545 [Hua XIX, 270f, 283-286, 369] and for the Sixth Investigation LI, 790 [Hua XIX, 678]. On Husserls different concepts of foundation cf. also T. NENON, "Two Models of Foundation in the 'Logical Investigations'", in *Husserl in Contemporary Context*, ed. B.C. Hopkins, Dordrecht 1997, 97-114.

evidence.

If we consider the realm of language, we might pose the problem of categorial intuition in the following way: what fulfills the elements of propositions which cannot be fulfilled by simple perception alone? In the first place this question points to those elements of propositions which Husserl named "Formworte", such as 'that,' 'one,' 'a,' 'some,' 'many,' 'is,' 'is not,' 'which,' 'and,' 'or' etc. (cf. LI, 774 [Hua XIX, 658]). If I claim 'This is a tree,' we might suppose that what is meant with 'this' and 'tree' can be fulfilled by sense perception (sensible intuition). But what specifically in sensibility fulfills the 'is' or the 'a' in this proposition? These elements must also be somehow fulfilled, otherwise the intention as a whole can not be fulfilled.[11]

In the most simple cases, the fulfilment of the categorical elements of propositions (like 'is', 'is not', 'and' etc.) is somehow connected with simple perception. Sometimes we even say: 'I see that this is a book,' while at the same time we know that we cannot see the matter of fact that this is a book in the same way that we perceive the book. In this respect the manner of speaking in sentences such as 'I see that it is a book' does not mean the same as 'I see the book'; rather, what is being stressed by this way of speaking is the intuitive character of categorial intuition.

Simple intuition, like perception, is not founded in other acts. Categorial intuition is founded in acts in which we intend the objects (or the aspects of objects) which we relate to one another in categorial intuition. Thus in categorial intuition we intend objects which cannot be intended in the simple founding acts, like 'being red,' 'being a book' (LI, 787ff [Hua XIX, 674ff]).

We could say that categorial objects are in relation to the objects of the founding acts. As Husserl says, they have a "gegenständliche Beziehung".[12] For example, 'A is greater than B' is founded in the simple perceptions of A and B. But these objects of simple perception only become objects of cognition in the founded act of categorial intuition which placed them within a synthetic relation. In the most simple cases, the categorial intuition cannot be fulfilled without the performance of the founding sensual perceptions. However, categorial intuition is not only a sum of all its founding perceptions; it is also directed towards an object which consists of a synthetic relation of the objects of perception.

There are different forms of categorial intuition, and each has its particular type of synthetic fulfilment. In the Sixth Investigation Husserl analyzes only some basic forms of categorial intuition to show that the concept of categorial intuition is justified,

---

[11] Thus the theory of categorial intuition implies the claim of a certain kind of parallelism between intuition and experession in speech: Each element of the proposition 'corresponds' to a certain element in intuition.

[12] With the help of the differences in this 'gegenständliche Beziehung' Husserl makes a distinction between synthetic and abstractive forms of categorial intuition. Synthetic categorial intentions are co-directed at the objects of their founding acts, as in 'A is bigger than B'. Abstracting intentions are not directed to the objects of the founding acts in the same way. In abstractive intentions the objects of the founding acts can only be a medium through which the intention is directed to something common, the eidos (etwas Allgemeines). The objects of the founding acts are only examples of this eidos. (cf. LI, 799, 788, 798 [Hua XIX, 690, 676, 688]).

and that these forms can serve as a pattern for analyzing the other forms of categorial intuition. Husserl analyzes the thematic identity of objects (LI, 791ff [Hua XIX, 679ff]), the relation of part and whole (judging about propositions and parts of objects), external relations, collection, the intuition of the general—that is, the so called 'Wesensschau'—the determined ('the A') and the undetermined intention of single objects ('an A') (cf. LI, 790f, 792f, 794f, 798ff [Hua XIX, 678f, 681f, 683f, 688ff]).

III. THE STRUCTURE OF THE CATEGORIAL ACT—THREE STAGES

In § 48 of the Sixth Investigation Husserl analyzes the stages of acts found in synthetic categorial intuition. Three clearly distinct steps or phases are to be distinguished. We will take the proposition "The door is blue" as an example.[13] The simple, founding perceptions must be those of the door and of the dependent moment of the color 'blue'. In the first step (1) we intend the object in one, unstructured glance. This is a simple act which is directed to the object as a whole; Husserl calls it a simple "Gesamtwahrnehmung" (LI, 793 [Hua XIX, 682]). The parts of the object are, however, also intended, but in this first unstructured intention of the whole of the object they are not yet explicitly intended (LI, 792ff [Hua XIX, 681ff]). Nevertheless these partial intentions are elements of the unstructured intention of the whole object, and are thus conscious as potential objects of an explicit intention.[14]

In the second step (2) the object is intended in an explicit manner by highlighting our interest with respect to the parts which, up to now, had only been implicitly intended. Husserl calls this kind of objectification a "subdividing act" ("gliedernde Akte", LI, 792 [Hua XIX, 681]). Parts of the object which had been implicitly intended now become the intentions of explicit acts. But this does not mean that in this new kind of objectification of the object there is an intention of a new object: it is still the door we are perceiving. The subdividing acts are special intentions within the simple act which is directed at the door. We might say that in the "gliedernde Akte" the door is intended through (or by way of) the medium of the blue color. There is no new object intended; rather the same object in a subdividing manner.

In the first unstructured perception of the object the parts of it were also intended, but only implicitly. In a subdividing, specifying intention ("gegliederte Sonderwahrnehmung") they are intended explicitly; they, so to speak, stand in the foreground. Our interest is directed to the sense contents in which the object is presented: I am attentive to the color and the smell of the rose, the rustle of the leaves.

---

[13] In the Sixth Investigation Husserl differentiates kinds of part-whole relations: The relation between whole and independent parts (Stücke) and the relation between whole and dependent parts (Momente), cf. LI, 792f [Hua XIX, 680f], 231, EU, §§ 50-52. In *Experience and Judgment* he interprets the two forms 'S has the part P' and 'S has the quality m' as equivalent in relation to the structure of their constitution, cf. EU, 262.

[14] In *Ideas I* Husserl will regard the possibility of making an intention explicit as characteristic of horizon-intentionality. Cf. Hua III/1, 57, 71ff, 212f.

In each continuous perception my attention wanders through the elements which present the object one after the other.

The shift from the unstructured perception of an object to the subdivided perception of an object might be interpreted as a 'double apperception' of the same sense contents, where we have the same object and the same intuitive mode of apperception. (That is, it is not a change of apperception which results in another object.)[15] Both are simple acts, but in the particular partial intentions ("Sonderwahrnehmungen") we intend the door by way of an intention of its color, while in the initial unstructured perception of the same object we are only implicitly directed at the color. In the first case the sense contents serve as representatives of an implicit partial intention, in the second the same sense contents are representatives of an explicit partial intention.

As we have already pointed out in the example of continuous synthesis, there is a so-called "synthesis of coincidence" in the transition from the unstructured intention of the whole to the explicit partial intentions. In this "synthesis of coincidence" we are aware both that we are intending the same object, and that this object, the door, not only has a color in general but that this color is blue. One important remark: both of these founding intentions are intuitively fulfilled and thus justify the thesis that the perceived object is a "real" object.[16] Thus the synthetic transition from the one to the other is also suitable for justifying the claim of "reality" with respect to categorial intuition. This constitutes difference between knowledge and mere hearsay.

This transition of founding acts and the 'synthesis of coincidence' which happens in this transition somehow offer everything we need for knowledge. But for actual knowledge there must also be a synthetic act which performs a categorial apperception of the 'synthesis of coincidence' itself. It is obvious that in every situation in everyday life we experience such 'syntheses of coincidence' and thus 'have everything needed for the performance knowledge,' but that nevertheless we only actually carry out such a performance to a very limited extent. Usually it is the importance of the object in question which is the decisive factor. Sitting in a train or in a car we might at each moment judge "This is a red car", "That is a green car." But if there is no relevant use in doing this we simply will not do it.[17] The acquisition of knowledge is acting ("Handlung"), and it is thus dependent on the structures of relevance in every day life.

In the third (3) decisive step of the process of categorial intuition we intend the objects of the particular subdividing perceptions ("gliedernde Sonderwahrnehmungen")

---

[15] There is also no change in the mode of apperception, for example between intuitive, pictorial, and signitive intentions.

[16] Cf. Ideas I, Hua III/1, 239.

[17] Nevertheless the opportunity for new insights does not disappear without a trace. In genetic phenomenology one of the prominent themes is the way in which this 'trace' (of knowledge experienced but not conceptualized) is kept or stored in the human subject in the different forms of pre-predicative experience (associations, types). Cf. the first section of *Experience and Judgment* and D. LOHMAR, *Erfahrung und kategoriales Denken*, Kap. III, 6-8.

synthetically in the new categorial intention. We can establish a relation between the objects of the founding acts, or between the object of the unstructured act as a whole and one of its dependent moments ("The door is blue"). In this founded act the elements which are synthetically connected in a categorial relation take on a new character: they are syntactically formed by the categorial act.

In all synthetic categorial intuitions we will find these three steps: (1) the initial, simple perception of the whole; (2) the particular, explicit subdividing perceptions; and (3) the actual categorially synthetic intention.

In the example of the door and its color, it is the "door" which takes on the categorial form of a "substrate" which bears qualities, while the "blue" becomes a "quality" of the substrate (substrate / accident). This categorial formation is not merely the performance of another type of simple apperception of the perceived object. The categorial act intends "that the door is blue" and is perhaps even the fulfilment of this matter of fact. Within categorial intention the "substrate capable of bearing qualities" and the "quality of the substrate" are dependent moments.

The categorial act is of an higher order, thus it must be differentiated with respect to intentional type: categorial acts either refer *synthetically* to the objects of the simple founding acts, or *abstractively* to an abstract moment of the object, which is meant only as an intuitive example of something general. (The latter is the so-called intuition of essences). Thus the fulfilment of a categorial intention is always dependent on founding perceptions and their intuitive fulfilment. But the dependence goes further: the fulfilment of perceptual intentions is in turn dependent on hyletic ("reelle") contents.

But the fulfilment of categorial intentions is not only dependent on the intuitive character ("Evidenz") of the founding acts.[18] Such a generalization, i.e., the thesis that the intuitive character of categorial intention is completely dependent on that of the founding perceptions, would lead to paradoxical results. For example, one of the consequences would be that axiomatic mathematics is not evident knowledge because its results are established completely within signitive intentions.

Thus sense perception can contribute to the fulfilment of categorial intentions at least in the most simple cases. But there are many objects of categorial intuition which have only a very loose connection with sense perception, for example the propositions of pure mathematics and algebra, where there is hardly any contribution of sensibility. But on the other hand, there are surely elements in categorial intuition which can be fulfilled with the help of sensible intuition—something like the "blue" of the door—and in each case there are elements which cannot be fulfilled in sensibility alone, like "being blue".

One of the decisive issues for this conception of knowledge concerns the function of the former stages of the categorial process in the intuitivity of the categorial act: to what extent is their performance in the third stage still "alive" or, alternatively,

---

[18] Husserl himself writes—though in the problematic Chapter 7 of the Sixth Logical Investigation—about the possibility of a functional dependence of the evidence of the categorial act from the evidence of the founding acts ("funktionalen Abhängigkeit der Adäquation (Evidenz) des Gesamtaktes von der Adäquation der fundierenden Anschauungen", LI, 811 [Hua XIX, 704]). Cf. D. LOHMAR, "Wo lag der Fehler der kategorialen Repräsentation?", 179-197.

"present"? On the one hand, this question concerns the intuitivity and the quality (respectively, thetic character, "Setzungsqualität") of the founding acts. But it also concerns the "synthesis of coincidence": we need to make clear what the founding acts are, and whether we can somehow keep their performance in play in the complex process of knowledge.

Let us turn once again to the details of our example of the blue door. After the simple perception of the whole is performed, the moment of the blue color of the door becomes the object of an explicit subdividing perception (LI, 793 [Hua XIX, 682]). But in the explicit perception of the "blue" we do not intend and perceive the "blue" for the first time. For an implicit intention, the 'blue' already occurs in the initial, simple perception of the whole. This implicit, partial intention corresponds to a possibility of an explicit intention. In the transition from the first simple perception of the whole to the explicit subdividing intention there occurs a "synthesis of coincidence" (LI, 765 [Hua XIX, 651] "Deckungseinheit", cf. LI, 697, 698, 764, 766 [Hua XIX, 569, 571, 650, 652]) between these two intentions. The coincidence occurs between the explicit intention of the moment 'blue color' on the one hand, and the partial intention implicit in the intention of the whole on the other.

It is decisive for the understanding of the concept of "synthesis of coincidence" that what is brought into coincidence are the intentional moments of the respective acts. The fulfilling coincidence is not based on equal or similar hyletic data ("reelle Bestände"). Such a coincidence may occur, but it does not support the intuitivity of categorial intuition. The bases of intuitivity in the case of categorial intuition are the coincidences of the intentional moments of acts, i.e., syntheses of coincidence between partial intentions.[19]

These syntheses of coincidence which occur between partial intentions now have a new function: they are apperceived as representing or fulfilling contents of the new synthetic categorial intention "The door is blue". The synthesis of coincidence which arises in the active process of running through the subdividing acts—making, so to speak, all the partial intentions of the object explici—are now representing the 'being blue' of the door.

At this decisive point in the phenomenological theory of knowledge we find the schema apprehension/apprehended content ("Auffassung"/"aufgefaßter Inhalt"). Thus we need to recognize that Husserl accepts this model of how to understand intuitivity for the categorial intuition as well as for sense perception. In the *Logical Investigations* as well as in many later writings we find this model introduced many times at decisive points of the argument (cf. EU, 94, 97-101, 103, 109, 111, 132f, 138ff).[20] For our limited purposes we do not need to take up Husserl's self criticism with

---

[19] Husserl writes: "Zugleich 'deckt' sich aber das fortwirkende Gesamtwahrnehmen gemäß jener implizierten Partialintention mit dem Sonderwahrnehmen.", LI, 793 [Hua XIX, 682]. It is important to stress that this 'synthesis of coincidence' can also occur between symbolic (and thus 'empty') intentions, which is of cruical importance for the foundation of mathematical knowledge. Cf. also Hua XXIV, 282.

[20] In the *Cartesian Meditations* Husserl speaks of analogizing apprehension ("analogisierenden Auffassung"), cf. Hua I, § 50.

respect to the model of apprehension/apprehended content, which in the first place only points out the limits of the schema but does not reject it.[21] Husserl criticizes the use of this model for the deepest level of constitution in inner time consciousness and for acts of fantasy (cf. Hua XXIII, 265f, Hua XIX, 884 (Handexemplar), Ms. L I 19, Bl. 9b). For acts constituting intentional objects and categorial objects it is not defective, but unavoidable.

But the model of apprehension and apprehended contents leaves some questions unanswered. For it is obvious that the very special character of the 'given' contents fulfilling categorial intuition, i.e., the syntheses of coincidence, requires a critical analysis.

Now I would like to analyze more closely what kind of contents synthesis of coincidence are. In relation to the special character of the synthesis of coincidence as a given content I will first present three negative insights. The discussion of these three negative insights will in turn reveal some positive insights into the character of the syntheses of coincidence which give intuitivity to categorial objects. 1. We cannot identify that which is the representing content of categoriality (i.e., the synthesis of coincidence) with the representing content of sense perception (neither with respect to the simple perception of the whole nor the explicit perception of the subdividing acts). 2. Syntheses of coincidence cannot be sense contents of outer perception at all. 3. Nor can it be a content of inner perception.

Concerning 1. One might think that a representing content of a perceived object could serve as a fulfilling content of a categorial intuition if it were apprehended in a new manner, i.e., in a 'categorial apprehension', where formerly it had only been used in a 'perceptual apprehension.' But I do not think that this is the case in categorial intuition. Consider the representing contents of the objects of explicit and subdividing acts in sense perception. If it were the case (that they could also serve as contents of categorial acts), then we would not be able to argue for three essential and necessary stages in the active performance of a categorial intuition. In principle we would already have (or would be able to have) categorial intuition on the basis of sense perception alone.

Concerning 2. The same argument shows that categorial intuition cannot be fulfilled with a perceptual content of outer perception.

Concerning 3. This argument rests only on the sense contents of outer perception; thus in order to cover all possible sources of representing contents we must consider inner perception and its contents. For a certain period in his development Husserl himself thought that such a solution might be promising. In the first edition of the *Logical Investigations*, precisely in Chapter 7 on "Studie über kategoriale Repräsentation", Husserl proposes the thesis that categorial intuitions can be fulfilled

---

[21] The insight that not every constitution has the structure of content/apperception is formulated in a footnote of the 1928 edition of the *Lectures on Inner Time-Consciousness*, cf. Hua X, 7, Anm.1.

by the apprehension of so-called "contents of reflection".[22] In this case, the content apprehended is the same content which represents the performance of the categorial act in inner perception. The shift of apperception takes the following pattern: in inner perception, sense contents represent the actual given performance of the act itself ("aktueller Vollzug"), and therefore may be called contents of reflection ("Reflexionsinhalt"). In categorial intuition these same contents are apprehended in a categorial manner, and thus can fulfill categorial intuition. So far the theory.

The main problem with this solution is that we always have to use *the same sense contents* (the experience of the "aktueller Vollzug" of the categorial act) for intuitively *different* categorial intuitions. For example, we would not be able to point out differences in the contents that fulfill the categorial intentions "The door is red" or "The door is brown". To solve this difficulty we must declare that the performance of the categorial act (the performance of the act itself!) is somehow dependent on sense givenness.[23] This is simply not the case, since we can have the same, but empty, categorial intention that performs the same categorial acts. Thus the inner perception of the performance of the categorial act does not solve the problem of the intuitivity of categorial intentions. Later on Husserl criticizes this attempt in the first edition of the *Investigations* as defective.[24]

We can now point to some positive aspects of the synthesis of coincidence. As we have seen in the example of the blue door, the representing contents of the door function in a double way: first in the simple perception of the whole object, then also in the explicit perception in which the color of the door is specifically intended. In the transition between these two acts there arises the synthesis of coincidence between the implicit intention and the explicit intention of the blue within the subdividing act that is aimed thematically at the color. This synthesis of coincidence now turns out to be able to function as a representing content for the categorial intuition of the "being blue" of the door (cf.LI, 793 [Hua XIX, 682]).

In this case the content which is apprehended is not a sense content at all—even if it rests on the coincidence of partial intentions fulfilled by sense contents, it is a synthesis between intentional moments of two or more acts which is imposed on us in the transition between the acts.[25] Experiencing the coincidence of the intentional

---

[22] Cf. LI, 814 [Hua XIX, 708] and D. LOHMAR, "Wo lag der Fehler des kategorialen Repräsentation?", 179-197. Tugendhat takes the view that the actual performance of the categorial synthesis fulfills the categorial intention. Cf. E. TUGENDHAT, *Der Wahrheitsbegriff*, 118-127.

[23] For this argument Tugendhat declares the 'sensuously dependent' actual performance (den "sinnlich bedingten" aktuellen Vollzug) to be the fulfilling representant of the categorial intuition. Cf. E. TUGENDHAT, *Der Wahrheitsbegriff*, 123f.

[24] Cf. the Preface of the 2. edition of the *Logical Investigations*, 663 [Hua XIX, 535].

[25] The concept of coincidence ("Deckung") has a double sense in Husserl's treatment of the problem of the fulfilment of intentions. In the *Logical Investigations* Husserl often uses the concept of coincidence to name the coincidence of intentions and the empty intentions they fulfill. But this is a trivial concept of fulfilment, for it does not answer the question how fulfilled intentions become fulfilled at all. The other context in which the concept of coincidence is used is in the analysis of categorial intuition as fulfilled

moments of 'blue' in the two acts at first only means that we 'experience' the equality of these intentions; it does not mean that we have the fact of equality or equivalence as a theme, nor that we have the matter of fact "being blue" as a theme. The synthesis of coincidence is somehow imposed on us in a passive manner, even if this happens in the framework of an actively performed activity. The content (the datum) is given to us—we must accept this seemingly paradoxical formulation—in a 'sense' which has nothing to do with sensibility, but which is an irreducible relation between the intentional moments of acts. It is the apprehension of such contents which fulfills the intention "The door is blue". Syntheses of coincidence are non-sensible representing contents.

Obviously the concept of non-sensible content is problematic within the framework of a phenomenology which begins its theory of knowledge with the analysis of sense perceptions. Yet we should not only dwell on the difficulties with this way of understanding categorial intuition, but also point to its advantages: the fact that non-sensible contents somehow fulfill categorial intuitions clearly justifies Husserl's extension of the concept of intuition beyond the realm of sensibility. Simple (founding) acts and founded, complex categorial acts do not only differ essentially in their structure, but also in the characteristics of the contents which make them intuitive. Besides this we have a clear hint of how to understand knowledge in mathematics with the same model (i.e., synthesis of coincidence) as in all other forms of knowledge. Moreover, we have a clear argument for the necessity of running through the complete three-staged process of categorial activity in order to reach intuitive fulfilment. Without the performance of the first two stages of categorial activity (i.e., the simple perception of the whole and the subdividing explication of the partial intentions), the necessary fulfilling syntheses of coincidence cannot occur. We may even suppose that in every case of categorial intuition there is a necessary contribution of non-sensible contents. I will now examine more closely this last thesis.

IV. THE FUNCTION OF SENSIBILITY IN CATEGORIAL INTUITION

After it turns out that one decisive contribution to the fulfilment of categorial intentions comes from non-sensible contents (which occur within a transition between acts), we need to make clear the positive contribution of the active performance of the founding acts—though we also need to make clear the limits of this performance.

In doing this, it is most important to be attentive to the differences between the forms of categorial intuition. For example, when we focus (later in this text) on the categorial form of collection it will turn out that there are some forms of categorial acts which are already fulfilled merely by the active performance of the categorial intention alone. This might lead to the suspicion that categorial intuition is some kind of esoteric 'super-sensible' kind of experience and knowledge. It looks as if categorial intuition is

---

by syntheses of coincidence between the partial intentions of the founding acts. This non-trivial use of the concept makes clear how the categorial intentions become fulfilled.

in this way completely independent from its founding basis, i.e., sense perception.[26] But this would obviously be an improper imputation of properties from special cases (collection) of categorial intuition to all forms. To ease this suspicion we must consider in more detail the function of sense perception within the fulfilment of categorial intuition.

The first task is to determine the contribution of the arbitrary active performance of categorial acts, as well as the limits of their contribution. On the one hand, the decisive syntheses of coincidence occur within arbitrary performed acts, but on the other hand they occur passively, i.e., we cannot arbitrarily reach the kind of fulfilment that we are looking for. There is a tension between arbitrary activity and passive givenness here which must be made more clear.

This tension can be felt even in the first example of unthematic identification (LI, 691f [Hua XIX, 678f]). The "flowing identification and coincidence" plays itself out passively; the synthesis of coincidence cannot be arbitrarily produced (cf. Hua XXIV, 279). On the other hand, if we want to have this identification in a thematic form within a categorial intuition of the identity, we must perform the acts again which had brought about the synthesis of coincidence. We have, again, a continuous perception of the thing in this arbitrary, active performance of the acts running through the different perspectives of the real object. Within this process, there is a synthesis of coincidence, but it is passive, i.e., it is not something reached by way of the arbitrary performance of acts alone. All we can do is to somehow 'direct' the series of acts, and it is within the transition between acts that there may occur a synthesis of coincidence; but this does not have to happen. We can arbitrarily direct the series of acts, but we cannot arbitrarily direct the syntheses which passively occur within the series of acts. Husserl mentions this difference in an lecture course form 1906/07: "Die Erscheinungen werden gleichsam in Deckungsstellung gebracht ..."(Hua XXIV, 283). We can somehow arrange acts in a situation in which the synthesis can happen, but we do not have the power to produce passive givenness. This setting of acts into a arrangement in which coincidence may occur does presuppose the attention of the ego; but arbitrary activity is not sufficient to ensure the coincidence (Cf. Hua XXIV, 283). After having dealt with the insight into the function of non-sensible contents for categorial intuition, we turn to the question: what function does sensibility have in the fulfilment of categorial intuition at all? On the one hand, one of the virtues of the concept of non-sensible contents was that it allowed for an understanding of knowledge in the case of formal axiomatic mathematics. Axiomatic mathematics is a case of knowledge in that it has the same structure as other cases of categorial intuition, and in that it rests on the same (non-sensible) contents. But on the other hand, it would be a clear disadvantage for a theory of knowledge if it were to have difficulties in making clear the dependence of knowledge on sensibility.

But this is not true for Husserl's analysis of categorial intuition: the

---

[26] Husserl's concept of categorial intuition has nothing in common with the concept of an 'intellectual intuition'. This misguided suspicion was initiated by some representatives of Kantianism. Cf. D. LOHMAR, *Erfahrung und Kategoriales Denken*, Kap. III, 2, c.

contribution of sensible intuition is found at a number of different junctures within the three stages of categorial intuition. The initial simple perception of the whole object is an apprehension of sense givenness. In genetic phenomenology, apprehension is assisted by empirical types based on sensible givenness. In most cases the complex, higher order structures of judgements (theories) lead step by step back to sensible intuition, which grounds the validity of the whole theory. The most simple intentions are fulfilled in sense perception.

The most important function of sensibility is in the legitimation of the thetic moment of (founding) intentions (real, possible, presupposed, dubious etc.). The justification of the thetic moment of acts is dependent on the sensible givenness of an object; only if the object is given intuitively can it make the claim to be 'real.' If the mode of givenness is deficient and the evidence of the givenness weakened, then we can only claim that the object is 'possible' or 'dubious'. If we make further judgments on the ground of such founding acts, then the judgments of objects that have such a thetic character can only be 'dubious' or 'possible' as well; it would not be reasonable to think that the state of affairs involving such objects is 'real'. We are familiar with this dependency of the thetic character of subsequent judgements on previous judgments from axiomatics: if the axioms are only 'presupposed,' then we are only able to arrive at the thetic character 'valid under the presupposition that, etc.'. Judging about a state of affairs that is 'real' demands that all founding acts directed to the objects in question have the thetic character 'real' as well.

We have seen how sense perception contributes to the categorial intuition by way of the thetic character of the founding acts. But there is also the possibility that sensibility can contribute directly to the intuitivity of categorial acts. Husserl makes a distinction between pure and mixed acts of categorial intuition; in the latter, the intuitivity of the categorial intention is also dependent on sense perception. If an object or realm A adjoins B (in a kind of direct communality) there is a sensed moment of 'adjoining' which connects the two realms in sensibility (cf. LI, 795f [Hua XIX, 684 f]). But in perceiving this sensed moment of adjoining the categorial intention 'A adjoins to B' is not thereby fulfilled; a categorial act is needed, one which is based on the founding acts directed to 'A' and to 'B' as well as to the 'adjoining'. In the transition from one founding act to the other there are syntheses of coincidence between partial intentions, but there are also sense contents which contribute to this 'mixed' categorial intuition. The intuitivity of pure categorial intuitions is completely dependent on the non-sensible synthesis of coincidence.

Up to this point we have only analyzed the most simple forms of categorial intuition. But we have also gained some insight into the character of categorial intuition in general. We have seen that the explicit, subdividing acts must have the form of simple, one-rayed intentions. If we now consider categorial intentions of a higher order, we are confronted with the question how categorial objects—for example judgments—can function in this way as founding acts for categorial intentions of an even higher order. From this point of view it seems to be necessary that we must be able to have simple, one-rayed intentions of all kinds of categorial objects. Husserl's solution for this one-rayed intention with respect to categorial objects is the so called act of nominalization.[27] I can refer to a judgement ("the brakes of the car are defective") with the one-rayed intention "this" and then judge with respect to this state of affairs "This is dangerous".[28]

There is a second difficulty which can be called the problem of practicability: it may turn out that categorial intentions—if they have the function of founding higher order judgments—must always be fully intuitive in order to guarantee the intuitivity of the founded intuition. In the case of a complex theory composed of judgments, we would have to perform all of the founding categorial acts of different levels down to the lowest founding perceptual acts. This turns out to be practically impossible, which is easy to see if we look at axiomatic mathematics. In order to prove a given proposition in an intuitive manner, I would first have to reproduce all the proofs of those propositions which contribute to the proposition in question.

Thus with respect to degree of intuitivity there must be a kind of functional surrogate (substitute) which also works with nominalized judgements; otherwise we would simply not be able to reach categorial knowledge of higher order. Without the surrogate, the attempt to reach an intuition of a single higher order judgement would be a task so complex that it would be impracticable. As we have already pointed out, one possibility is that the thetic character of the founding act may be useful as a surrogate. Sensible intuition justifies a certain thetic character of the founding acts, for example 'real'. Then the founded acts which for example intend states of affairs would also assume the thesis 'real'.

Our understanding of categorial intuition will become more precise and lucid if we discuss two further forms of categorial intuition: eidetic intuition ("Wesensschau") and collectivity.

V. EIDETIC INTUITION—HUSSERL'S "WESENSSCHAU"

Husserl's theory of eidetic intuition begins with the fact that the human mind has the ability to become aware of common features in different objects. In § 52 of the Sixth Investigation Husserl analyzes this form of knowledge as a particular form of categorial intuition. Within this context Husserl names this form of categorial intuition "ideierende Abstraktion"; in other contexts he uses the term eidetic intuition or, in German, "Wesensschau". The phenomenological method of eidetic intuition is the attempt to work out and enforce the original ability of the human mind to become aware of common features. Husserl wants to work out a method for a priori knowledge that is based upon features of acts of consciousness and objects of thinking and perceiving.

---

[27] For the concept of nominalization, cf. LI, 796f [Hua XIX, 685f] and EU, § 58.

[28] Husserl treats the one-rayed backward intention of complex categorical intentions under the concept of 'secondary sensuousness'; cf. for example Hua XVII, 314-326 (Beilage II). Secondary sensuousness is the already mentioned functional substitute for the intuitivity of the categorical object.

The method of eidetic abstraction or "Wesensschau"[29] is of crucial importance for the claim of phenomenology to be a philosophical science. In the *Logical Investigations* Husserl still interprets his phenomenology as a version of "descriptive Psychology"—at least he uses this denotation—but on the other hand phenomenology is not meant to be an empirical discipline that only collects arbitrary facts. Thus, phenomenology has to find and establish methods which make it possible to arrive at a priori insights independent from the given particular factual case. Armed with eidetic intuition developed as a phenomenological method, Husserl claims that phenomenology does not only collect insights with respect to individual cases or limited sets of individual cases, but that it is capable of arriving at universal a priori insights concerning every possible case. For example, phenomenology claims to reach universal knowledge concerning the features of consciousness in general; Husserl has to show that this is possible with the phenomenological method of eidetic intuition.

Thus the claim of phenomenology to be science depends on whether eidetic intuition can be established as a justified form of categorial intuition. We may also look at this from the point of view of the idea of self-justification that Husserl pursues for phenomenology: to establish eidetic intuition as a justified form of categorial intuition is a decisive aim of the *Logical Investigations*.

Eidetic intuition (Wesensschau) is founded in simple intuition in a way similar to other forms of categorial intuition we have seen. We are only able to have an intuition of general features like 'blueness' or 'human' by running through a whole series of blue objects in perception or fantasy (cf. LI, 337-40, 391ff, 431f, 799-802 [Hua XIX, 111-115, 176ff, 225f, 690-693]). The aim of the theory of eidetic intuition is to make clear not only how it is that we can gain general concepts of objects, but also how the intuition of general features works, i.e., how it is that we can have an intuition of the characteristics held in common by different objects. We may speak in this respect of 'common objects,' and insofar as we usually identify such common objects with 'concepts,' it is also an investigation into the legitimating source of our intuition of concepts. Thus in performing the eidetic intuition of 'blueness,' we must run through a series of perceived or imagined blue objects in order to have the intuition of the common 'blueness'. This process is not circular, because in the founding acts the theme is single blue objects while in the founded eidetic intuition we apprehend the common feature of blue on the basis of the synthesis of coincidence which, as we already know, is a non-sensible content.

A detailed analysis of eidetic intuition as a form of categorial intuition is found in § 52 of the Sixth Investigation. The analysis runs along the lines of the three stages found in every form of categorial intuition: first the simple perception of the object as a whole; then the explicit, subdividing acts; finally the categorial synthesis. In the second stage, that is, in running through the subdividing acts explicitly pointing to the

---

[29] The designation 'Wesensschau' for eidetic intuition seems to be a wrong choice in terminology in that it suggests a proximity to Platonism that is not Husserl's intention. Cf. R. BERNET, I. KERN, E. MARBACH, *Edmund Husserl. Darstellung seines Denkens*, Hamburg, 1989, 74-84, J. N. MOHANTY, "Individual Fact and Essence in E. Husserls Philosophy", *Philosophy and Phenomenological Research* XIX, 1959, 222-230; E. TUGENDHAT, *Der Wahrheitsbegriff*, 137-168.

moment of color with respect to different perceptive or imaginative objects, there occurs a synthesis of coincidence with a particular style.

In order to arrive at an intuition of general objects it is of decisive importance that we have intuitive or imaginative acts for the subdividing acts during the second phase. Eidetic intuition cannot be founded on signitive acts alone (cf. LI, 728ff [Hua XIX, 607ff]). But on the other hand, eidetic intuition is also possible if only one intuitively present object is given, for we can vary this example in imagination.[30] In the *Logical Investigations* Husserl states that it is insignificant for the intuitivity of eidetic intuition whether the subdividing acts of the second phase are intuitive acts or imaginative acts; that is, imaginative acts are admissible (cf. LI, 800ff, 784 [Hua XIX, 691ff, 670]). In the further development of his theory Husserl arrives at the insight that the imaginative acts are not only to be tolerated but that they are to be preferred—he even asserts that imaginative or "free" variation is necessary for eidetic intuition.[31] It is free variation that assures us that in the procedure of eidetic variation we do not adhere to a limited realm of cases which may carry only contingently common features (cf. EU, 419-425).[32]

In the third stage of the process of eidetic intuition we apprehend the synthesis of coincidence which occurs in running through the different acts of the second stage. We apprehend this synthesis as a representation of the common feature, i.e., the general object that we intend. As in the act in which a real thing is thematically identified, the synthesis of coincidence which occurs at the second stage between the subdividing acts is the apprehension of the coincidence as an identity. But now it is apprehended as representing not the identity of a particular real thing, but that of the general feature. The general feature, the (same) color, is intuitively given through the series of blue objects and the synthesis of coincidence between the acts directed at the moment of color. In eidetic intuition we find a particular type of synthesis of coincidence between the subdividing acts of the second phase. The special properties of such syntheses are difficult to describe. They exhibit a kind of 'center' of clear coincidence with a halo of loose coincidence mixed with divergences (cf. EU, 418f). This halo results from the individual differences among the blue objects which are the theme of the subdividing acts.

We can understand higher order eidetic intuitions in the same way: we can perform eidetic intuitions founded in categorial acts. For example, we can have an

---

[30] In the process of variation within eidetic intuition the range of arbitrary variability has to be limited. One limitation is performed by the intuitively present object, for example a tree, which works as a 'Leitfaden' (guideline) for the possible variations. But this is not sufficient. A second source of limitation stems out of our vague everyday understanding of a concept like tree. As the eidetic method is a means to reach an intutitively fulfilled, clear intention of concepts, we usually start with such vague concepts and in the variation they serve also as a limiting 'Leitfaden'.

[31] Cf. Hua III/1, 146ff, where Husserl speaks of a priority ("Vorzugsstellung") of imagination, also Hua XVII, 206, 254f and EU, 410ff, 422f. Seebohm points out that imaginative variation is already found in the *Logical Investigations* (TH. SEEBOHM, "Kategoriale Anschauung", 14f.).

[32] The factual reality of single cases in eidetic variation is irrelevant in this respect. Cf. Hua IX, 74.

intuition of the general aspect 'color' based on the intuition of different colors, and we can have an intuition of the concept 'act of consciousness' by running through eidetic intuitions of different forms of consciousness (remembering, perceiving, wishing etc.).

There are also problematic aspects of eidetic intuition, which is above all an experimental form of reflection. With the help of eidetic intuition we can supposedly have a clear idea about the limits of our concepts: by imaginative variation of particular cases of a general concept we might discover the point at which a degree of variation exceeds the limits of the concept, and at which we are imagining something else.[33] We can thus learn to recognize the limits of our concepts—and experience them as non-arbitrary. But even in recognizing them as something fixable, it is not clear how their limits are determined.

The full extent of this problem is only realized in the attempt to intuit the essence of objects which carry some cultural meaning. Whereas in one culture we may intuit the essence of the divine as plural, in another we might intuit the essence of the divine as singular. The same turns out to be the case with the essence of woman, honor, justice etc. There is no way of finding a common answer.

To partially solve this problem we might try to draw a distinction between 'simple' objects which carry no cultural meaning and those which do. Acts of consciousness—the preferred theme of Husserl's phenomenology—may turn out to be objects of the first class. On the other hand, complex objects which can only have their full sense in the intersubjective constitution of the community—objects such as cultural world, myth, religion etc.—all exceed this limit. Most everyday concepts are learned by each of us in a long process of formation within the intersubjective consensus of our community. In this way our everyday concepts have a genesis and a 'history' closely connected to the convictions of our respective community.

VI. COLLECTIONS (SETS)

The analysis of the categorical intuition of collections involves special problems. The fulfilment of the categorical form 'a and b' is dependent on the performance of founding acts directed at 'a' and 'b', whereby the members of the collection have been made an explicit theme. But this is not sufficient as long as the synthetic intention of both together, the 'and', is not performed. In this case the fulfilling factor will not be found in a synthesis of coincidence, because we can combine objects in a collection that have no partial intentions in common.

One may object that this describes only artificial forms of collections. We might also argue that in the realm of sensual givenness there may be prefigurations ("Vorformen") of collectiva that occur independently of the categorial form of a

---

[33] In his genetic phenomenology Husserl analyzes the acquisition and determination of the limits of concepts in his theory of types. Cf. D. LOHMAR, *Erfahrung und kategoriales Denken*, Kap. III, 6, d. To this problematic cf. also K. HELD, "Einleitung", in E. Husserl, *Die phänomenologische Methode. Ausgewählte Texte I*, Stuttgart, 1985, 29; and U. CLAESGES, *E. Husserls Theorie der Raumkonstituion*, Den Haag, 1964, 29ff.

collection. Such speculation could be motivated by the fact that in reality there are syntheses of coincidence among similar objects that form groupings that are somehow independent of our synthetic activity, like a row of trees along an avenue. This model of a passive prefiguration of collections in sense perception implies that objects can somehow form a group on their own accord.

Husserl analyzes this model of collection already in his *Philosophie der Arithmetik*: "sensuous marks of multiplicity" or "figurative moments" ("sinnliche Mehrheitsanzeichen" resp. "figurale Momente") are groupings in accordance with configuration, similarity, or common motion that form "sensual signs of unities" ("sinnlichen Einheitscharaktere", Hua XII, 689), as for example in swarms, rows, or avenues (cf. Hua XII, 193-217 and LI, 799 [Hua XIX, 689]). In the Sixth Investigation, Husserl makes very clear that such sensuous signs of multitudes are only clues or weak signitive indications and do not represent the categorial form of a colletion (cf. Hua XII, 689). These weak signitive indications cannot take on the character of intuition, which requires categorial synthetic activity (cf. Hua XII, 690).

From the point of view of genetic phenomenology we might understand sensuous signs of multiplicity ("Mehrheitsanzeichen") as a pre-predicative form of collection that can guide the performance of the categorial act which 'revitalizes' the pre-predicative form.[34] But not every collection has a pre-predicative predecessor, for we are completely free to collect completly different objects into a collection. Besides, we have to realize that even the syntheses of coincidence that occur between acts directed at similar objects (like swarms of birds, trees along avenues, etc.) are not sufficient to fulfill the categorical intention of the multiplicity. We might, for example, on the basis of a synthesis of coincidence judge that the birds or trees are similar, but that in itself it is not an intention of the collection 'a and b'.

It turns out that in cases like collections we cannot do without the contribution of the synthetic categorial intention 'and' itself. Collections owe their intuitivity solely to the fact that we synthetically combine objects, that we collect them. Only while synthetically combining the 'a' and the 'b' do we have the collection intuitively. But this leads to the strange result that the categorial act contributes to its own intuitivity. This at least enables us to understand why we are completely free to combine objects into collections even from different realms of being—for example: '7 and justice and Napoleon'—, for we are not dependent on partial intentions held in common.

The idea of an intention that contributes to its own fulfilment might give the impression of circularity. But we need to be precise: it is the synthetic activity of combining the objects of the founding acts into a new object, the collection, that brings about the fulfilment. This strange case raises questions about what kind of fulfilling or 'representing' contents are found in collectiva. We might suppose that what serves as a representant is the experience of the performance of the act of collection (in inner perception). But it seems more reasonable to accept the fact that the categorical intention 'and' itself can be viewed as a non-sensible content (like syntheses of coincidence), one that can serve as the fulfilling content of the intention of the

---

[34] Cf. D. LOHMAR, *Erfahrung und kategoriales Denken*, 187ff.

collection.

It is clearly a very special case—in fact an important exeption—in the realm of intentions and categorical intentions that the will to perform a synthetic intention is enough to fulfill an intention. But it remains an exception, for the fulfilment of intentions that counts as knowledge in the narrow sense is dependent on syntheses of coincidence that occur passively in the transition from one founding act to another. A collection is therefore itself not a contribution to knowledge at all, though it can be an important element in knowledge if we continue to perform judgments with respect to the collectiva (or set). The contrast between collectiva and acts of knowledge in the narrow sense will be more lucid if we consider the hint Husserl gives in the *Logical Investigations* with respect to the particular lack of independence on the part of collectiva: the statement that collectiva are not 'states of affairs' ("nicht selbst Sachverhalte") (cf. LI, 798 [Hua XIX, 688] and EU, 254). The elements of collections can be completely alien to one another and even stem from different realms of being ('red and triangle'). In *Experience and Judgment* Husserl states more precisely why these forms lack the independence of knowledge (state of affairs): there are no syntheses of coincidence that fulfill the categorical intention ("Es tritt hier nicht jene Synthesis partialer Deckung ein") (cf. EU, 135, 254, 297, 223). The intuitivity of a collectiva is not rooted in the character of the objects that are synthetically combined.[35]

I hope that my analyses have shed some light on the strength as well as on the problems of Husserl's concept of categorial intuition.

---

[35] Cf. the statement that collection is "keine sachlich, in den Inhalten der kolligierten Sachen gründende Einheit" cf. E. HUSSERL "Entwurf einer 'Vorrede' zu den 'Logischen Untersuchungen'", edited by E. Fink, *Tijdschrift voor Filosofie* 1, 1939, 106-133 and 319-339, especially 127, and Hua XII, 64f.

FREDERIK STJERNFELT
University of Copenhagen

CATEGORIES, DIAGRAMS, SCHEMATA
THE COGNITIVE GRASPING OF IDEAL OBJECTS
IN HUSSERL AND PEIRCE

The question of the status, the presentation, and the representation of ideal objects has received new actuality in recent years as the result of various scientific and philosophical developments. In cognitive science and computer science, concepts like scripts, schemata, frames, diagrams have received renewed attention as opposed to supposedly purely formal logical representations;[1] in complexity theory, it has been suggested that all sufficiently complex adaptive systems must include a general, schematic representation of aspects of its environment;[2] in the renaissance of Austrian philosophy and phenomenology in general, new attention has been paid to a priori structures and their representation.[3] As all of these developments show, the grasping of ideal objects pertains not only to mathematics and logic—even if they form an important case—but also to everyday cognition, as most cognitive acts are not simple and involve general, ideal elements in what Husserl calls "sinnlich gemisschte" form.

In light of this, it is natural to look at the major modern philosophical theories of ideal objects and the means of gaining access to those objects. Two systematic accounts of this problem are here worth mentioning: Husserl's ideas of abstraction and "categorial intuition" which were first developed in his early work and which played an important role in *Logical Investigations* and later in *Experience and Judgment*[4] and elsewhere; and Charles Peirce's notion of "diagrams" which was crucial in his last attempt to construct a philosophical system in the first years of the twentieth century. In this paper, I shall compare these two accounts of ideal object access. This is not the place for a general comparison of Husserl and Peirce (however much this could be wished for); let it suffice to mention the following similarities (among many others), relevant to the problem of ideal objects.

• the conception of meaning as being general (as a species (Husserl) or a type

---

[1] For instance in the cognitive semantics tradition in linguistics, cf. G. LAKOFF, *Women, Fire, and Dangerous Things*, Chicago: Chicago University Press, 1987; and the diagrammatic reasoning interest in computer science, cf. J. Glasgow, et al. (eds.) *Diagrammatic Reasoning. Cognitive and Computational Perspectives*, Menlo Park, Cal.: AAAI Press/MIT Press, 1995.

[2] See for instance M. GELL-MANN'S and B. MARTIN'S papers in G. A. Cowan et al. (eds.): *Complexity. Metaphors, Models, and Reality*, Reading Mass., etc.: Addison Wesley, 1994.

[3] See for instance B. SMITH, *Austrian Philosophy*, Chicago: Open Court, 1994, especially the last chapter; or A. PERUZZI, "An Essay on the Notion of Schema", in L. Albertazzi (ed.), *Shapes of Forms*, Dordrecht: Kluwer, 1999, 191-244.

[4] E. HUSSERL, *Erfahrung und Urteil*, Hamburg: Felix Meiner, 1985.

(Peirce, at least with respect to sufficiently complicated and interesting signs))
- the striving for a phenomenological solution to the problem of how logic and mathematics—and universal, objective knowledge in general—can be shared by subjective acts of knowing.
- the central role given to intuition and evidence in epistemology
- the introduction of variables as empty "slots" in logic and semantic expressions
- the claim to the reality of species and our intuitive access to them (eidetic phenomenology and "Wesenserschauung", Husserl; the "pragmatic maxim" and diagram experimentation as means of clarifying a concept in Peirce)
- the positive redefinition of the synthetic a priori (as "pure laws including material concepts" (Husserl, Third Logical Investigation) or as "universal propositions relating to experience" (Peirce))
- a criticism of empirist and psychological theories of abstraction in favor of a formalizing or "ideierende Abstraktion" (Husserl) or Peirce's complex of abstraction types—and even the close connection between abstraction and mereological part-whole description (Husserl's Third Logical Investigation; Peirce's definition of his three types of distinction)
- the attempt at giving a rational exposition of the loose Kantian idea of a schematic mediator between "Sinnlichkeit" and "Verstand" in epistemology (Husserl: "kategoriale Anschauung" and the intuitive fulfilment of signitive acts, Peirce: diagrammatical representation).

The aim of this article is to compare Husserl's account of categorial intuition in the Sixth Investigation (and its prerequisites elsewhere in the book) with Peirce's notion of diagram and diagrammatical reasoning. I shall investigate Husserl's ideas more closely in what follows, so let me begin with a short summary of the mature Peirce's notion of *diagrams*.[5] Peirce's doctrine of diagrams is not very well known, not even among Peirce scholars. Peirce's graphic logic formalizations[6] are comparatively well-known, but his general teachings on diagrams as such not so. Husserl radically expands the concept of intuition ("Anschauung") in such a way as to involve the grasping of states-of-affairs, of essences, of linguistic syntax, etc. Similarly, Peirce extends the concept of diagram considerably in order to encompass exactly the same features. According to him, a diagram is a special type of icon, that is, a sign which signifies by means of similarity

---

[5] Peirce's doctrine of diagrams must be reconstructed from scattered quotes in C. PEIRCE, *Collected Papers*, I-VIII, London: Thoemmes Press, 1998 [1931-58], and *Elements of Mathematics* I-IV, The Hague: Mouton, 1976. For a detailed discussion, see F. STJERNFELT, "Diagrams as Centerpiece of a Peircean Epistemology, in *Transactions of the Charles S. Peirce Society* XXXVI/3 , 2000, 357-84.

[6] Known as Alpha-, Beta-, and Gamma-graphs, they formalize (a) propositional logic, (b) first order predicate logic, and (c) various brands of modal logic, speech act logic etc.

with its object.[7] A diagram is a relational, skelettal picture of an object with the special requirement that it is built from relations which have a rational character, be it explicit or not. Thus, a diagram is a type, it is a general sign, and this makes it possible for it, in turn, to signify general objects. Its generality is stated in an accompanying symbol which determines what object it stands for and in what respects. These requirements makes it possible to undertake experiments on the diagram. The symbol governing it involves certain rules, explicit or not, by which the diagram may be manipulated in order to reveal new information about its object. Thus, an equation may be solved; on a map a distance may be measured; on a model, a future behaviour may be predicted; a linguistic articulation may be rephrased—to take a series of different diagram experiments. Thus, the diagram concept in Peirce includes all instruments which may be used for necessary reasoning, a priori as well as a posteriori. By the "more information" criterion, the diagram category thus includes much more than the prototypical diagrams consisting of interrelated lines on a sheet of paper: they include algebra, maps, graphs, logic, mereology, linguistic syntax—all these formal structures permit information-gaining manipulation. In addition to such pure diagrams come applied diagrams in which these formal instruments are given material content in empirical use. In the overall picture of Peirce's epistemology, diagrammatic reasoning occurs at a specific phase in every investigation. All research takes place in a three-part rhythm, beginning with abduction which makes a guess at the reason for some unexplained phenomena. The second phase formalizes this guess and infers some deductive consequences from it. The third phase inductively checks these consequences against reality. Diagrammatic reasoning pertains to the second phase and thus concerns the structure of (hypothetical) a priori knowledge.

The idea of this paper is to focus on the similar roles played by diagrams and categorial intuition in Peirce and Husserl around 1900—and to introduce the cross-fertilization between those two concepts to enhance the actual understanding of the cognitive ability to grasp, understand, and manipulate ideal objects.

I. MEANING AND INTUITION IN THE *LOGICAL INVESTIGATIONS*

In Kant, of course, we find the idea that a crucial problem of epistemology is the possible mediation between what he considers two faculties of mind, *Verstand* and *Anschauung*, respectively. A simple meeting between the two in an "intellectual intuition" is deemed impossible and the belief in its possibility leads into the "transcendental illusion". The possible mediation between these two is only deemed possible in the construction of rule-bound schemata (the arch examples being arithmetic (addition), geometry (the triangle) in the realm of pure schemata, and the concept of the

---

[7] Or, to give Peirce's definition of what such similarity implies: an icon is a sign which permits us to get more information about the object than what lies in the construction recipe for the sign. Cf. F. STJERNFELT, "How to Learn More. An Apology for a Strong Concept of Iconicity", in T. D. Johansson et al. (eds.) *Iconicity. A Fundamental Problem in Semiotics*, Copenhagen: NSU Press, 1999, 21-58

dog in the realm of empirical schemata). Each in their way, Husserl and Peirce strive to clarify the more precise relationships behind the sketchy Kantian deliberations.

In the *Logical Investigations*, this problem is highlighted in the second section of the Sixth Investigation, involving close ties to various other chapters throughout the book. The prerequisite to understanding the ideas given in the Sixth Investigation is, of course, the structure of the intentional act as outlined in the Fifth Investigation. Here, Husserl distinguishes between the act itself, its content and its object. The content is the act's meaning conceived of as species, and it, in turn, includes three dimensions: the quality of the act (its character of being propositional, imperative, wishing, or whatever), the matter of the act (the way the object is presented), and the representative content of the act (the degree of fulfilment to which the object is presented: intuitive vs. signitive acts). In the intuitive acts—of which perception is the prototype—the object is immediately given, but in other, more distant acts, the object is merely intended in a symbolic fashion, the so-called signitive acts, which prototypically comprise linguistic expressions (but not only, cf. below). The meaning of signitive acts has no intuitive character, but, on the other hand, they aim at being fulfilled by synthesis with decidedly intuitive acts. This more complicated, founded act forms the "Erfüllungssynthese", that is, it fulfils an immanent striving present in the merely signitive acts. This very tension between signitive and intuitive acts forms Husserl's version of *Verstand* and *Sinnlichkeit*, respectively, and it is at stake in any linguistic and symbolical act in general as well in science more specifically. This fulfilling of an empty signitive act is thus a higher-order act, involving the *Leervorstellung* of the signitive act, its intuitive fulfilment, as well as the act founded upon the two which unites them.

A host of problems are implied here. For in sufficiently complicated acts, the signitive act contains lots of elements not immediately present in the fulfilling perception. Husserl's introductory example of these categorial elements in the *Logical Investigation* is sentential structure; all the *unselbständige* moments of the sentence (apart from the material presented in the nominals serving as subject and predicate), including quantifiers, conjunctions, numerals etc.—the syncategorematica of the Fourth Investigation. This leads to the idea of the "categorial intuition". The basic claim of phenomenology: that the justification of any kind of knowledge ultimately derives from the possibility of grasping it in intuition, is extended to include categorial aspects of meaning. Thus the concept of intuition is generalized to encompass categories. The categorial content of the act also aims at its own fulfilling intuition, that is, the idea that the object of the logical and formal apparatus of the expression can in some sense be grasped intuitively as it is in itself, in perfect analogy with the perceptive fulfilment of the parts of the expression referring to sensible objects. Categorial intuition thus comes to bear an immense weight in Husserl's epistemology: it becomes responsible for the grasping of everything that is not simply sensuous.[8] In short, categorial intuition is what

---

[8] Compared to this central role in Husserlian epistemology, categorial intuition has hardly received the interest it deserves. Among the most important contributions to its clarification are the following: R. SOKOLOWSKI, *The Formation of Husserl's Concept of Constitution*, The Hague: Martinus Nijhoff, 1964; *Husserlian Meditations*, Evanston: Northwestern University Press, 1974; "Husserl's Concept of Categorial Intuition", in J.N.Mohanty (ed.), *Phenomenology and the Human Sciences 1981*, Norman, Okl.

makes Husserl differ from a crude sensualism. Thus, it involves not only syncategorematica, but all kinds of ideal objects taken in a broad sense of the word: states-of-affairs, logic, mathematics, formal ontological categories, material ontological categories, all sorts of natural and cultural kinds, word meanings.[9] Thus the different essences grasped by eidetic variation (already introduced in the *Logical Investigation*) are intended by categorial intuition which thus includes *Wesenschau*. And thus the ideal objects grasped by categorial intuition include Ingarden's so-called "purely intentional objects"[10] involving the objects of linguistic meanings in general and literary works in particular. In introducing the new distinction between signitive and categorial, Husserl clarifies aspects which were mixed up in the Kantian outline: on the one hand, we have merely signitive meaning aiming at its intuitive fulfilment. On the other hand, we have two different forms of intuition, sensuous and categorial, respectively—and the categorial intentions possess their own type of intuitive fulfilment, more or less remotely founded upon sensuous intuition. This gives a combinatorial table as follows:

	signitive act	intuitive act
sensuous object		
categorial object		

1982; *Introduction to Phenomenology*, Cambridge: Cambridge University Press, 2000. D. LOHMAR, "Husserls Phänomenologie als Philosophie der Mathematik", Köln: Lohmar 1987; "Wo lag der Fehler der kategorialen Repräsentation? Zu Sinn und Rechweite einer Selbstkritik Husserls", *Husserl Studies* 7, 1990, 179-197; *Erfahrung und kategoriales Denken*, Dordrecht: Kluwer, 1998; "Husserl's Concept of Categorial Intuition", this volume. E. STRÖKER, "Husserls Evidenzprinzip", *Zeitschrift für philosophische Forschung* 32, 1978, 3-30. R. BERNET, "Perception, Categorial Intuition and Truth in Husserl's Sixth 'Logical Investigation'", in J. Sallis et al. (eds.), *The Collegium Phenomenologicum*, Dordrecht: Kluwer, 1988, 33-45; "Husserl's Theory of Signs Revisited", in R. Sokolowski (ed.), *Studies in Philosophy and the History of Philosophy*, vol. 18, Washington: Catholic University of America Press, 1988, 1-24. T. SEEBOHM, "Kategoriale Anschauung", in Th. Seebohm et al. (eds.), *Logik, Anschaulichkeit und Transparenz*, München: Karl Alber, 1990, 9-47; R. COBB-STEVENS, "Being and Categorial Intuition", *Review of Metaphysics* 44, 1990, 43-66. Most of these accounts aim at a reconstruction of Husserl's views (and are very useful, even fertile in so doing) and do not attempt to go into comparisons with other accounts of the problem. I suspect, however, that such comparisons might cast new light over the problem itself.

[9] Husserl's own examples of the higher-order objects grasped in categorial intution in the Sixth Investigation include the identity of an object, the relation of part to whole, relations, collections, the "ideierende Abstraktion" and its intuition of essences, the determinate and indeterminate grasping of single objects ("das A", "ein A"). Sokolowski's "Husserl's Concept of Categorial Intuition" presents a thorough analysis of the steps from an unanalyzed experience to its categorial articulation in subject and predicate. Lohmar's *Erfahrung und kategoriales Denken* articulates a general 3-step structure for categorial intuition: "Gesamtwahrnehmung, Sonderwahrnehmungen, kategoriale Synthesis".

[10] R. INGARDEN, *Das literarische Kunstwerk*, Tübingen: Max Niemeyer, 1972.

There are two possible sides to the signitive act; one side which requires fulfilment in a categorial intuition, another side requiring fulfilment in a sensuous intuition. Apart from very simple cases, most acts include categorial components (as soon as perceptual judgments are passed, for instance, or natural kinds are invoked, in perception, categorial meaning is implied). A pure intuition is possible, it should be added, only in the cases of certain types of objects (i.e., mental acts and certain species and universals[11]), but emphatically not in the cases of empirical objects, in which only partial fulfilments are possible due to their appearance in adumbrations.

The first axis (signitive-intuitive) is complicated by the fact that other types of approaches to the object are possible: intuitive acts comprise also imagination which presents its object through (partial) similarity, but without allowing immediate fulfilment. (Here, imagination should probably be taken to include imagery, phantasy, and memory alike, which were subsequently distinguished in Husserl's writings in the years after the *Logical Investigations*).[12] Finally, the combinatorial table given above is complicated by the fact that signitive intentions typically involve categorial meaning;[13] only signitive intentions with neither syntax nor generality (exclamation of simple word meanings) might constitute a limit case.

This ingenious construction leaves open one question: how is the fulfilment of a signitive act (a categorial form, respectively) performed? As Jocelyn Benoist has remarked, "Le paradoxe est qu'une forme catégoriale signitive ne peut être remplie que par une intuition déjà elle-même catégorisée."[14]

The problem is that no positive determination of the meaning part of the signitive intention, taken separately, is undertaken. On the one hand, signitive acts are distinct from mere indexical *Anzeichen*;[15] on the other hand, meaning is distinguished from all kinds of psychological imagery, representations, "Vorstellungen". Meaning is seen as the species whose instantiations are the single mutually synonymous meaning acts, but this does not indicate how the meaning can be characterised in each specific

---

[11] This is, of course, what makes transcendental phenomenology possible as a project: the idea of taking the essences of consciousness as an object of eidetic study. It seems possible, however, to retain the idea of the possibility of fulfilment of (certain) intentions aimed at eidetic phenomena as well as phenomenology as an anti-psychologist science of consciousness, without assuming the constitutive nature of the latter. This would preclude (or, at least, bracket) the possibility of a transcendental phenomenology, but preserve eidetic phenomenology.

[12] Cf. Hua XXIII.

[13] Later, in his drafts of a new version of the Sixth Investigation, Husserl took the position that they *always* involve such meaning, cf. U. MELLE, "Husserl's Revision of the Sixth Logical Investigation", this vol.

[14] J. BENOIST, *Phénoménologie, sémantique, ontologie*, Paris: P.U.F., 1997, 136

[15] We find in the three degenerate act types (imaginative, indexical, and signitive, respectively) a not coincidential parallel to Peirce's three different ways of signifying an object (icon, index, symbol). This has been noted by D. MÜNCH, *Intention und Zeichen*, Frankfurt am Main: Suhrkamp, 1993, 218.

case.[16]

But without any further positive determination of the meaning concept, it remains difficult to describe precisely why a specific meaning finds its fulfilment in the exact set of perceptions it does.

II. CATEGORIAL MEANINGS AND OBJECTS

The meaning and object sides of the act are easily distinguished in the prototypical categorial case of logic. Logic categories include *subject, predicate, proposition*, etc., and the corresponding object categories include *object, property, state-of-affairs*, etc. In general, logical categories refer to object categories pertaining to what Husserl calls *formal ontology*, the general science of objects without regard to their material qualities. This apparently simple duality between logic and formal ontology hides some complications. Both are species concepts, but meaning species and object species are not identical, even if the grasping of the second by means of the first plays a crucial epistemological role. Both, consequently, are species made explicit by the ideational abstraction described in the Second Investigation. At the same time, categorial meanings form a crucial part (that is, moment) of sufficiently complex, "sinnlich gemisschte" empirical meaning species in general (cf. below), just as categorial objects form parts (that is, moments) of empirical object species. This forms the central link in Husserl's solution to the problem of epistemology: by means of the dependency calculus in terms of parts and wholes, complex objects characterized by specific sums of interrelated parts may be represented in signitive meanings characterized by analogous interrelation systems between their parts.[17] This implies the possibility for manipulating with empty, signitive meanings without constant reference to their intuitive fulfilments: the (partial) isomorphism of the manipulation rules guarantee the fulfilment possibility. This basic idea is analogous to Peirce's general diagram concept in which the crucial feature is that the diagram is a sign representing its object by a schematic figure connecting parts by means of rational relations, that is, precisely a mereological analysis of the object in terms of ideal relations graspable by abstraction. This analogy leads to the main question of this paper: what precisely, does categorial meaning comprehend? It goes without saying that the basic logic categories form prototypical categoriality, but as categoriality is present wherever we rise from a purely sensous perception fulfilment,

---

[16] An analogous point is made by R. SOKOLOWSKI, *The Formation of Husserl's Concept of Constitution*, 59, when he complains that the account given of meanings in the *Logical Investigations* is "severely limited" because "their origins are not explained."

[17] This point and its relation to the transcendence issue is not always clearly emphasized; a strong exception is D. WILLARD, "Wholes, Parts, and the Objectivity of Knowledge", in B. Smith (ed.), *Parts and Moments*, München: Philosophia, 1982, 379-400.

logic is not sufficient for describing categoriality.[18]

A whole series of problems is connected with this issue: the role played by categoriality in fulfilment of signitive intentions; the status of different pictorial signs (and the categoriality inherent in them) in relation to the grasping of ideal objects; the principle of variation in the determination of species in general.

III. MEANING AS THE DETERMINATION OF A RANGE OF POSSIBLE INTUITIONS

Let us take a closer look at what meaning is supposed to *do*. In the beginning of the Sixth Investigation it is laconically stated that "The 'generality of the word' means, therefore, that the unified sense of one and the same word covers (or, in the case of a nonsense word, purports to cover) an *ideally delimited manifold of possible intuitions*, each of which could serve as the basis for an act of recognitive naming endowed with the same sense."(LI, 691-92 [Hua XIX, 563], our italics). This is exemplified as so often before in the word "red": "To the word 'red' corresponds the possibility of both knowing as, and calling 'red', all red objects that might be given in possible intuitions. This possibility leads, with an *a priori* guarantee, to the further possibility of becoming aware, through an *identifying synthesis* of all such naming recognitions, of a sameness of meaning of one with the other: this *A* is red, and that *A* is *the same*, i.e., *also* red: the two intuited singulars belong under the same 'concept'." (ibid.). The bound variation of the species meaning in question may singularize it in particular instantiations. Thus, it is the opposite operation of the variation undertaken in the abstraction process's isolation of the species in the first place.

This eidetic variation procedure can allegedly be applied in the most simple as well as in the most complicated cases; in the *Prolegomena*'s conclusive and ambitious outline of a "theory of theories" focusing on theoretical form, we find the same idea at the level of whole theories: to substitute for its given parts undetermined variables so as to leave only the formal categorial structure of the theory behind as invariant (§ 67).[19] Furthermore, the variation can be extended to involve the formal structure itself: by the variation of basic factors in the theory, the conditions for the transposition of one theory into another may be made clear (§ 69). Correlatively, on the object side of the theory, the domain of knowledge corresponding to the purely formal theory will be the idea of pure mathematics in general, the *Mannigfaltigkeitslehre* (§ 70). If space, writes Husserl, is the categorial form of cosmos, studied by geometry, then this is only a part of a genus of categorially determined manifolds describing space in

---

[18] In fact, if categoriality were identified with formal logic only, then some version of logical positivism might be the outcome. But it is not necessary to identify categoriality nor the propositional stance with logic or language. Rather, language is one (prominent, to be sure) instrument developed on the basis of the cognitive potentials of abstraction and categoriality. A very broad definition of categoriality—comprising all higher-level acts founded on perception—is proposed in B. SMITH, "Logic and Formal Ontology", in *Manuscrito* (forthcoming).

[19] The intimate connection between categorial intuition and this "theory of theories" is highlighted in COBB-STEVENS's "Being and Categorial Intuition".

a generalized meaning of the word. Here, the categorial form of the theory is strictly correlated with its object side. To the formal logic of the former corresponds the formal ontology of the latter.

In the Second Investigation, Husserl returns to the question in the famous discussion of the general triangle in the British empiricists. He refutes Locke's claim that the non-existence of the general triangle should imply that it is only a mere invention of understanding, and he critizises Hume's psychologistic and nominalist idea that a singular representation becomes general merely by means of the addition to it of a general name. On the other hand, Husserl is close to Berkeley at this point: the universal is a singular idea used to represent all other singular ideas of the same sort, provided that representation here is read as implying meaning rather than reference, as triggering rather than substituting.[20] The single sign can not refer to an infinity in extension, rather it means "any triangle, no matter which one".[21] Thus, the role of singular illustrations for universal concepts should be, Husserl repeats over and over, taken as trigger ("Anhalt") rather than substitute ("Stellvertreten"). So it is a *means* of grasping the thought rather than a *substitute* for it, but it is not necessarily a less prestigious role to be *Anhalt* than *Stellvertreter*. For the role of the trigger seems to be an illustration—an ilustration subsequently to be read in an eidetic fashion, and, in turn, to be varied eidetically in order to yield "any triangle".[22]

IV. VARIATION AND ABSTRACTION

We know from the criticism of the empirical abstraction theories in the Second Investigation that the way we make an "ideierende Abstraktion" is analogous to what Husserl later in *Experience and Judgment* calls 'eidetic variation'; that is, we substitute for all non-essential parts of the phenomenon empty, algebraic variables, making it

---

[20] Calling the illustration, the diagram token, a "representation" takes up Husserl's terminology for the way the act content represents its object. In J.-M. ROY, "Saving Intentional Phenomena: Intentionality, Representation, and Symbol" in J. Petitot et al. (eds.), *Naturalizing Phenomenology*, Stanford, Stanford University Press, 1999, 111-47, Husserl's distinction between signitive and intuitive based on different representations is taken as the point of departure for a detailed argumentation leading to the claim that "Repräsentation" must not in this context be read symbolically as in the normal Anglo-Saxon use of "representation". If such a reading is preferred, intuitive representations will lose their direct connection to their object. Husserl's solution is to take the representational content to be identical and the difference between the two to lie in the "Auffassungsform". Consequently, diagrams will be categorial representations characterized by an intuitive form of apprehension.

[21] In Peirce, this problem is solved by taking general meaning to have a continuum of merely possible (but vague) referents as its extension.

[22] Here, Husserl is on a par with Peirce for whom the diagram is not the particular drawing on the page nor the reader's perception of it. Peirce thus distinguishes between the diagram token—the particular drawing on the page, corresponding to Husserl's "Anhalt"—and the diagram type which we are able to grasp through a reading of that token, governed by a symbolic sign (which, in Peirce's terminology, implies generality).

possible to focus upon the invariant species left.[23]

In the conclusion to the Second Investigation's eidetic abstraction theory, Husserl explains the extended meaning of abstraction as follows: "Thus we directly apprehend the Specific Unity *Redness* on the basis of a singular intuition of something red. We look to its moment of red, but we perform a peculiar act, whose intention is directed at the 'Idea', the 'universal'. Abstraction in the sense of this act is wholly different from the mere attention to, or emphasis on, the moment of red; to indicate this difference we have repeatedly spoken of *ideational or generalizing abstraction*."(LI, 432 [Hua XIX, 226]).

In this two-tier account for abstraction (emphasis—generalization) there is a surprising similarity to Peirce's abstraction theory, in which he puts great weight on distinguishing various types of abstraction having to do with the distribution of attention to selected aspects of the object on the one hand (involving three types of "distinctions"), and the so-called "hypostatic abstraction" on the other. The seminal attention focussing abstraction, which enables us to distinguish parts which can not act as distinct unities, is "prescission".[24] But this focussing mecanism, however important, does not by itself lead to higher degrees of abstraction. The property focussed upon must, in turn, be made subject to "hypostatic abstraction" which makes of it a general noun as a subject for a new proposition with predicates to be determined. This two-step abstraction mechanisms seem to correspond to what Husserl outlines in the Second Investigation in the quote given with its distinction of the "Hervorheben" and the "generalisierender Abstraktion".

To return to the issue of the 'illustrative' aspect of meaning, this abstraction account seems to clarify more precisely what we more exactly do when we use a picture as "Anhalt": first, we emphasize the moment of it in question ("Red", "Triangle"), second, we generalize this moment of it by variation which is what, third, permits us to give it a specific, nominalized name ("Redness", "Triangularity").[25] But once this has been achieved, there is, conversely, a way "back"; by using variation we may now devise the "ideally delimited manifold of possible intuitions", that is, we may, by variation, produce any particular triangle. The variation principle delimits the manifold. The question here is: what is the part played by categoriality in this relation of variation between signitive intention and intuitive fulfilment?

---

[23] As is evident, this variation procedure is modeled upon function analysis in mathematics, even in Husserl's terminology.

[24] On Peirce's abstraction theory in relation to wholes and parts, see F. STJERNFELT, "Schemata, Abstraction, and Biology" in B. Brogaard and B. Smith (eds.),*Rationality and Irrationality*,Vienna: öbvhpt, 2001, 341-61; on mereology in Husserl, Peirce, Jakobson, and Hjelmslev, see F. STJERNFELT, "Mereology and semiotics", *Sign System Studies* 28, 2000, 72-98.

[25] As has been studied by the cognitive semantics tradition (G. LAKOFF, *Women, Fire, and Dangerous Things*), this variaiton procedure may be subject to complicated and conflicting constraints in empirical concepts giving rise to a "radial" concept structure with highly variable variation possibilities departing from at prototypical center.

V. HUSSERL'S EXAMPLES IN THE *LOGICAL INVESTIGATIONS*

Husserl's general description of categorial intuition suffers from the same defects as does the analogous description of sensuous fulfilment—we do not know the precise road from signitive categorial intentions to fulfilled categorial intentions presenting categorial intuitions. But unlike the case in the perceptual counterpart, we do not even have a clear idea of what the relevant fulfilment looks like. Husserl's own primary examples involve formal logic and its use in linguistic syntax of empirical languages as for instance when he considers the example of conjunction ("und"). He writes, in a famous passage, that the act of conjunction is different from simple—non-categorial—perceptions of sensously given unitary sets, series, swarms etc., because it is a distinct act adding the contents of two former acts to mean the compound content "A and B". So this conjunction is a founded, categorial act requiring its own intuitive fulfilment.[26]

Some of the more complicated examples given in the course of the *Logical Investigations* may throw some light upon this issue—e.g., the mathematical expression to be calculated; the map of England; the recognition of Goethe's handwriting; the model of the steam engine. Husserl does not draw any categorial conclusion from this variety of examples, but taken together, they make it possible to outline what we may regard categorial intuition as involving. Not all of these examples are given in the relation to the Sixth Investigation's chapters on categorial intuition, but still they involve different aspects of it.

The first example concerns the mathematical expression $(5^3)^4$ and is concerned with mediate fulfilment. It is not the case that the meaning of a complicated expression is of the same kind as a simple word meaning. On the contrary, the complicated expression facilitates "... the possibility of *fulfilment-chains built member upon member out of signitive intentions*. We clarify the concept $(5^3)^4$ by having recourse to the definitory presentation: Number which arises when one forms the product $5^3 \times 5^3 \times 5^3 \times 5^3$." (LI, 723 [Hua XIX, 601]). In the same manner, this expression takes us back to simpler definitions, and every step in this operation is an act of fulfilment, prescribed by the signitive representation: "A remarkable property of the cases just discussed, and of the class of significative presentations which they illustrate, lies in the fact that in them the *content* of the presentations—or, more clearly their 'matter'—*dictates a*

---

[26] D. LOHMAR ("Husserls Phänomenologie als Philosophie der Mathematik", "Wo lag der Fehler der kategorialen Repräsentation?", *Erfahrung und kategoriales Denken*) highlights this example in order to correct an error which Husserl himself later detects (E. HUSSERL, "Entwurf einer "Vorrede" zu den "Logischen Untersuchungen" 1913", *Tijdschrift voor philosophie* 1/1, 1939, 106-33; 1/2, 1939, 319-339; cf. K. SCHUHMANN, "Forschungsnotizen über Husserls "Entwurf einer 'Vorrede' zu den 'Logischen Untersuchungen'", *Tijdschrift voor filosofie* 34/3, 1972, 513-24). Husserl's idea in the *Logical Investigations* was that the categorial act of collection by means of the "und" operator could only reach fulfilment by a 'reflection upon the act itself', because it is the very act that constitutes the collection of entities envisaged (all possible entities whatsoever may be such collected). As an alternative to this strange idea where the performance of an act becomes the intuition fulfilling that same act, Lohmar points to fulfilment as *Deckungssynthesis* between partial intentions. Thus, collection would be so to speak a zero-degree *Deckungseinheit* and is probably involved in all more complicated acts because it simply co-localizes its entities in one and the same categorial place.

determinate order of fulfilment a priori."(LI, 724 [Hua XIX, 602]). What can be learnt from this example is that certain expressions allow their contents to be constructed by a stepwise operation with increasing fulfilment. If we generalize this to other mathematical expressions we can add that it is far from always the case that the procedure to be undertaken is unanimous nor clear. An equation may be solved in different ways, in different variables; maybe it may not be solved at all; maybe it is not even known whether it may be solved. Similarly, a theorem may be proved in different ways, maybe it is undecidable, maybe its not known whether it may be proved or not (Goldbach's conjecture). In short, in expressions like these, a (to some extent) rule-bound but otherwise free operation can be performed in order to seek fulfilment, but only in some cases is it clear that stepwise fulfilment is able to reach its goal.

This may be compared to an example given a couple of pages earlier on an intuitive series of fulfilment: "Another example of an intuitive fulfilment-series is the transition from a rough drawing to a more exact pencil-sketch, then from the latter to the completed picture, and from this to the living finish of the painting, all of which present the same, visibly the same, object."(LI, 721 [Hua XIX, 599]). This fulfilment series has a slightly different character from the mathematical case—also apart from involving imaginary rather than signitive intentions. In the painting series, the earlier stages may be left behind, once the latter more fulfilled ones are reached. But this is not so in the mathematical example where it is important to remember the problem which the number 244140625 is in fact a solution to. Here, conversely, $(5^3)^4$ might as well be a fulfilment of this number, in an intention pointing the opposite way, given the signitive intention (much more difficult, to be sure) to resolve it into prime factors.

A peculiar case concerns what Husserl calls "signitive intentions outside the meaning function"—referring to acts of classification without the relevant word being invoked. The examples may be the recognition of a thing as a Roman roadstone or of a tool as a drilling machine—but separated from the uttering of the corresponding word. The classification of a phenomenon as belonging to a species seems thus to be the pure function of the signitive intention.[27] "Objects are, strictly speaking, only 'known', as they are given in their actual intuitive foundation, but, since the unity of our intention ranges further, objects appear to be known as what they are for this total intention. *The character of knowing is accordingly somewhat broadened.* Thus we recognize (know) a person as an adjutant of the Kaiser, a handwriting as Goethe's, a mathematical expression as the Cardanian formula, and so on. Here our recognition can of course not apply itself to what is given in perception, at best it permits possible application to intuitive sequences, which need not themselves be actualized at all."(LI, 716 [Hua XIX, 593]). With the signifier of the expression placed in brackets, this paragraph in fact presents the signitive intention *in nuce*: it concerns the pure species and the problem of how, given a concrete perception, this perception is classified as instantiating the species: a piece of handwriting identified as Goethe's. This, in fact, is to our day still a problem hard to solve: how is it possible to identify a style of writing? From a general

---

[27] This corresponds to Peirce's semiotics where the classification of objects in types do not require symbols, while the opposite is the case.

point of view, this question may be of the same kind as those about the emperor's servant and Cardan's theorem, but from a detailed cognitive science point of view, there is a huge difference. The simple version of variation is certainly not possible in the Goethe's handwriting example: there are no simple parts which may be replaced with algebraic variables. Rather, the species are grasped through the variation of the whole with certain stylistic features kept constant: the variation of the type of ink and the type of paper is easily performed, but the variation of the written expression with the style kept invariant is more difficult. We can not seriously assume a variation which *de facto* covers all possible texts in the world, rewritten using Goethe's handwriting, rather we implicitly grasp the idea of such a variation and judge it possible in principle. Goethe's style is grasped as a set of certain, typical, stable variative aberrations as compared to a normal zero handwriting.[28] This is an adaptation to intuition processes which need not be actualized themselves: we need not see for our inner gaze other examples of Goethe's handwriting in order to recognize an example of it, this variation is presumably undertaken without being explicit in consciousness.

From this example, two things can be inferred: that the main problem resides not in the (mostly arbitrary) relation between word expression and meaning, but in the relation between meaning and its fulfilment; and that the variation process involved in classification may vary the content continually while keeping general moments invariant which characterize the whole of the object and which are hard, maybe impossible, to make explicit as such.

A further example is the map of England, a prototypical diagram example. Husserl mentions it as an example of an indirect representative serving as partly fulfilling intuition: "... as when the use of a geographical name calls up the imaginative presentation of a map, which blends with the meaning-intention of this name ..."(LI, 727 [Hua XIX, 606]). When the fulfilling of the name "England" is performed by a map (instead of by the object itself), it sure is an indirect object. "The analogy of what appears and what is meant, which may be present here, does not lead to a straightforward presentation by way of an image, but to a sign-presentation resting upon the latter. The outline of England as drawn on a map, may indeed represent the form of the land itself, but the pictorial image of the map which comes up when England is mentioned, does not *mean* England itself in pictorial fashion, not even mediately, as the country pictured on the map. It means England after the manner of a mere sign, through external relations of association, which have tied all our knowledge of land and people to the map-picture." (ibid.) The map referring to England is seen as a complicated expression with several levels; the iconic qualities of the map in relation to England is

---

[28] A strong case, built on an analogy to Gödel's theorem, can be made for the claim that the set of possible writing styles is so large that it cannot be exhausted by computational algorithms (cf. D. HOFSTADTER, *Metamagical Themas*, Harmondsworth: Penguin, 1986; F. STJERNFELT, "Buchstabenformen, Kategorien und die Apriori-Position", in H.U. Gumbrecht and L. Pfeiffer (eds.), *Schrift*, München: Wilhelm Fink, 1992, 289-310. Thus, the very concept of writing style cannot be the result of a variation procedure limited to computational strength. Thus it points to the fact that the variation implied in grasping essences does not always—if ever—proceed to completion through all possible variants. Rather we intuit the fact that such a variation may go on indefinitely.

superposed by the use of it as a sign referring to England as the object, including the associative connections to our diverse knowledge of that country. So the map is not a mere picture, even if is indeed built on iconic qualities. It must be considered as a diagram, which implies two things: a similarity between map and object, plus the use of the map as a sign for the object.

What can be learnt from this example is that the map has a double foundation: it is composed of a moment of similarity on the one hand and of a signitive intention on the other.

The last of Husserl's scattered examples concerns the most typical diagram example in the *Logical Investigations*: the steam engine model. The example occurs in the context of the chapter of the Sixth Investigation which concludes the exposition of sensuous and categorial intuitions. The chapter introduces the crucial distinction between (1) the categorial synthesis of simple perceptions (e.g., particular states-of-affairs)—and (2) general intuitions with general objects. The categorial syntheis and the general intuitions give rise to *synthetical* and *abstractive* categorial intuitions, respectively. In the former, the founding acts' objects are included in the founded acts, not so in the latter—but both are categorial acts. Accordingly, we may distinguish at least three types of involvement of categorial intuition: one is present in the categorial moments of simple perception judgments, e.g., of concrete states-of-affairs. Another is the pure grasping of categorial structures in specie, in logic and mathematics. And yet another is the use of categorial means to grasp general empirical objects.

A crucial observation here is the following: "Talk of 'perception' presupposes the possibility of correspondent imagination: a distinction between them, we held, is part of the natural sense of our ordinary talk about 'intuition'. But it is just this distinction that we cannot here draw. This seems to stem from the fact that abstractive acts do not differ in consonance with the character of the straightforward intuitions which underlie them; they are quite unaffected by the assertive or non-assertive character of such underlying acts, or by their perceptual or imaginative character."(LI, 800 [Hua XIX, 691]). The fact that the distinction between imagination and perception becomes irrelevant in the case of categorial intuition is very important: it implies that when talking about categories, an imaginative fulfilment is as good as any. This brief statement is ripe with consequences. The function of imagination as access to ideal structures is implied, just as the role of thought experiments in science and thought in general. This implies, moreover, that merely imaginative representatives of categorial structures may be used as completely fulfilling signs for them. As to the categorial structure of an object, it is an image of a special, general kind (or, as Peirce calls it, a diagram) which permits us to directly grasp the very category in specie. This includes a general categorial "reading" of a particular example, cf. the discussion of Locke's triangle above. An individual object can not serve as an analogy of itself, Husserl writes, but "It is quite different in, e.g. the case where mathematical analysis has given us an indirectly conceived Idea of a certain class of curves of the third order, though we have never *seen* any curve of this sort. In such a case an intuitive figure, e.g. of a familiar third-order curve, perhaps actually drawn, perhaps merely pictured, may very well serve as an intuitive image, an analogon, of the universal we are intending: our *consciousness of the universal is here intuitive, but analogically intuitive, in its use of an individual intuition.*" (LI, 801 [Hua XIX, 692], our italics). This interesting claim is what is exemplified in the steam engine example: "And does not an ordinary rough drawing function analogically in comparison with an ideal figure, thereby helping to condition the *imaginative character of the universal presentation?* This is how we contemplate the Idea of a steam-engine, basing ourselves on a model of a steam-engine, in which case there can naturally be no talk of an adequate abstraction or conception. In such cases we are not concerned with significations [In solchen Fällen haben wir es mit keinen blossen Signifikationen zu tun], but with universal representations by way of analogy, with universal imaginations, in short." (ibid.)

This characterization of the model of the steam engine[29] thus unites iconicity and generality—Peirce's two major characterizations of the diagram. Unlike the merely signitive word "steam engine", the model implies a general imagination of the idea of such a machine—and the act of imagination is in abstract, categorial cases a complete fulfilment. But implicitly, it also displays the third major feature of diagrams: the possibility for experimenting. A model of a steam engine reveals the idea of the working of this apparatus only when conceived of in a temporal, operational, and experimental fashion. The model gives rise to a thought experiment, letting water be heated, steam to be produced and suddenly cooled with the characteristic working process of the machine as a result. Mobile parts of the object which are possible to manipulate physically may add to the efficiency of such thought experiments. This feature of the diagram is only implicitly present as a necessary feature in Husserl's steam engine example, but in the mathematical example above it was made explicit in the idea of a stepwise, operational *Erfüllungsreihe*.

To sum up: categorial intuition and its use in the direct "erschauen" of meaning

---

[29] We can ask, then, what is implied in the *mere* signification of the word "steam engine", before the analogical fulfilment by the general imagination of the model? "Steam engine" is a compound noun, that is, it means an engine somehow concerned with steam. Depending on the underlying schema chosen, such an engine could work by steam, produce stem, fight against steam, etc. The syntax of noun composition tells us only that it is an engine in some way concerned with steam (thus founded upon simpler signitive acts aimed at "steam", and "engine", respectively; but these acts are both concerned with general objects and thus already presupposing categoriality in the form of generalizing abstraction.). The same structure characterizes Descartes' famous "chiliogon"-example which Husserl uses to argue against the representative use of diagrams in geometry. True, we can not imagine such a figure in its finished shape, and thus the understanding of the P-S structure of the word, literally "thousand-edge", rests on our categorial understanding of the syntactical structure as well as our categorial understanding of each of the composite elements: a figure with a thousand edges. A further step in the *Erfüllungsreihe* may now prompt us to try to construct the figure in imagination. We still cannot imagine it as a figure, but we may imagine the procedure to construct it (take a rectangle and subdivide the sides until you get a number close to thousand, then add or subtract sides until you get thousand.). An analogous case is the well-known "round square" with its impossibility of intuitively construing such an object. All such composite expressions prompt an *Erfüllungsreihe* prescribed both by their syntactical structure, by their founding acts. The compound noun problem forms a center of the discussion of grammatical "blending" in Turner and Fauconnier's cognitive semantics (cf. M. TURNER & G. FAUCONNIER, *The Way We Think* (in press); P. BUNDGAARD, F. STJERNFELT, & S. ØSTERGAARD, , "Dolphin Safe Fire Stations" (in press).).

as species constitutes a strikingly close parallel in the *Logical Investigations* to the mature Peirce's diagrammatic epistemology. Peirce's distinctions between pure and applied diagrams find a counterpart here in the distinction between pure categorial intuition (in which categories are grasped in abstraction from the acts they spontaneously appear in) and categories put to use in the grasping of empirical species (such as the steam engine) or empirical states-of-affairs. Furthermore, Peirce's extrapolation of logic from formal inference schemata to cover a much wider range of diagrammatic signs finds its (implicit, that is) counterpart in these (few, but) widespread examples in Husserl's text. These examples make it clear that not only logic, but also geometry and the whole "Mannigfaltigkeitslehre" of the *Prolegomena* form the content of pure categorial intuitions, that are possibly to be put to use in applied—"sinnlich vermisschte"—categorial intuitions.

Finally, it must be the more or less perfect grasping of categorially formed species that allows for the mysterious route leading from signitive intentions to intuitive fulfillings. How should the passage from the word "steam engine" to the perceptive fulfilling of it be possible if not via the intermediary (maybe only parts or aspects of) a general, imaginative model of it?[30]

VI. THE AMBIGUOUS STATUS OF PICTURES IN THE *LOGICAL INVESTIGATIONS*

Taken as a whole the *Logical Investigations* remain ambiguous as to the role of pictures. It seems as if two tendencies are *verschmeltzt*—fused together—in the early Husserl: one is the phenomenological turn against psychologism; the other is the formal turn against imagination in favor of formal calculi, and I believe there is a tendency in Husserl to confuse the two. This can be seen in his repeated arguments against "phantasies" in the question of semantics—all at the same time as the steam engine example admits the crucial role of imagination in categorial intuition fulfilment. But this confusion is has dire consequences. There are two strands in this argument. One is the

---

[30] However, a problem remains concerning the purely sensuous species concepts. Husserl distinguishes three cases: sensuous abstraction giving sensuous concepts, categorial abstraction yielding pure categorial concepts, and a large group of mixed concepts (with "color", "house", "judgment", "wish" as examples of the first ones, "unity", "plurality", "connection", "concept" as examples of the second ones, and "coloredness", "virtue", "parallel axiom" as examples of the mixed group. The latter two can of course be seen as direct parallels to Peirce's pure and applied diagrams, respectively. Peirce also admits the existence of concepts not (yet?) analyzable in diagrams and mentions "murder" as an example. Still, I would argue, even concepts as these are not without diagrammatic content. Both Husserl's "house" and Peirce's "murder" are founded concepts; both presuppose a schema of willful, human action oriented towards a goal and towards eliminating certain factors opposing that goal. I have argued for the existence of a teleological schema of this sort in F. STJERNFELT, "Biosemiotics and Formal Ontology", *Semiotica* 127-1/4, 1999, 537-66. The reason why Peirce will not consider "murder" a diagram is that its semantics contains no rational relations. But this only implies that it is a "stiffened" diagram: it is not possible to perform any information-yielding experiments on it. But it is still a diagram in so far as it is a schematic relation able to subsume instantiations by variation. Thus, I believe that the field of pure sensuous concepts is probably narrower than both Husserl and Peirce suppose; they seem to be restricted to primitive sense qualities and even then, the categorial apparatus of variation is necessary for isolating them from phenomenological experience.

anti-psychological argument: semantics is not psychology and meaning must be conceived of as an ideal, phenomenological species and should not be taken to rely on more or less contingent, individual, mental phantasies. But this does not entail that semantics is formal—in the sense of lacking intuition—rather it necessitates a concept of phenomenologically pure, eidetic pictures, the "allgemeine Imaginationen" that Husserl points to at the end of the central chapter in the Sixth Investigation—that is, diagrams.

The ambiguous attitude towards pictures is mirrored in a similarly ambiguous attitude towards space. Husserl writes for instance (LI, 455 [Hua XIX, 256]), when discussing the redefinition of analytic/synthetic concepts, that ideal objects comprise two types, the essences to which "...correspond the concepts or propositions which have content, which we sharply distinguish from purely formal concepts and propositions, which lack all 'matter' or 'content'. To the latter belong the categories of formal logic and the formal ontological categories mentioned in the last chapter of the *Prolegomena*, which are essentially related to these, as well as to all syntactical formations they engender. Concepts like Something, One, Object, Quality, Relation, Association, Plurality, Number, Order, Ordinal Number, Whole Part, Magnitude etc., have a basically different character from concepts like House, Tree, Colour, Tone, Space, Sensation, Feeling, etc., which for their part express genuine content", the two categories of concepts giving rise to formal and material ontologies which are analytical and synthetical disciplines a priori, respectively. Here, surprisingly, space is classified along with the other material species that belong to different material ontologies. This classification of it apparently runs counter to what is said in the conclusion of the *Prolegomena* where we find the idea that the correlate to a purely formally conceived theory is a field of experience in general. This field is, in turn, to be studied by Husserl's general conception of mathematics, the "Mannigfaltigkeitslehre". But here, this study *includes* space, placing it on the purely formal level, far from the "sachhaltige" rendering of it in the quote above: "... if we mean by 'space' the categorial form of world-space, and, correlatively, by 'geometry' the categorial theoretic form of geometry in the ordinary sense, then space falls under a genus, which we can bound by laws, of pure, categorially determinate manifolds, in regard to which it is natural to speak of 'space' in a yet more extended sense."(LI, 242 [Hua XVIII, 252]). Thus, the specific concepts of space pertaining to each material ontology are but species of a formal genus of space belonging to formal ontology. But this general space category implies that space is also among the categories finding fulfilment in the categorial intuition. This allows for the Husserlian counterpart to Peirce's pure diagrams (requiring space) with no reference to any actual existence.

With this insight, we can return to the issue of the possible role of pictures in the fulfilment of signitive intentions. As a geometer, Husserl agrees completely with the formalist tendencies of his time: "It is a well-known fact that no geometrical concept whatsoever can be adequately illustrated. We imagine or draw a stroke, and speak or think of a straight line."(LI, 302 [Hua XIX, 70]). The picture drawn is no representative of the geometrical object—cf. Locke's triangle—but is a mere "Anhalt", a trigger for a more precise fulfilment, just like Peirce's diagram token is not in itself a representation but merely a precondition for the diagram type to be grasped. Now, given the possibility of a stepwise fulfilment with an increasing degree of fulfilment, this role of "Anhalt" may be given a more detailed description: the picture is read in an eidetic manner, governed by the signitive intention present (for instance, the picture of a triangle accompanied by the word "triangle"—as opposed to the very same picture accompanied by the word "manifold", "polygon", "Jourdan-curve", etc., emphasizing other moments in it). This eidetic reading of the concrete picture is a higher-level categorial act, founded on the signitive and pictorial acts alike, and it makes possible the eidetic imagination of the general picture. The concrete drawing is not general, but the categoriality of the signitive intention prompts such a reading. Husserl himself does not consider further this interplay between pictorial and signitive intentions leading to eidetic imagination, but Peirce's diagram concept does just that. It emphasizes the diagram's double determination: it is an icon in so far as it is a (skelettal) picture of its object, but it is governed by a symbol permitting the emphasizing of the relevant aspects of the picture intended. To that extent, the interplay between symbol and icon, signitive and pictorial intentions, prompts eidetic abstraction permitting us to imagine the pure species. This species may now, in turn, be used to map the relational structure of widely differing empirical objects (triangle trade, erotic triangles, triangulation in navigation, etc.). The diagram category thus makes evident that the mereological dependency calculi of the sort laid down in the Third Investigation are necessary but not sufficient for formal ontology. Mereology needs supplementation by other branches of mathematics; geometry, topology, and category theory are prominent candidates, but only ongoing investigation will show which formal disciplines will be needed adequately to map the categorial properties of diagrams and the corresponding categorial objects they depict.

VII. HUSSERLIAN CATEGORIAL INTUITIONS AND PEIRCEAN DIAGRAMS

To sum up, in the relation between signitive and intuitive acts, categorial intuition plays the following roles:

- it permits the synthesis of contents into all kinds of nominal objects and states-of-affairs
- it permits that the eidetic variation be a crucial step in grasping species, that is, meaning. Once the species is constituted, the variation procedure may work in the other direction furnishing the species with possible particular instantiations
- it permits the rule-bound, stepwise fulfilment of certain signitive acts (the mathematical and the sketch examples)
- it permits the adequate grasping of formal logical structures in formal ontology. As J. Petitot points out, this implies the necessity of geometrising the

basic structures in formal ontology.[31]
- it permits the grasping of the content of complicated empirical species (the steam machine example) by permitting rule-bound operations involving its parts in specific configurations.

All of these points make categorial intuitions play roles very similar to if not exactly identical with those played by the diagram in the mature Peirce's theory of knowledge. Here, diagrams are similar to their objects in two crucial aspects: they perform relational, mereological analyses of their objects, and what is most important, they are subject to Peirce's operational criterion for iconicity: one phenomenon is an icon for another if and only if experiments or manipulations on the former may reveal new insight into the latter ("new" in the sense that the information in question is not explicity expressed in the icon). This implies that diagrams are the vehicles for all deductive reasoning—such reasoning simply being defined as manipulations on diagrams.

This procedural aspect of the diagram's iconicity is not explicitly thematized in Husserl's account of categorial intuitions, but it is, as shown, present in his examples. The crucial variation procedure itself is nothing but an operation on a diagram; the steam engine model permits us to imagine the working of the machine in an operational procedure; the rule-bound transformation of the mathematical expression is another operation on a diagram.

In Peirce, this operational criterion for iconicity is tied to a metaphysics of continuity: to perform an operation on the diagram implies the continuity between the single diagram instances which the operation connects—which facilitates the corresponding continuous unity of the depicted object in space and time.[32] From a

---

[31] Thus, I perfectly agree in his insistence that it is a mistake for Husserl to claim that the "vague morphologies" principally resist mathematization (cf. the introduction to J. Petitot et al., *Naturalizing Phenomenology*). It is interesting to note that this was not unanimously Husserl's contention in the first version of the *Logical Investigations* where he still claims the ideal that "Die vagen Gebilde der Anschauung mittels exakter Begriffe möglichst deutlich zu charakterisieren, ist überhaupt eine phänomenologische Aufgabe ...", even if he immediately admits that this task "... lange nicht genug angegriffen und auch in Beziehung auf die vorliegende Untersuchungen nicht gelöst ist" (Hua XIX, 249). My English translation: "To characterize the vague forms of intuition in the most clear way by means of exact concepts, this is in general a phenomenological task ..." which "... has not, for a long time, been sufficiently investigated, and it is not solved in connection with the present Investigation."). The second version replaces this contention with a longer argumentation to emphasize that "Offenbar sind die Wesensgestaltungen aller anschauliche Gegebenheiten als solcher prinzipiell nicht unter "exakte" oder "Ideal-Begriffe", wie es die mathematischen sind, zu bringen." (ibid.). In the English translation: "The descriptive concepts of all pure description, i.e. of description adapted to intuition immediately and with truth and so of all phenomenological description, differ in principle from those which dominate objective science. To clear up these matters is a phenomenological task never yet seriously undertaken and not carried out in relation to our present distinction" (LI, 451).

[32] Of course, discontinuous operation procedures are possible, e.g., the stepwise construal of $(5^3)^4$. But discontinuity is dependent on continuity, Peirce would argue: the only way we are able to synthezise the single components of a discontinuous procedure into one state-of-affairs is by embedding them in a continuous space. Thus, discontinuous phenomena are always embedded into continuous ones, and discontinuous objects or calculi presuppose (explicitly or not), continuity.

Husserlian point of view, this central property in diagrams is related to several important issues. One is the idea clearly brought to the fore in *Ding und Raum*,[33] that the very prerequisite for the unity of a logical entity is the continuum of *Abschattungen* of an object which makes their schematic synthesis possible. This forms the very basis of the founding of logic on phenomenology in Husserl, and it implies, as Jean Petitot remarks, that the categories of object and logic both presuppose continuity.[34] This casts a Husserlian light on the operational icon definition in Peirce's diagrams: it is because the object *itself* is defined by a range of continuous operations that a formalized icon may depict it by repeating (parts of) these operations. Furthermore, it connects time-consciousness intimately to diagrams—as well as to categorial intuition: it is only through the synthesis of temporal experience with the fulfilment series involved in diagram manipulation that the corresponding insight into its object becomes possible.

VIII. DIAGRAMS AS WHOLES WITH SENSUOUS MOMENT OF UNITY?

Having argued for the contributions which Peirce's diagram concept may add to categorial intuition and the *Logical Investigations,* we may now let Husserl's conception throw a refining light back on Peirce's ideas. For why is it that diagrams are so apt at capturing ideal objects? As Elmar Holenstein argues,[35] Husserl's arguments in §§ 60ff of the Sixth Investigation places him at a delicate intermediate position with respect to the different schools of Gestalt Theory. Husserl claims, of course, that categorial acts are founded upon sensuous acts—but, then again, he does not claim the same for acts intending sensuos Gestalts which are grasped immediately. In the first claim, Husserl agrees with Meinong's and the Graz school's "theory of production"; in the second claim, though, Husserl is on a par with the Berlin School led by Koffka, claiming that the Graz view reintroduced sense data not pertinent in experience and invoking the direct perception of Gestalts instead. If Husserl is correct on this point, this may throw some light upon the efficacy of diagrams: they permit to grasp categorial contents *by the representation of them in sensuous Gestalts,* provided with signitive, categorial reading instructions. True, as we have seen, the sensuous Gestalt is by no means sufficient in itself (Locke's triangle) and it needs to be supplemented by general rules for its eidetic reading, for its variation, as well as for the experimenting upon it. The diagram (or, at least, the simplest significant part of it) must be graspable *in one glance* in order to represent the relevant species or type. There must be a minimum of

---

[33] Hua XVI.

[34] J. PETITOT, "Morphological Eidetics for a Phenomenology of Perception", in J. Petitot et al. (eds.), *Naturalizing Phenomenology*, 330-71.

[35] In E. HOLENSTEIN, *Phänomenologie der Assoziation*, Den Haag: Martinus Nijhoff, 1972, 288. Husserl's argument rests on § 22 in the Third Investigation, where he notes that not every whole requires a specific moment of unity, only the "zerstückbare" wholes requires that. All which is really uniting consists of relations of foundation, and unity is a categorial predicate, even though this unity is given directly, sensuously in Gestalts.

spontaneous Gestalt grasping for the mind to be able in any way to construct more complicated Gestalts or to abstract features from the Gestalt in order to represent categorial properties.[36] This would give a further Husserlian support to Peirce's claim that all necessary reasoning proceeds by diagrams.

Peircean diagrams and Husserlian categorial intuitions—both suggest that the necessity of the intuitive access to ideal objects is a prerequisite for a phenomenologically conceived realism. Categories and diagrams give such intuitive access to idealities and so makes possible the recognition of empirical objects instantiating analogically formed properties. The central role of a de-mentalized, eidetic notion of icons, of *allgemeine Imaginationen*, must be recognized, in all degrees of generality, and their role in categorial fulfilment must be further investigated.

Thanks to Berit Brogaard, Barry Smith, and Dan Zahavi for helpful comments.

---

[36] This fact is, of course, what gives rise to the attempts to find a vocabulary of simple schemata, e.g., the "kinaesthetic image schemas" in G. LAKOFF'S, *Women, Fire, and Dangerous Things*, or the schemata in A. PERUZZI's, "An Essay on the Notion of Schema". The precise amount of such schemata which the human mind is able to process is no doubt governed by empirical psychological regularities—but an eidetic, phenomenological corollary is that *any* possible mind will have to do with some finite vocabulary or other of such simple diagram atoms. This will, in fact, be the phenomenological equivalent of the impossibility of "intellectual intuition": if we possessed such a faculty, we could process infinitely complicated diagrams would be possible to process momentaneously.

IV

Semiotics, Alterity, Cognitive Science

ROBERT SOKOLOWSKI
Catholic University of America

SEMIOTICS IN HUSSERL'S *LOGICAL INVESTIGATIONS*

Husserl begins the first of his *Logical Investigations*[1] by examining what he calls "The Essential Distinctions." The first distinction he makes is between two kinds of sign, indications and expressions, *Anzeigen* and *Ausdrücke*. Notice how he proceeds here at the start of his phenomenology, at the point where he is analyzing consciousness and defining his terms for the very first time. He does not begin his philosophy by looking inward at consciousness. His access to intentional acts is not by introspection. Rather, his access is through the public, palpable, and worldly phenomena of signs, both indicative and expressive. Signs are public things, they are "outside" the mind: they are sounds, marks, arrangements of objects, a wave of the hand, a pile of stones. It is by examining such public things that Husserl gains access to intentionality and makes distinctions within it.

However, signs are not simple public things like rocks or trees; besides being material things, they involve the presence of mind, they involve and therefore reflect the activity that lets them be signs. By starting with signs, Husserl begins his philosophy in the most felicitous way possible, with something that is a material entity but is also saturated with the presence of thinking.

To describe how things can become signs for us, Husserl appeals to a concrete, ordinary experience. Both in the Fifth Investigation and in an essay he wrote in 1894, Husserl presents the following situation: we are looking at some arabesques and admiring their intricacy. Suddenly we realize that these elegant marks actually are words; they spell out someone's name or make some statement.[2] For this change to occur, we must have begun to "intend" differently; we no longer simply perceive, we now read or interpret the marks as saying something. Our new intention is different from the one we were engaged in until that change occurred: the new intention goes beyond what is immediately present; it begins to intend not just these marks but, say, Winston Churchill or the Gare St. Lazare, and this same new intention changes the marks from being fascinating curlicues to being words.

The new kind of intention that establishes a sign as such is not something we feel; we do not somehow palpate the difference between signifying and perceiving. Signifying and perceiving are two kinds of intentionality, but they become visible in what they do, not in themselves. When we try to analyze, philosophically, the difference between a sign and a percept, we do not look at the intentions directly, we do not look at the signitive act and then the perceptual act, we do not introspectively discover

---

[1] Citations will be from E. HUSSERL, *Logical Investigations*, trans. J. N. Findlay, London: Routledge and Kegan Paul, 1970, 2 volumes (abbreviated as LI).

[2] See *LI*, 566, and E. HUSSERL, "Psychological Studies for Elementary Logic," trans. R. Hudson and P. McCormick, in *Husserl. Shorter Works*, ed. P. McCormick and F. Elliston, Notre Dame: University of Notre Dame Press, 1981, 137.

qualitative differences among our intentionalities. We get at the intentionalities by looking at signs and contrasting them with ordinary perceived objects; the differences between signs and perceived things allow us to discover differences in the intentionalities that are correlated with them. To put it into Husserl's later terminology, we first register a noematic difference and thereby become able to discover a noetic difference. This approach remains with Husserl throughout his philosophical career and it also remains with phenomenology throughout its history. Contrary to widespread opinion, phenomenology is not introspective. It gets at the mind not directly but through the mind's presence in and with things.

After he distinguishes between indication signs and expressions, Husserl spends the first pages of *Logical Investigations* talking about indication. I will not follow him in this. I will begin with the study of the other branch of the distinction, with expression, and will turn to indication later on.

I. WORDS AND WHAT THEY EXPRESS

The paradigm of expression is the linguistic sign, the word. When we recognize some sounds or marks as really being words, many new dimensions come into play. Let us suppose that we are surrounded by mere background noise and suddenly realize that somebody is saying something in that noise; or, let us say that we are looking at what seem to be random marks on paper and suddenly we realize that there is a message written into them. The physical sounds or marks now "contain a meaning," and they are being used to "refer" to something. They embody both meaning and reference, but they do so not by themselves, by their own material weight or by their own independent being. They contain a meaning and exercise a reference because *we* are signifying and referring through them, and because we realize that *someone else* has signified and referred through them. The change from being a mere sound or mark into being an expression thus involves the presence of a signifying activity, along with the introduction of a meaning and a reference. Thus, the sign is not just there all by itself; it could not stand alone; surrounding it, radiating from it, are three essential components: the signitive act that makes it a sign, the meaning, and the reference.

Incidentally, Husserl's doctrine of the signifying act as establishing meaning is elegantly confirmed by Paul Bloom in his book, *How Children Learn the Meanings of Words*.[3] Bloom shows that association alone is not sufficient to explain how children learn to use words. If a mechanical sound were to be regularly produced when a child experiences a certain kind of object, the child would not take the sound to be the name of the thing. Instead, children learn what words are and what they mean when they grasp the fact that someone is intending the object through the use of the sound: "young children will make the connection [between sound and object] only if they have some warrant to believe that it is an act of naming—and for this, the speaker has to be

---

[3] P. BLOOM, *How Children Learn the Meanings of Words*, Cambridge: MIT Press, 2000.

present."[4] Bloom speaks of "the child's own ability to infer the referential intentions of others."[5] In Husserl's terminology, the child accepts certain sounds as words when he takes them to be animated by a speaker's signitive intentionality.

One of the first points that Husserl makes concerning expressions is that they can occur in the absence of the thing to which they are used to refer. I might look out the window and say, "There's a police car in the driveway." I perceive the police car, but you, who hear me say these words, may not be looking out the window; you don't see the car, and yet you understand what I have said. You can possess the meaning even if you don't perceive the referent. The meaning, therefore, cannot be located in the perceptual or intuitive activity associated with the expression. The meaning must lie in another act, in what Husserl calls the signifying or meaning-bestowing act. In this way, he works out another of his "essential distinctions," that between the signifying act and the intuition, or between the empty intention and the fulfillment. He says, "Let us take our stand on this fundamental distinction between meaning-intentions void of intuition and those which are intuitively fulfilled."(LI, 281).[6] Once again, a distinction is achieved not by somehow looking at two different kinds of acts and seeing differences among them, but by looking at what the acts have done or accomplished or achieved. Husserl looks at how we interact with the world and how we communicate with one another, and in this wider context he distinguishes between empty and filled intentions.

The next step is to investigate the expressions themselves and to ask how they are structured. Husserl insists that the expression is not just the physical sound or mark; rather, it is the composite made up of the physical phenomenon and the meaning. He says, "The word 'expression' is normally understood . . . as the *sense-informed expression*."(LI, 281).[7] Thus, the expression *four legged animal* is made up of both the phonemic stratum and the meaning contained in it.

Expressions, therefore, according to Husserl, are composed of both sound and sense. Let us go on to ask one more question, one that will play a strategic role in our argument. The question is: What do expressions express? At first glance, the answer to this question might seem obvious. We would probably be inclined to say that expressions express their meaning, the meaning that informs them. But Husserl does not accept this reply; he explicitly rejects it, even while recognizing how natural and obvious it might seem: "One should not, therefore, properly say (as one often does) that an expression *expresses its meaning* (its intention)."(LI, 281). But if an expression does not express its meaning, what does it express?

---

[4] P. BLOOM, *How Children Learn the Meanings of Words*, 64.

[5] P. BLOOM, *How Children Learn the Meanings of Words*, 84.

[6] This contrast is more clearly drawn in the Sixth Investigation (LI, 680).

[7] Ferdinand de Saussure has a similar idea, claiming that the sign is composite, and the signifier and the signified are its two components. However, he works primarily not with the public expression but with the mental image and hence with a private language or mental speech. For him, it is the *image acoustique* that is the signifier, not a publicly uttered sound, and the concept is the signified. See F. DE SAUSSURE, *Cours de linguistique generale*, ed. C. Bally and A. Sechehaye, Paris: Payot, 1962, 99.

At this point, things get complicated. Recall the distinction between the signitive act and the intuitive act that fulfills it. If I say, "There's a police car in the driveway," you can understand what I say even when you are not looking at the driveway or the car. The car and driveway are absent to you, and yet you intend them in an empty intention and you possess the meaning that is part of this expression. However, your empty intention can be fulfilled. You can turn around and look into the driveway, and you then see the car. The intuitive act by which you do this is intrinsically related to the empty, signitive act you carried out when you understood my words. The intuitive act fulfills the empty intention, and the empty intention, in principle and by its nature, is geared toward fulfillment, even though in fact it may never be fulfilled. Both acts, of course, intend the same object; they have the same reference.

Husserl then says that there is a content to the fulfilling, intuitive act. The content of the intuitive act is, obviously, the police car's being in the driveway. It is the same content as the meaning found in the signitive act, but it has a different modality in that it is part of an intuitive act, a perception, not part of a signitive act. And now we come to the central point. According to Husserl, *what the expression expresses is the content of this intuitional act*. The expression does not express its own meaning; rather, it expresses the content of the act that fulfills the signitive act that constitutes the expression. Husserl says this in the following way: "One might more properly adopt the alternative way of speaking according to which the *fulfilling act* appears as *the act expressed by the complete expression*: we may, e.g., say that a statement 'gives expression' to an act of perceiving or imagining."(LI, 281). This statement of Husserl's, however, is still incomplete, because it only says that the expression expresses the fulfilling act. Later on in the First Investigation, Husserl more precisely says that "the essence of the meaning-fulfillment is the *fulfilling* sense of the expression, or, as one may also call it, the sense expressed by the expression."(LI, 290). He goes on to say that we must assert "that a statement of perception expresses a perception, but also that it expresses the *content* of a perception."(LI, 290).[8]

Husserl's argument is tortuous and highly condensed, and it is made even more complicated in his text because he discusses reference as well as sense, and he adds the notion of ideal meanings, or meanings taken *in specie* and transcending their realization in any intentional act, whether empty or filled. I would like to simplify his argument, to simplify his response to the question, What do expressions express? What he says can be more directly stated, and its importance can be more effectively brought out, in the following way.

---

[8] One might raise the further question: What is the relationship between the meaning and the content of the perception? Husserl does not answer this question in *Logical Investigations*, but he does answer it in *Formal and Transcendental Logic*, The Hague: Martinus Nijhoff, 1969, §§44–46, where he says that the meaning or sense just is the objective content, the state of affairs, but taken as proposed or supposed. This clarification in *Formal and Transcendental Logic* is a major philosophical discovery and it has been insufficiently treated by commentators on Husserl. See R. SOKOLOWSKI, *Husserlian Meditations. How Words Present Things*, Evanston: Northwestern University Press, 1974, 43–54, 275–82; *Presence and Absence. A Philosophical Investigation of Language and Being*, Bloomington: Indiana University Press, 1978, 51–62; *Introduction to Phenomenology*, Cambridge: Cambridge University Press, 2000, 99–100.

An expression does not express its own meaning; an expression expresses the content of the perception or intuition that would present the thing or state of affairs corresponding to the meaning of the expression. That is, an expression expresses something we can find in the world; it expresses an object as it can be given in a certain way. An expression expresses not a meaning but a part of the world, as that part can be given to us through a perception or intuition. If I say, "A police car has driven into the driveway," my expression expresses a small—but important and perhaps even urgent—part of the world, the police car's being in the driveway, the state of affairs that you would see if you turned around and looked out the window. My expressions, my words, do not form a closed circle of signifiers and signifieds, they do not live only in intertextuality or interverbosity. They express something that is not merely verbal; they bring something in the world to light. They articulate a part of the world.

This expressive function occurs even when we are not in the presence of the thing being expressed. The words still express the world even when we are in the absence of that part of the world that the words are used to refer to. Expressions always keep their teleological ordering toward the way things are, toward the evidencing of things, even when they are just passed back and forth among speakers in the total absence of the things being spoken about. The signifying acts that establish the expressions as such remain always geared toward the intuitive acts that saturate them.

Husserl further spells out this realistic understanding of words in the Sixth Investigation, where he describes how we intuit things we have named. He says that "the expression seems to be *applied* to the thing and to clothe it like a garment."(LI, 688). He also says that when I call something my inkpot, "the name 'my inkpot' seems to *overlay* the perceived object, to belong *sensibly* to it."(LI, 688). He then adds the remark, "This belonging is of a peculiar kind." Husserl insists, however, that in such recognition, we do not just have the word and the thing or the word and the intuition; we also must have the signitive act that enlivens the word and finds fulfillment in the intuition and is blended with it. The signifying act, the act that makes the word to be an expression, comes between the word and the intuited thing, between the formation of the word and the intuition. Husserl also says that recognition does not mean that we somehow stand back and register a relationship between the thing named and the expression; nor do we merely associate the name and the thing. Rather, recognition is more elementary and more direct; we go right through the expression to the thing and we recognize or classify the thing immediately. As Husserl says, "In this mode of naming reference, the name appears as *belonging* to the named and as one with it."(LI, 690). He says that the word and the intuition are not just two things added to one another: "Phenomenologically we find before us no mere aggregate, but an intimate, in fact intentional unity...."(LI, 691). And of course, although names belong with things and can "clothe them like a garment," they can also function in the absence of things, when they are supported only by their signitive acts, and hence we can speak about things in absence as well as in presence. To prolong the metaphor, you can have the garment just hanging in the closet and not clothing anything, but still it belongs to what it clothes, and it longs to clothe it. The garment may be just hanging there in an empty, signitive intention, but the empty intention longs for fulfillment in intuition.

These descriptions of Husserl bring out the special mode of being of words. They show that words are transparent, that when we hear someone speak or when we read a text or even when we see someone using sign language, we go right through the words to the things being signified and expressed by them. The word, as Husserl says, "is one with" the thing it names, it fits that thing, it belongs with it in a special kind of belonging that is not like any other relationship. Some people have even thought of a person's name as containing that person's soul, and they would keep the name secret lest someone use the name to gain power over the person or to injure him. Our sense of the being and manifestation of things is more subtle and less credulous, but there is something to that primitive belief. When the name is spoken the thing comes to light, the looks of the thing arise, whether in the thing's presence or absence. This transparency of words will be even more vividly shown when we discuss, in the third section of this paper, not just simple words but words pervaded by syntax.

II. WORDS AND WHAT THEY INDICATE

Let us now turn to the other branch of Husserl's original distinction, to indication-signs, *Anzeigen*. I would like to introduce another English word as a translation of this German term; besides "indication" I will use the term "signal" to name this kind of sign. Indications, like expressions, have a bodily dimension. Examples of indications are a whistle that signals a foul in a basketball game, a gesture that indicates that I am going to turn left, a blinking yellow light that signals caution, a gunshot that indicates the start of a race. A flag flown at half mast indicates that someone has died, a flag flown upside down signals distress. In contrast with expressions, such signs do not articulate the thing they signal; they merely show its presence, its proximate existence.[9] They turn our minds to the thing in question, they make us aware of it, but they do not say anything about it.

Husserl says, furthermore, that indication is established by association, and this claim allows him to comment on the nature of association. He says that association establishes a relationship between two things, so that when one of the things appears, we are led to think of the other. He says, "If A summons B into consciousness, we are not merely simultaneously or successively conscious of both A and B, but we usually *feel* their connection forcing itself upon us, a connection in which the one points to the other and seems to belong to it."(LI, 274). He speaks of the "felt mutual belongingness" between the associated items and speaks of the "new phenomenological *character*" that we experience in such cases. He says, "That one thing points to another, in definite arrangement and connection, is itself apparent to us."(LI, 274).

---

[9] Many interesting questions arise. Suppose we have a flag of something that no longer exists, such as a flag of the Soviet Union. It is still a sign, but no longer an actualized one. It is something like a dead body. It might be seen as a latent or potential sign, one that could come to life again if the Soviet Union were to be revived. The phenomenon of retiring the colors of a regiment would be an interesting intermediate case.

The only kind of indication signs Husserl talks about are those based on association or convention. He does not want to include the stronger kind of relationship that occurs when one thing is a sign of another because it is caused by that other thing, as smoke is seen as a sign of the fire that causes it, or wet streets are a sign that it has rained. Such things, according to Husserl, could be considered as indication signs only if their causal connection were left out of consideration. The sign and object must be connected *just* by association. Husserl does not want his indication signs to be based on reasoning, inference, or insight of any kind. He wants to exclude the case in which we might think, "The streets are wet everywhere in the city, so it must have rained."[10] Indication signs must be based on the more external relationship of mere association. Husserl says, "When one says that the state of affairs A indicates the state of affairs B, . . . one's mode of speech implies no objectively necessary connections between A and B, nothing into which one could have insight."(LI, 272). Wet streets could be an indication that it has rained, and smoke could signal that there is a fire, but only if we take these relations as mere associations, as mere signs, not as effects from which we can infer a cause.

Let us explore the difference between indications and expressions. Indications or signals obviously have a signification—the pistol shot "means" the start of the race—but they do not have meanings in the way that expressions do.[11] Signals do not possess a meaning that can be quoted, paraphrased, or communicated to someone else by the use of other signs; there is something abrupt and concrete and singular about signals. They just bring something to mind, they just show that it is present in some way. They don't say anything about it. It is true that signals can be explained, but when that happens we are not paraphrasing them; we merely turn them into objects to be expressed. Furthermore, signals or indication signs do not possess a meaning that could be fulfilled by an intuition. We do not try to verify or falsify them as we do statements made by a speaker. Truth and falsity mean something else in the case of signals: they mean the genuine versus the fake, not the correct versus the erroneous or the mendacious.

But although indications and expressions are different, they become related in an important and interesting way in the case of speech. Expressions, as we have seen, contain a meaning and express a state of affairs, but they also serve to indicate something. The physical aspects of speech, the sounds or marks or, in the case of sign language, the gestures, besides expressing something and putting it on record as what is said, also serve to indicate, to a listener, that the speaker is carrying out the intentional acts that establish the expressions as expressions. As Husserl says, ". . . One sees that all expressions in *communicative* speech function as *indications*. They serve the hearer

---

[10] The exclusion of proof and reasoning occurs in §3 of the First Investigation, where Husserl says indications should involve *Hinweis* but not *Beweis*.

[11] Speaking about signs such as facial movements or gestures, Husserl says, "Such 'utterances' are not expressions in the sense in which a case of speech is an expression. . . . They 'mean' something to [an onlooker] in so far as he interprets them, but even for him they are without meaning in the special sense in which verbal signs have meaning: they only mean in the sense of indicating." (LI, 275).

as signs of the 'thoughts' of the speaker, i.e., of his sense-giving inner experiences. ... This function of verbal expressions we shall call their *intimating function.*"(LI, 277). Husserl also says that "the hearer *intuitively* takes the speaker to be a person who is expressing this or that, or as we certainly can say, *perceives* him as such."(LI, 277). He says that when I hear someone speak, "I perceive him as a speaker, I hear him recounting, demonstrating, doubting, wishing, etc. ..."(LI, 278).

We should try to appreciate the full and rich picture that Husserl offers us here. The center of focus is the living word, the spoken sound. When words stream by, the things that they express are being manifested and parts of the world are coming to light. Whether the issue is important or trivial, the world and the things in it are being disclosed: we are being told about the condition of a house, the health of a patient, the status of the stock market, the legal significance of what someone has done. Parts of the world are flashing on and off as the words move by. But while a part of the world is being expressed in a speech, something else is also coming to light, namely the speaker whose words the words are. He and his performances, his more or less responsible speaking and thinking, are being manifested, but not in the way the world is shown up by him; he appears in another, more oblique manner. He and his thinking are not being expressed but signaled or indicated. While we focus on what he expresses (say, the water overflowing the sink), we also marginally know and perceive that *he* is expressing this, that he is the responsible manifester, the agent of truth thanks to whom the thing is showing up as it is. He brings the thing to light, and he shows up precisely as the one who is doing so, as the agent of disclosure. His minding appears on the margin of what he minds, but not as part of it. The interplay of expression and indication, all occurring within the words that are being spoken, achieves this double manifestation, of world and speaker, through the functions of expression and indication. Husserl here presents a very dynamic, appealing description of how language works.

I have one more point to make about the interaction between expressions and indications. Expressions, such as the names of persons and things, are different from indications. Expressions express the things they refer to. However, expressions do possess within themselves a layer of indication. Even in their referential function, they retain a level of association or indication. The name *Peter Quince* is an expression and it is used to name Peter Quince, but it could also degenerate into being a mere signal for Peter Quince, a mere indication associated with him. If Peter Quince suddenly appears and I am jolted by his presence, I might blurt out the sounds, "Peter Quince!" My words may be more an exclamation than a name. A phrase like, "Here's Johnny!" is a signal more than a name with reference, or at least it oscillates between the two modes of semiotic being. This level of indication in names comes to the fore when we have forgotten someone's name and are trying to remember it. We try to bring the name to mind by means of association; we think of the person, we imagine meeting him and saying, "Hello. . . ." We hope that the image or even the actual presence of the person will call up the name for us. This is sheer association and sheer indication. It shows us that the "name" could come to mind not really as a name but only as an associated sound. Now, this same sound, this associated signal, can be turned into a name and an expression. What turns it into a name is the use we make of it; we have to activate a signitive, meaning-bestowing act, we have to use the sounds to refer to Peter Quince, and then—and only then—the sounds become a word and a name with a meaning. Until that transformation happens they are more a response to a stimulus than a name of a person or thing. They are something we are simply used to uttering when this entity appears. This indicational layer remains operative in all words as a substrate for their verbal functioning, and sometimes, perhaps in moments of emotional distress, this lower layer breaks through and disrupts the expressive function of the words. Association takes over and smothers both the meaning and the logic involved in it.

III. Syntax and Articulated Displays

It is time to speak about syntax. We have been discussing words, but we have not distinguished the grammatical aspects of speech from the merely appellative aspects. Syntax, whether found in particular words, in inflections, or in word placement, is what changes animal sounds and cries into human speech. Syntax is what allows us to make definite, discrete statements, statements that can be true or false, that can be quoted, repeated, and communicated, and that can be tested for meaningfulness, consistency, and coherence. Syntax allows definite wholes to be built up out of specified parts. It enables us to achieve sentences and propositions. It allows articulation in the speech itself, in the meaning contained in the expression, and in the state of affairs disclosed in the world. It allows us to signify relationships of all sorts. Syntax permits the Chinese-box kind of enclosing that only language can achieve: where one statement or term can be embedded in another, where statements can be moved from one part of an argument to another, where extremely complex wholes of sense can be built up, not only in science and mathematics but also in literature, journalism, history, and law, as well as in ordinary discourse, story-telling, rhetorical arguments, and emotive articulation.

Before discussing syntax, which Husserl examines under the rubric of categoriality, I would like to mention its involvement with the two kinds of signs we have discussed, indications and expressions. Syntax is essential to expressions. It is only because expressions have syntax, and their meanings have logical form, that expressions can be what they are. Words are made to be words by the presence of syntax; there are no single words just by themselves. Words don't come one by one. When we do find a name just by itself, it is recognizable as a name only because it normally comes with syntax. It is a name only on the margins of grammatically articulated speech. When we name a thing, we normally do so in view of saying something about it; we are prepping it for predication. When we say that words are transparent and serve to express things in the world, we imply that the words have been articulated into linguistic wholes and parts, and that correspondingly the things being displayed—the contents of the fulfilling act, in Husserl's terminology—are being articulated into wholes and parts as well.

Although syntax is essential to expression, it is not found in indication signs. Signals are abrupt and single, they are one-shot affairs, and they are not coordinated into larger wholes that could be formulated in many different ways. We don't *say* anything when we signal something; we don't set up a referent and assert something about it. One signal might follow another—the gunshot at the start of the race is followed later on by a flag's being waved to signal the winner—but this sequence is not grammatical. To make use of Husserl's terminology, there is categoriality in expressions but not in indications, not in signals. Husserl himself recognized this fact. He writes in a manuscript, "Im Reich der Signale gibt es keine Grammatik," "In the domain of signals there is no grammar."[12]

How then does syntax or categoriality function in expressions? There is no systematic treatment of categoriality in the First Investigation, even though the term is used here and there, especially in relation to some remarks about formal logic. Categoriality is treated in the Sixth Investigation, specifically in the second section, entitled, "Sense and Understanding." Chapter 6 in that investigation is entitled, "Sensuous and Categorial Intuitions." I should mention that the theme of categoriality makes much use of the Third and Fourth Investigations, entitled respectively "On the Theory of Wholes and Parts" and "The Distinction between Independent and Non-independent Meanings and the Idea of Pure Grammar."

Let us distinguish different levels in the combinatorics of speech. The first, easiest, most obvious, and least controversial level is that of linguistic expression itself, where the ordinary grammar of the various languages serves as the organizing element in words. The second level is that of the meaning or the propositions, where logical grammar functions. The third and most controversial level is that of the things or states of affairs being presented through language. Are there syntactic elements here? What is it in the states of affairs or relationships among things that corresponds to logical syntax and linguistic grammar? If I say, "This paper is white," is there anything in what I perceive that corresponds to the grammatical parts of speech? I obviously can perceive the paper and I can perceive the whiteness, but is there anything else corresponding to the *joining* of the terms *paper* and *white*, and to the words *this* and *is*?

If we were to limit perception just to the sensible qualities that are presented to us, we would have to say that there is nothing in the thing that goes beyond the paper and the whiteness. Husserl writes, "... it is hopeless, even quite misguided, to look directly in perception for what could give fulfillment to our supplementary formal meanings."(LI, 779). And yet we are not limited to saying that we see only the paper and the whiteness; we do say that we see *that* the paper is white. We do claim to perceive or intuit states of affairs, relations, and groups, and not only things and features. As Husserl puts it, "We do not merely say 'I see this paper, an inkpot, several books,' and so on, but also 'I see that the paper has been written on, that there is a bronze inkpot standing here, that several books are lying open, and so on'."(LI, 773). In a famous phrase, Husserl says that "a surplus of meaning remains over" in the signitive intention, something more than the mere sensible percepts (LI, 775). The syntactic dimension is that surplus, and we must ask what corresponds to it in the things

---

[12] The passage is quoted by U. MELLE in "Signitive und signifikative Intentionen," *Husserl Studies* 15, 1998, 170. The manuscript reference is A I 18, 39a.

we express. As Husserl observes, "The 'a' and the 'the,' the 'and' and the 'or,' the 'if' and the 'then,' the 'all' and the 'none,' the 'something' and the 'nothing,' the forms of quantity and the determinations of number, etc.—all these are meaningful propositional elements, but we should look in vain for their objective correlates ... in the sphere of *real* objects, which is in fact no other than the sphere of *objects of possible sense-perception.*"(LI, 782).

What then do the categorial parts of speech express in things? They express the modalities of presence in the things being presented or intended. They correspond to the way things and features are related, presentationally or intentionally, to one another. They express the dimensions of articulation in things, the formal-ontological relationships that are also given when things are given. Here are some formulations of Husserl. He says that the categorial parts of speech "relate to the object itself *in its categorial structure.*"(LI, 785). He says that the object "is set before our very eyes in just these forms," and that "*aggregates, indefinite pluralities, totalities, numbers, disjunctions, predicates, states of affairs,* all count as 'objects' ..."(LI, 785). Categorial articulation is the work of intelligence as opposed to sensibility, and so Husserl says, "The working of synthetic thought, of intellection, has done something to [our objects], has shaped them anew, although, being a categorial function, it has done this in categorial fashion, so that the sensuous content of the apparent object has not been altered."(LI, 796). In a similar vein, he says, "Categorial forms leave their primary objects untouched...."(LI, 820).

Another way of describing what categorial acts establish is to say that they explicitly articulate wholes and parts in the things we experience: "It is clear ... that the apprehension of a moment and of a part generally *as* a part of the whole in question, and, in particular, the apprehension of a sensuous feature *as* a feature, or of a sensuous form *as* a form, point to acts which are all founded. ... This means that the sphere of 'sensibility' has been left, and that of 'understanding' entered."(LI, 792). Husserl speaks about objective categorial structures as being "specific forms of the relation between a *whole* and its *parts*. All such relationships are of categorial, ideal nature."(LI, 794). We could also describe categorial intentions as bringing out various kinds of identity within the objects of consciousness, various realizations of the old Platonic forms of "sameness" and "otherness." In a categorial object, a thing is identified in a special way with one of its features, several objects are collected into one identifiable group or number, or a thing is recognized in its identity with itself under alternative descriptions. In all such cases, to use Husserl's phrase, "The identity itself is now made objective. . . ."(LI, 791).

One of the best passages about categoriality in *Logical Investigations* is the following. It expresses in a colorful way how intellection differs from sensibility. Husserl turns to the phenomenon of picturing things. He says that when I paint or draw two things together, "I can paint *A* and I can paint *B*, and I can paint them both on the same canvas: I cannot, however, paint the *both* nor paint the *A and* the *B*. Here we have only the one possibility which is always open to us: to perform a new act of conjunction or collection on the basis of our two new single acts of intuition, and so *mean* the *aggregate* of the objects *A* and *B*."(LI, 798). In both the real world and the painting, the categorial form cannot be the target of a sensory perception; in both cases, I must *think* the two things together, I must execute the intellectual activity of conjoining them if I am to have the objective correlate of the terms *both* and *and* presented to me. The syntactic parts of language, the parts that make speech human and differentiate it from animal sounds and cries, has as its correlative the part-whole compositions, the recognized identities, and the categorial objects that make up an intelligible and intellected world. The syntactic parts of speech express the presentational combinatorics of the things we thoughtfully articulate, whether in their presence or their absence.

The objective side of intellection are the categorial objects that we present or intend. The subjective side is the execution of higher-level intentional acts that constitute such objects. The acts are complex and consist essentially of various identifications and part-whole intentionalities. We will not follow Husserl as he carries out his descriptions of these acts and their interlacement, but we will emphasize one point. We have seen that the syntactic parts of speech can be said to *express* the categorial formation of the objects being presented to us. These same syntactic parts of speech serve as *signals* of the categorial acts that are the substance of human intellection. That is, when we listen to someone speak, and when we follow the speech and turn our minds to the things and states of affairs being disclosed in that speech, we also experience, obliquely, the speaker as carrying out acts of intellection, and his thoughtful, categorial activity is *indicated* to us by the very grammatical terms that help express the objects of his discourse. We accept the speaker who addresses us as thinking, as carrying out categorial intentions, as articulating the things he is speaking about, and his thinking is signaled to us specifically by the grammar of his speech. Discussing the word *or*, Husserl says, "The word *or* is accordingly no name, and likewise no ... appellation of disjoining; it merely gives voice to this act."(LI, 838). The grammatical term does not name the thoughtful act of conjoining, it just gives voice to, or signals, that act. The exquisite interplay of expression and indication, the semiotics of *Logical Investigations*, thus reaches its apogee in categorial intentionality and in the speech that publicizes it. The one stream of words manifests parts of the world and simultaneously brings to light the thoughtful activity of the person responsible for the manifestation.

There is, however, one item in the treatment of signs that Husserl overlooks. He shows that expressions signal the intentional acts of the speaker and thus make the speaker visible as such. But he does not notice that these same expressions also serve as signals to the listener to perform the same thoughtful acts himself. The expressions serve not only as signals *of* but also as signals *to*. Husserl focuses on the speaker but overlooks the audience. Syntax does not only disclose the speaker and his thinking but also leads the listener to think in concert with the speaker: words link the speaker and listener in one common train of thought.[13] What the speaker thinks—the way the world appears to him—is made public because it is shared with the listener through the presence of words. The receptivity of the listener should be added to the dimensions of

---

[13] See R. SOKOLOWSKI, *Presence and Absence*, 48–49, 99–115.

speech that are so well described in Husserl's *Logical Investigations*.

BERTRAND BOUCKAERT
Chargé de recherches du Fonds National Belge de la Recherche Scientifique

THE PUZZLING CASE OF ALTERITY IN HUSSERL'S *LOGICAL INVESTIGATIONS*

The following paper deals with the question of alterity or intersubjectivity[1] in Husserl's *Logical Investigations*.[2] The research is broken down into five main parts. First I will examine the present scholarly consensus to focus the study of Husserl's intersubjectivity on his writings done at Freiburg from 1917 until 1938, and not on those from Göttingen (1901-1916) or Halle (1887-1901). Then the reasons which seem to be at the origin of this present consensus will be critically examined. This will lead to the search for a kind of "intersubjective structure" in the *Logical Investigations* themselves. It will be shown that in this text, as in *Cartesian Meditations*, that such an "intersubjective structure" is present; however, from one text to the other this structure is—so to speak—"reversed". Finally, I will try to formulate some hypotheses to explain this development.

I. THE CONSENSUS IN FAVOUR OF A READING FROM FREIBURG

Schematically, it can be said that the consensus which favours the writings of the Freiburg period is based on two dominant forms of motive: external or heuristic reasons on the one hand and internal or phenomenological reasons on the other. The external reasons are either "materials" when they have to do with the quantitative importance of the texts from Freiburg (in particular the *Cartesian Meditations*) or are "interpretative" *stricto sensu*. More precisely, certain precepts of reading promoted by Eugen Fink are here to be considered. The internal reasons, firstly, have to do with the impact of Husserl's discovery of phenomenological reduction on his elaboration of an investigation on intersubjectivity, and, secondly, with the originality and the novelty of the signification Husserl gave to the word "Intersubjektivität".

Since the publication in French of Husserl's *Cartesian Meditations*,[3] a consensus has gradually come about in phenomenological literature that the question of intersubjectivity in Husserl must be considered from the point of view of his writings

---

[1] Cf. B.BOUCKAERT, "Geistiger Verkehr et für wen immer Geltung: figures de l'intersubjectivité dans les *Recherches Logiques* de Edmund Husserl," in *Etudes phénoménologiques* 25, 1997, 77-104. In this article, I was not yet aware of the ambiguity in the concept of intersubjectivity.

[2] Husserl's works are cited according to the *Husserliana: Edmund Husserl Gesammelte Werke* (abbreviated as Hua). When an English-language edition of the cited text is available, this reference is given first, followed by the original reference, cited in brackets. I use Findlay's translation of Husserl's *Logical Investigations*, London: 1970; other translations are my own.

[3] HUSSERL'S *Cartesian Meditations*, written in 1929, were first published in French, the translation having been attributed to G. Peiffer and E. Levinas, even though A. Koyré also contributed to a large extent. This translation was published by Armand Colin in Paris in 1931.

of the 1930s, the *Cartesian Meditations* occupying among these a prominent situation. Several factors encouraged this heuristic position. Above all, there is the indisputable fact that the fifth *Cartesian Meditation* constitutes the only lengthy and uninterrupted text dedicated to the problem of transcendental intersubjectivity by Husserl. Besides, he had himself announced in *Formal and Transcendental Logic* that the *Cartesian Meditations* would reveal the answer to this sensitive question (*FTL*, 243 [Hua XVII, 250]).[4] Even the most reliable secondary sources seemed to support it, since Fink, the faithful disciple of the older Husserl, had explicitly asserted that the best way to understand his master's thinking was indeed "to move back" from his last texts to the early ones, starting with the *Krisis* and finishing with *Philosophy of Arithmetic*.[5] This process inevitably grants a position of eminence to the writings from Freiburg. Later, Fink also suggested that the difficulties raised by the problem of intersubjectivity were finally solved in Husserl's latest manuscripts,[6] a statement which definitively encourages the *a priori* in favour of a reading of Husserl's texts on intersubjectivity from Freiburg.

Beside these, so-to-speak, "external" factors, reasons which are inherent in things themselves seemed also to be influential. Most important is the fact that the problem of intersubjectivity seemed, in a way, to appear in Husserl as the result of the development of phenomenological reduction. Consequently, it seemed pointless to search for a theory of intersubjectivity in Husserl at any time earlier than the full development of his reductive method—which means, at the earliest, not before Husserl's writings from Göttingen. Additionally, there is a more subtle and nearly ontological factor for why it was believed intersubjectivity has been elaborated only in the later texts. This factor has to do with the originality of the Husserlian concept of intersubjectivity. In the French language, the term "intersubjectivité" appears very late, in 1931, at the time of the publication of *Cartesian Meditations*. This lexicographical originality endows this text with a certain kind of phenomenological primacy. Even though the term "Intersubjektivität" was already used in *Ideen I*, and even though it already existed in German before Husserl used it, its appearance in French was understood as a radical novelty, which, actually, is not completely false. Anyway, phenomenological ontology was not likely to have entered the territory of intersubjectivity before the 1920s at the earliest, and consequently it did not seemed worthwhile even to search for the idea of intersubjectivity in earlier texts.

---

[4] It is interesting to note that Husserl also made reference in his notes to his 1910 lectures titled *Grundprobleme der Phänomenologie* and that he addresses the question here in a radically different way than how he does in *Cartesian Meditations*.

[5] Cf. E. FINK's introduction to: E. HUSSERL, "Entwurf einer 'Vorrede' zu den 'Logischen Untersuchungen'." *Tijdschrift voor Filosofie* 1, 1939, 106-109. (English translation by Ph. J. Bossert and C. Peters, The Hague: Martinus Nijhoff, 1975).

[6] Cf. E. FINK'S discussion of A. SCHÜTZ'S paper, "Le problème de l'intersubjectivité transcendantale chez Husserl."*Philosophie 3*, 1959, 373. And: E. FINK, "Die Spätphilosophie Husserls in freiburger Zeit," in *Nähe und Distanz. Phänomenologische Vorträge und Aufsätze*, Freiburg/München: Alber, 1976, 221-222.

II. CRITICISM OF THIS CONSENSUS

First of all, it must be observed that from a hermeneutic point of view the consensus regarding the question of intersubjectivity has given rise to a curious reading of the texts. Intersubjectivity has been considered as a fixed problem. Neither its meaning nor its history have been considered problematic. The problem seemed to be only one of the consistency of the formal structures canonically established by the *Cartesian Meditations*: reduction to the *Eigenheitsphäre*, *Körper* here, *Körper* over there, *Leib* here, analogy, double pairing, *Leib* over there, *Einfühlung*, and so on. From this point of view, the other texts only appeared as useful, sometimes illuminating, complements, but nevertheless peripheral to the *Meditations*. Even the 1973 publication of volumes XIII, XIV and XV of the *Husserliana* series has in effect made little change in this orientation. Yet, an analysis devoid of *a prioris* should normally proceed in a very different manner. It should start with determining the meaning of the word "Intersubjektivität" in the German language before Husserl took over the term. Then it is necessary to see if the term's original meaning matched the use made of it by Husserl. If in fact Husserl re-defined the term, then the differences between the two usages should be examined. In the light of such a research, the real question to be asked would be the following: "What are the real phenomenological motives that forced Husserl to develop his own theory of intersubjectivity?".

It is not possible here to disentangle the whole story of the concept of intersubjectivity, but the scientific literature clearly attests to a kind of semantic duality in the use of this concept.[7] It is necessary to acknowledge that the concept of intersubjectivity appeared relatively late in western countries.[8] It did not appear until 1885, in German, in a work of the neo-Kantian Johannes Volkelt entitled *Erfahrung und Denken*.[9] The terminology used by Volkelt and in which the qualifying adjective "intersubjektiv" appears was particularly clumsy since it qualified as intersubjective "alles ... was jeder in seinem Bewußtsein unmittelbar vorfindet": "Anything that is directly apprehensible to everyone in his consciousness". Such a conception appears strange today and is even contrary to the present understanding of what is intersubjective. It must be pointed out that Volkelt had forged the word "intersubjektiv" to oppose it to the word "transsubjektiv", a term he defines as follows: "Ich bezeichne als transsubjektiv alles, was es ausserhalb meiner eigenen Bewußtseinsvorgänge etwa gegeben mag". It is important to notice that Volkelt introduced this terminology to clarify the Kantian notion of objectivity. Kant, one knows, had defined universal objectivity by saying that it retains its worth "for us always and in the same way for whomever" [*vor Jedermann*]. Put otherwise, in the first *Kritik*, Kantian objectivity is

---

[7] Cf. "Intersubjektivität." In *Enzyklopädie Philosophie und Wissenschaftstheorie* 2, ed. J. Mittelstrass, Mannheim/Wien/Zürich: B.I. Wissenschaftsverlag, 1984.

[8] Our reference source here is chiefly the *Historische Wörterbuch der Philosophie*, Band 4, I-K, eds J. Ritter and K. Gründer, Basel/Stuttgart: Swabe & C° Verlag, 1976.

[9] J. VOLKELT, *Erfahrung und Denken. Kritische Grundlegung der Erkenntnistheorie*, Leipzig: Verlag von Leopold Voss, 1885.

universal, and it is such because it is tied to a concept of pure understanding. Historically, the neo-Kantian notion of intersubjectivity appears to be a deepening of the Kantian notion of universality.

The terms introduced by Volkelt, although a little awkward, were meant to clarify a fundamental philosophical difficulty. Therefore, this terminology was not forgotten. On the contrary, it was very quickly taken up and adopted by his contemporaries, but in a simplified version and with a meaning that, with the perspective of time, can be said to be "classic". The first appearance of the word "intersubjective" in English testifies eloquently to this simplification. In a talk given for the *Giffords Lectures* in 1896 and published thereafter in *Naturalism and Agnosticism* in 1899, James Ward affirms: "... Descriptive conceptions plainly imply intersubjective intercourse; in other words, universal, or, as it has been called, transsubjective experience".[10]

Slowly, a "classical" signification of the word "intersubjectivity" appeared. According to it, one qualifies as intersubjective everything that is independent of every consciousness whatever it may be and is, therefore, objective. Although with this definition it is difficult to distinguish intersubjectivity from universality, one frequently meets this conception of intersubjectivity as subjective invariance in positivist philosophies, in the thought characteristic of the Vienna Circle, as well as in N. Hartmann and K. Popper for example.

It remains to be seen if this "classical" concept is compatible with the Husserlian use of the term "Intersubjektivität". He, of course, had carefully read *Erfahrung und Denken*, but he had not received *Naturalism and Agnosticism* before late in the 1920s and to all indications he never read it. Anyway, it is of little importance since his own conception of the word "Intersubjektivität" differs profoundly from the classic conception. For Husserl, we know, objectivity is said to be intersubjective because it depends constitutively on a plurality of subjects.

At first sight, the "classical" concept and Husserl's concept of intersubjectivity cover similar areas of concern; it appears that both of them attach objectivity to a plurality of subjects. However, in spite of this apparent overlap, these two concepts are not only distinct but they are ontologically conflicting. While the classic conception qualifies as intersubjective what is *independent* of every subject whatever it may be, Husserl calls "intersubjective" what is constitutively *dependent* on a plurality of subjects. Between the dependence and the independence there is an opposition that the lexical confusion can perhaps conceal but not eliminate.

It must be asked why phenomenologists have neglected taking into account the ambiguity inherent in the concept of intersubjectivity. It seems to me that, besides factors that we have already discussed which lead to a privileging of the only meaning expounded by Husserl during his time in Freiburg, an important explanation is due, once again, to Eugen Fink's interpretation of Husserl's work. More precisely, Fink repeatedly claimed that difficulties surrounding the interpretation of intersubjectivity in the *Cartesian Meditations* were to be solved, in the late manuscripts, by grounding

---

[10] J. WARD, *Naturalism and Agnosticism*, London: Adam and Charles Black, 1899, 154.

intersubjectivity on a primary life, an absolute ego that pluralizes itself into a multiplicity of transcendental egos. This thesis, which actually grounds Husserl's intersubjectivity in a "suprasubjective" universality, even though it leads to a confusion between the two types of intersubjectivity that we described above, was and still is greatly popular among Husserl's scholars.[11] Dan Zahavi, however, rightly showed that it is not faithful to—and finally contradicts—Husserl's requirement of an intersubjective constitution of objectivity.[12]

In a nutshell, the present preliminary review of the question of intersubjectivity shows that, by virtue of material and interpretative criteria, the privileged position granted to the Freiburg period for the study of intersubjectivity is not decisive. On the one hand, the *Cartesian Meditations* and the texts published by Kern in general reflect on only one aspect of intersubjectivity and therefore skip over a large portion of the problem. On the other hand, the interpretation decreed by Fink is far from faultless on this point and leads to ontological contradictions. What remains to be done now is to consider the most important aspect of the question, namely: the internal or phenomenological criteria *stricto sensu*.

Basically, these criteria are derived from the following two assertions: 1) "The question of intersubjectivity in Husserl is a direct consequence of the use of the reductive method" and 2) "The Husserlian concept of intersubjectivity is a radically new one". It has, therefore, in a way, no history.

To respond to these two assertions it must be said that, firstly, it is not really the discovery of phenomenological reduction that drove Husserl to elaborate the concept of intersubjectivity, but rather the objection of solipsism that this method apparently implies. Secondly, it seems to me that in view of the duality inherent in the meaning of the concept of intersubjectivity, the challenge is not to understand this or that conception of intersubjectivity, conceived independently of the other, but to understand the nature of the "intersubjective structure" that is the result of the interplay between these two concepts. In other words: which intersubjectivity grounds the other?

After this long introduction, it seems, then, that two questions must finally be asked. 1) Is there an objection of solipsism in the *Logical Investigations*? 2) If yes, what "intersubjective structure" answers this objection? Let us try to give these questions an answer.

---

[11] Cf. J.R. MENSCH, *Intersubjectivity and Transcendental Idealism*, New York: SUNY Press, 1988.

[12] D. ZAHAVI, "The Self-Pluralization of the Primal Life. A Problem in Fink's Husserl-Interpretation." *Recherches husserliennes* 2, 1994, 3-13.

III. THE PUZZLING CASE OF ALTERITY IN *LOGICAL INVESTIGATIONS*

a) Individual relativism and supersubjectivity

In distinction to the fifth *Cartesian Meditation*, the main stake of the *Prolegomena to Pure Logic* is not to answer an objection of solipsism, but rather to refute psychologisms of all types. However, there exists an exacerbated form of psychologism that is also the most extreme of solipsisms. Husserl studies it under the title of "individual relativism". According to this point-of-view, every logical law depends upon a particular empirical individual. In *Logical Investigations*, then, evidence of an objection to solipsism is clearly present. To illustrate it, Husserl sometimes evokes the hypothesis of a "mathematical angel" or a "logical superman" who would have logical laws (and would therefore possess a rationality) made for him alone, and shows the practical and ethical absurdities to which such a hypothesis leads (cf. LI, 163 [Hua XVIII, 155], Hua XXIV, 147). However, Husserl's most acrid criticism concentrates on the internal incoherence of this position. We will gather a better understanding of the nature of these objections by looking at a precise example.

Indisputably, one of the most fundamental logical laws is the principle of non-contradiction. This principle states that two contradictory propositions can not both be true at the same time. In the fifth chapter of his *Prolegomena*, Husserl criticises the psychologistic interpretations that this principle has been given.

John Stuart Mill, for example, viewed the principle of non-contradiction to be "one of our earliest and most familiar generalizations from experience".[13] For him, the value of the principle of contradiction would rest therefore on an *empirical* and not on an *ontological* incompatibility between contradictory acts of belief. Husserl's objection on this point is especially interesting in the context of this present paper. He observes indeed that if two acts of judgment which are really incompatible can not simultaneously exist in the consciousness of one individual, nonetheless they can exist at the same time in the consciousness of two distinct individuals. According to the definition of J.S. Mill, the principle of non-contradiction therefore would be valid for an individual consciousness only. Such a conception of the principle of non-contradiction would be, as Husserl points out, obviously relativistic. More precisely, it would even undoubtedly be solipsistic. In distinction from the approach followed in his later writings, Husserl's refusal of a solipsistic foundation of objectivity leads by no means to the explicit affirmation of a constitutive intersubjectivity. To qualify the logical laws of "intersubjective" in the meaning that Husserl will give to this term later on would, therefore, be excessive. Not being solipsistic, logical laws are also not intersubjective in the strict meaning of the term; actually, they are unconcerned about this question of intersubjectivity.

> The validity of these laws is, however, absolutely unrestricted, nor does it depend on our power, nor on anyone's power [*wer immer*], to

---

[13] Cf. J. ST. MILL, *Logic*, Book II, chap VII, § 5. Cited by HUSSERL in LI, 111 (Hua XVIII, 79).

achieve acts of conceptual presentation, nor to sustain or repeat such acts in the consciousness that they have the same intention. (LI, 128 [Hua XVIII, 109])

This indifference of the logical principles to the question of plurality as well as to the question of subjectivity itself is intimately bound up with the fact that Husserl tries to answer the criticism of a solipsistic foundation of objectivity by stressing the opposition between reality [*Realität*] and ideality [*Idealität*], and not the distinction between private subject and intersubjective plurality.

According to Husserl, the relativism of a psychologistic approach is the result of a confusion between the real and the ideal (LI, 193-196). Consequently it is important to maintain firmly that the laws of logic belong to the domain of ideality and not to that of reality.

> The logical pattern of connection is the ideal form for the sake of which we speak *in specie* of the same truth ... by whomsoever [*für wen immer*] these "same things" may be thought. (LI, 186 [Hua XVIII, 182])

It is therefore on the basis of a bringing to the fore of the domain of ideality that Husserl, during the Halle period, manages to extricate himself from the peril of solipsism that he denounced at the heart of psychologistic conceptions under the name of "individual relativism". The laws of logic, he says, don't rest on real mental acts but on ideal relations that are indifferent to every subjective consciousness and which are consequently objective.

In Halle as in Freiburg, Husserl sets solipsism against objectivity. In doing so, he already anticipates the fundamental questions that will preoccupy him in his later writings on transcendental intersubjectivity. This later conception, indeed, will be at the same time the answer Husserl will formulate to the objection of transcendental solipsism and the constitutive origin of objectivity. However, this does not imply that Husserl, in his early writings, explicitly binds objectivity to the constitutive acts of plurality of subjects. On the contrary, Husserl claims an indifference of ideality regarding the individual as well as the plurality of subjects, and this indifference is the direct result of a fundamental separation between ideality and reality.

We can conclude from all this, firstly, that what Husserl qualifies as "für wen immer Identität" in the *Logical Investigations* corresponds actually to the so-called "classical" neo-Kantian conception of intersubjectivity, initiated before him by Volkelt: a conception that classifies as "intersubjective" all that is indifferent to every subject whoever he is. To express this idea, Husserl will prefer to use the term "Übersubjektivität" (cf. Hua XXIV, 41, 141, 142, 143, etc.) or suprasubjectivity. The term "Intersubjektivität" will appear only later in his writings, with a different meaning. A second conclusion of note is that during his Halle period Husserl replies to the objection of solipsism that is the result of individual relativism by a theory that is not yet the theory of intersubjectivity described in the *Cartesian Meditations* but another one, based on the suprasubjectivity of idealities which are intuitively grasped. But this isn't the end of the matter. It must still be decided if this aspect of intersubjectivity is the only one presented in *Logical Investigations*. If this is not the case, then the "intersubjective structure" that appears in this text will have to be sketched out.

b) The geistiger Verkehr and the grounding of intersubjectivity in suprasubjectivity

With the supersubjectivity of idealities, the *für wen immer Identität*, we have described a first aspect of intersubjectivity in the *Logical Investigations*. There is however, in this text, a broaching of intersubjectivity that is much nearer to Husserl's later work on the *Einfühlung*. This is the analysis of the *geistiger Verkehr*, the mental commerce that occurs in linguistic communication.[14] This example is particularly interesting because suprasubjectivity of meaning plays a main role in it as well. Consequently, by studying the Husserlian conception of language it must be possible to answer the following question: "Which of the two forms of intersubjectivity grounds the other in Husserl's *Logical Investigations*"?

Deriving the problem of the experience of others from Husserl's study of linguistic communication necessarily implies that we also consider the suprasubjective identity of the meaning that is exchanged in it.[15] Therefore, communication and ideality can not be treated separately from each other. Husserl is perfectly conscious of the intertwining of these two dimensions in linguistic communication. However, whereas his study of expression privileges the ideal dimension of language (the meaning), his study of communication favours the real dimension: the indication.

Husserl's philosophy of language lies in his conception of the sign [*Zeichen*] and, more precisely, in the important distinction between "expressions" [*Ausdrucken*] and "indications" [*Anzeige*]. Expression is characterised by the fact that it possesses meaning [*Bedeutung*] while indication is presented as being deprived of it. The indication just refers back upon [*Hinweisen*] its object in a contingent and subjective manner. Husserl notes that the common element to all indicative processes is that actual knowledge of one real state of affairs motivates the presumption, or the conviction, of

---

[14] Cf. I. KERN, "Einleitungen des Herausgebers," in Hua XIII-XIV-XV; N. DEPRAZ, "Les figures de l'intersubjectivité. Etude des Husserliana XIII-XIV-XV Zur Intersubjektivität." *Archives de philosophie* 55, 1992, 479-498; J.-L. PETIT, *Solipsisme et intersubjectivité. Quinze leçons sur Husserl et Wittgenstein*, Paris: Cerf, 1996.

[15] We are definitely talking of the suprasubjective and not of the intersubjective. See, for example, R. MCINTYRE & D.W. SMITH, "Husserl's Identification of Meaning and Noema." *The Monist* 59, 1975, 118; J.N. MOHANTY, "Husserl's Thesis of the Ideality of Meanings," in *Readings on Edmund Husserl's Logical Investigations*, Den Haag: Martinus Nijhoff, 1977, 77; D. ZAHAVI, *Intentionalität und Konstitution. Eine Einführung in Husserls Logische Untersuchungen*, Copenhagen: Museum Tusculanum Press, 1992, 71; R. BERNET, "Bedeutung und intentionales Bewusstsein. Husserls Begriff des Bedeutungsphänomen" *Phänomenologische Forschungen* 8, 1979, 34; J. J. DRUMMOND, *Husserlian Intentionality and Non-Foundational Realism. Noema and Object*, Dordrecht/London/Boston: Kluwer Academic Publishers, 1990, 36, etc.

the existence of another state of affairs. However, what is essential to indication is not so much that there is a relationship joining one bit of knowledge to another. Such relationships can be found in other phenomena, like causality or demonstration, for example. What is important here is the particular nature of this relationship: the motivation.

> This relation of "motivation" represents a *descriptive unity* among our acts of judgment in which indicating and indicated states of affairs become constituted for the thinker. ... It is in it that the essence of indication lies. (LI, 270 [Hua XIX/1, 32])

It appears, then, that motivation establishes a mental unit between the acts of judgments constituting the indicating states of affairs and those constituting the indicated states of affairs. It is necessary to specify that even though Husserl's text is ambiguous the unity under discussion here is established between acts and not between states of affairs. It is in this sense that it is said to be "descriptive". From here on out, what is constituted are not merely real states of affairs but states of affairs *inasmuch as they indicate and in as much as they are indicated*. Motivation is constitutive of indication itself. It is in this sense that Husserl refers it as the "essence of indication".

Furthermore, Husserl specifies this point by writing that "[t]he motivational unity of our acts of judgment has itself the character of a unity of judgment; before it as a whole an objective correlate, a unitary state of affairs, parades itself, is meant in such a judgment, appears to be in and for that judgment" (LI, 270 [Hua XIX/1, 32]), expressing that the unity constituted between the act constitutive of the indicating and the act constitutive of the indicated is itself an act whose objective correlate is what he calls the "since" or the "because" [*weil*] of indication, that is the typical backward reference [*Hinweis*] of motivation. The essence of indication, the motivation, is therefore a synthetic act constitutive of a state of affairs of the second degree: the "because".

This descriptive analysis of indication having been made, we are still in ignorance of how, genetically, this synthesis occurs.

To understand it, it is necessary that a mental fact which falls under the historical rubric of the "association of ideas" intervene (LI, 273-274). The association as Husserl presents it in *Logical Investigations* does much more than to link acts of consciousness together under the requirement of a necessary logical law. The association possesses, in addition, a certain dimension of "liberty". Certainly, the association cannot oppose the formation of unities according to the rules of material logic; however, "it can create additional phenomenological characters and unities which do not have their necessary, law-determined ground in the experienced contents themselves, nor in the generic forms of their abstract aspects." (LI, 274 [Hua XIX/1, 36]). The association that make indication possible imposes, therefore, an *excess* with regard to logical demonstration. While in demonstration it is an *interconnection of being* that is brought into play, an ideal interconnection, in indication it is a felt connection [*ein fühlbare Zusammengehörigkeit*] that is experienced.

It appears that we have now arrived at the deepest point of Husserl's description of indication in *Logical Investigations*. The present attempt to delve deeply into the character of indication in Husserl has been done only as a preparatory work for the consideration of another question. We want to understand the status of indication in the simple case where it intervenes in that particular structure of signs which is communicative language.

> The articulate sound-complex ... first becomes a spoken word or communicative bit of speech when a speaker produces it with the intention of "expressing himself about something" through its means; he must endow it with a sense in certain acts of mind, a sense he desires to share with his auditor. (LI, 276 [Hua XIX/1, 39])

When we read this text, it seems at first sight that Husserl transfers to the intention of expressing what makes in the case, in the first place, that a sound-complex becomes a communicative bit of speech. Only the intention of expressing oneself, would transform the sound-complex into a communicative bit of speech or into a spoken word. More deeply, the particularisation of an ideal meaning in the content of an expressive act would be the only reason for the communicative value of indicative speech.[16] Such a reading probably would be too facile. It is more exact, I think, to say that it is only the transformation of the sound-complex into pure and simple speech that is, in the first place, the result of the intention to express. The value of this speech as a "communicative bit of speech" requires, in addition, understanding. "Such a sharing becomes a possibility if the auditor also understands the speaker's intention." (LI, 277 [Hua XIX/1, 39]).

In his attempt to describe the phenomenon of understanding of communicative bits of speech, Husserl will explicitly describe the functioning of linguistic communication:

> What first makes mental commerce possible, and turns connected speech into discourse, lies in the correlation among the corresponding physical and mental experiences of communicating persons which is

---

[16] The major difference between the theory of ideality developed in *Logical Investigations* and that developed in later texts such as *Formal and Transcendental Logic* consists chiefly in that Husserl, during his time in Halle, believed that idealities become particularised in experiences like species, whereas later texts describe a noematic constitution of these idealities. This difference is important for our problem, but we cannot develop it more deeply here. Cf. TH. DE BOER, *The Development of Husserl's Thought*, Den Haag: Martinus Nijhoff, 1978, 252-255 and 443-445; R. SOKOLOWSKI, *Husserlian Meditations*, Evanston: Northwestern University Press, 1974, 113; J.N. MOHANTY, "Husserl's Thesis of the Ideality of Meaning". in *Readings on Edmund Husserl's Logical Investigations*, Den Haag: Martinus Nijhoff, 1977, 77-78; R. BERNET, "Bedeutung und intentionales Bewusstsein. Husserls Begriff des Bedeutungsphänomens." *Phänomenologische Forschungen* 8, 1979, 31-64; J. S. HEUER, *Die Struktur der Wahrheitserlebnisse und die Wahrheitsauffassungen in Edmund Husserls Logische Untersuchungen*, Anmersbek: Verlag an der Lottbek, 1989, 84-106; etc.

effected by the physical side of speech. (LI, 277 [Hua XIX/1, 39])

It would be the understanding by someone of the other as "speaking to him", that is to say, as intentionally "expressing" something to him, which would makes the mental commerce possible. This dimension of understanding, which only makes the communication, as a *geistiger Verkehr*, possible, would therefore reside in what Husserl calls a "correlation". It is of fundamental importance to know of what this correlation consists and between which acts it is established. The question is certainly not, for Husserl, to give a new name to association as he had described it earlier. The correlation which is brought into question in linguistic communication is not established between the mental and physical experiences of one subject only (either the listener or the speaker), since these experiences are already associated through a mutual connection. The correlation we are speaking of is presently established between the associated mental and physical experiences of the listener (meaning and heard word) and the associated mental and physical experiences of the speaker (meaning and spoken word).

Husserl, specifying what this correlation is, wrote: "If one surveys these interconnections, ones sees at once that all expressions in *communicative* speech function as *indications*." (LI, 277 [Hua XIX/1, 40]). This correlation is therefore described as being an indication of a particular type, not of the second but of the third degree. We already saw that motivation was a synthetic act, constitutive of a state of affairs of the second degree: the "because" of motivation. We further specified that what distinguishes logical demonstration from indicative reference has to do with the fact that association does not establish a connection of being but a felt connection. From then on, it appears that the descriptive unit, the state of affairs of the second degree constituted by motivation, is precisely this felt connection but that the correlation is constituted in a third intentional step.

In conclusion, Husserl describes mental commerce as an indicative structure comprising four terms.[17] These four are, to review them: 1) the speaker's mental act, 2) the speaker's physical act, 3) the listener's physical act, 4) the listener's mental act. If one keeps in mind that the descriptive unit grounded in motivation is constituted between acts and not between states of affairs, then at first sight, two "felt connections" only can be established: namely, *the speaking* (in which the mental act of the speaker is associated with the physical act of the speaker) and *the listening* (in which the listener's mental act is associated with the listener's physical act).

What is typical of the linguistic correlation is the establishment between these two connections of the second degree of yet another connection, a connection of the third degree: the understanding.

We are now able to advance an answer to the question of whether in his description of communicative language Husserl does or does not grant suprasubjectivity

---

[17] In this sense there is a certain similarity of structure between this correlation and Husserl's *Einfühlung*. In this text, four terms are tied together by an analogous relationship: my body here, my body over there, my flesh here, and the flesh of another being over there. In addition Husserl points out this similarity in *Ideas II*.

a privileged position. At first sight, the simple fact that "all expressions in communicative speech function as indications." (LI, 277 [Hua XIX/1, 40]) seems to suggest that the communicative dimension of language is independent of the ideality of meaning. It is necessary to avoid overly hasty judgments and to rather go back to the things themselves. It is possible that *understanding*, which is a necessary condition for true communication to be accomplished, grants more importance to suprasubjectivity than would initially appear to be the case.

Husserl has a very precise conception of what he calls communication. Communication implies two things: on one hand, it is necessary that the speaker give a meaning [*Sinn verleihen*] to an empirical complex with the aim of sharing this meaning with the person listening to him; on the other hand, it is necessary that the listener understand this intention.

> He does this inasmuch as he takes the speaker to be a person, who is not merely uttering sounds but *speaking to him*, who is accompanying those sounds with a certain sense-giving acts, which the sounds reveal to the hearer, or whose sense they seek to communicate to him. (LI, 277 [Hua XIX/1, 39])

In other words, communication occurs only when the indicative side of the discourse manifests an act of sense-giving to a listener who, to the extent he understands, grasps this ideal meaning.

Otherwise put, understanding seems to have the hardly comprehensible requirement that each time it happens an ideation is performed.[18] If the linguistic sign does not motivate an intuitive grasp of the species, there is no mental commerce. Certainly, there are nuances to this position since the association that constitutes motivation includes some kind of creativity and interpretation. However, this does not alter the fact one has to accept, which is that in *Logical Investigations* the suprasubjectivity of meaning grounds the communicative function of language. For communication to have occurred, it is not enough if the discourse is pronounced and heard by an attentive person who knows the language being used. The listener must understand what the discourse means, its ideal meaning, and this understanding cannot come about except when an ideation is performed.

IV. CONCLUSION

Our survey has taught us that in Husserl's *Logical Investigations* we are presented with an intersubjective structure in which suprasubjectivity grounds intersubjectivity. The later texts, *Cartesian Meditations* for example, present a structure which is a reverse of the earlier one, since there it is the transcendental intersubjectivity which grounds suprasubjectivity. Why has Husserl made such a turnaround?

---

[18] Cf. R. BERNET, "Le concept husserlien de noème," in *La vie du sujet*, Paris: P.U.F, 1994.

There is no easy answer to this question. First of all, it is important to realise that this turn-about could not have happened except through the pressure of unavoidable phenomenological evidence. Indeed, the structure proposed in *Logical Investigations* which gives primacy to suprasubjectivity is the result of Husserl's intimate conviction that psychologism can only be avoided if one recognises the objectivity of a domain of idealities. Any link between idealities and subjectivity appeared to Husserl to be like a door dangerously opening onto relativism.

To abandon his position, therefore, Husserl had to have been confronted with powerful and unavoidable evidence that showed that in *Logical Investigations* there were, as Husserl later admitted, elements of psychologism. A first element of explanation of this move is perhaps that the theory advanced in *Logical Investigations* is itself, in a certain way, solipsistic. In this theory, the subject reaches the other only to the extent that he grasps universal meanings, so that in effect there is no true intersubjective commerce but only an individual capacity to grasp supraindividual idealities. Another aspect of the answer is probably that Husserl became conscious that his phenomenology could no longer be considered to be a descriptive psychology (cf. LI, 47, Hua III, 4, Hua XXIV, 441). Nevertheless, there also must have been deeper and more radical reasons for Husserl's turn-about. At least two may be suggested, which I will briefly outline here.

The first reason concerns the paradoxical status of ideality in the general structure of intentionality in Husserl. What can be the phenomenological origin of idealities if they are identical for all subjects and allow for the constitution of sensory materials? Are they metaphysical unities of a Platonic type or are they rather, like every object, the result of an intentional constitution? We know that Husserl could not accept the former hypothesis, but the latter one made him face incredible difficulties. He wrote: "Isn't this an enormous problem? ... How can the ideal be introduced into the real, how can suprasubjectivity enter into subjective act?" (Hua XXIV, 142). These questions, which soon lead Husserl to distinguish between the noetic idealities and the noematic idealties, seem to be of central importance in the about-face under discussion (cf. Hua XXVI).

A second difficulty concerns the internal structure of presentations [*Vergegenwärtigungen*]. Presentations are distinguished one from the other because of their static characteristics and their genetic motivations. However, *Einfühlung*, that is a founded presentation related to the field of *Phantasie*, shares the characteristic of being positional and simultaneous to its act with an other presentation related to the field of *Phantasie*: the hallucination (cf. Hua XXIII). These two presentations therefore appear to be phenomenologically indistinct, which is already a significant problem. Truly, the paradox is even more fundamental because *Ideas II* states that the only way to become conscious of a hallucination is to pass from the stage of solipsistic objectivity to that of intersubjective objectivity. This inescapable paradoxical situation leads to the necessity of grounding intersubjectivity constitutively.

It seems to me that there are enough reasons to explain the development in Husserl's thought, but the detailed tracing of the steps in this development will have to await another paper.

DIETER MÜNCH
Technische Universität Berlin

THE RELATION OF HUSSERL'S *LOGICAL INVESTIGATIONS* TO DESCRIPTIVE PSYCHOLOGY AND COGNITIVE SCIENCE

Husserl's *Logical Investigations* can be characterized as an attempt to determine the relation between idealities and contingent facts. According to ancient tradition, in which, as Husserl points out in his *Crisis*, the idea of science originated, philosophy deals with idealities. Ordinary experience is quite rough. Everyday experience shows, for instance, that ravens are black, but that there are also albinos which are white. Normally, summers are dry and hot and winters are cold, but we all know that this is not really certain. Thus we have to admit that judgments of ordinary experience are valid only with a certain kind of probability. It was therefore a great discovery when philosophers realized that there are also judgments which have the character of certainty. Such judgments were first developed by mathematics. Socrates, the first philosopher, who asked for definitions, extended it to linguistic analysis. Plato systematized it in his dialectics and his doctrine of ideas, and his pupil Aristotle invented formal logic which allowed the drawing of conclusions from true premises which are necessarily true. The problem is, however, that we gain certainty not in regard to contingent facts but only in regard to idealities. This leads to the conception of ideal essences which are conceived as the reliable structure on which the contingent appearances grow. In this early stage in the history of science, genuine science was conceived as dealing with such ideal essences.

The first book of Husserl's *Logical Investigations* is a penetrating study which insists on this old philosophical insight that ideal entities and structures exist. Every attempt to reduce them to contingent peculiarities of our nature, as, for example, psychologism with its thesis that the validity of logical laws can be reduced to empirical psychological laws governing the process of our cognitive acts claims, is untenable. But idealities cannot be found merely in formal logic. Rather, Husserl is convinced that the whole realm of meaning belongs to this sphere. This means that the proper study of meaning cannot be the task of psychology or any other empirical science since they have no direct access to idealities, and therefore to meaning. What is needed is an 'eidetic' science which describes the ideal structures and the laws valid in the realm of ideality.

It is obvious that, according to Husserl, philosophy is not based on psychology. Nevertheless there is still the problem of how it is possible for contingent entities such as you and me to grasp idealities. The key concept Husserl introduces in the second volume of his *Logical Investigations* in order to solve this problem is the concept of intentionality. According to this concept, psychical acts are directed towards an object 'outside' of consciousness. These intentional objects do not necessarily belong to the region of reality as does the contingent person performing the intentional act. Thus intentionality is a kind of mediator between contingency and ideality. Phenomenology as introduced in the *Logical Investigation* is primarily the study of the psychical acts which leads to an elucidation of the fundamental logical concepts and to a theory of knowledge.

The concept of intentionality, the insight that psychical acts are *about* something, is also fundamental for cognitive science. Cognitions, which are the subject of this interdisciplinary research project, have a representational content which is also *about* objects or states of affairs. Moreover, there are not only empirical sciences, which participate in cognitive science, studying contingent reality, but also formal sciences such as logic, computer science, or formal linguistics. The reason for this is that cognitive science is not only interested in the actual cognitive processes of a certain class of contingent entities, human beings, but also in 'ideal' processes such as reasoning, without presupposing that a person or an artificial system actually performs these processes. Cognitive science is not merely physiological psychology, from which Husserl, as we shall see, dissociates phenomenology, but to some extent also an ideal science. Thus, these considerations show that there are at least some parallels between cognitive science, which is an important part of our philosophical and scientific context, and phenomenology. Since the centennial of Husserl's *Logical Investigations* is a challenge to evaluate this work from our present perspective, it is an urgent task to clarify its relation to cognitive science.

In the next paragraph I shall discuss the relation of Husserl's early work to cognitive science. I shall defend the thesis that Husserl in his *Logical Investigations* supports a version of the 'language of thought' hypothesis. In the third paragraph I shall examine the relation of phenomenology to descriptive psychology. This investigation is necessary since Husserl says in the first edition that phenomenology is descriptive psychology, whereas he rejects this characterization in the second edition. I shall show that this change took place because there were new developments in psychology—expecially the development of cognitive psychology in the Würzburg School—which asked for a different descriptive system in order to structure the psychological landscape. In the fourth paragraph I shall discuss several concepts of description which can be applied to the *Logical Investigations*. It shall result in the claim that Husserl's attempt to dissociate phenomenology from empirical psychology, which characterizes the transcendental turn, is a tilting at windmills. Reading the *Logical Investigations* as a contribution to cognitive science is suggested.

I. HUSSERL AND COGNITIVISM

Edmund Husserl's early work is an important contribution to cognitive science.[1] Thus

---

[1] For a detailed discussion of the relation of the early Husserl (i.e., before the *Logical Investigations*) to cognitive science see D. MÜNCH, "The Early Work of Husserl and Artificial Intelligence", *The Journal of the British Society for Phenomenology* 21, 1990: 107-120; *Intention und Zeichen. Untersuchungen zu Franz Brentano und zu Edmund Husserls Frühwerk*, Frankfurt: Suhrkamp, 1993; "The Early Husserl. Forerunner and Critic of Cognitive Simulation", in *Handbook—Phenomenology and Cognitive Science*, edited by E. Baumgartner et al., Dettelbach: Röll, 1996, 199-210.

in his *Philosophy of Arithmetic*[2] Husserl anticipated the program of cognitive simulation, as has been formulated by Newell and Simon.[3] This anticipation was possible since Husserl realized that arithmetic and all higher cognitive processes are based on "mental mechanisms" (cf. Hua XII, 349f) Arithmetical devices, for instance, are neither typically applied with evidence, nor have they been invented on the basis of arithmetical insights: our mind, in using them, becomes rather like the working of a machine, which uses "blind-mechanical" or "logical-mechanical" devices (Hua XII, 364). According to Husserl the blind mechanical devices with their "blind causality", i.e., the unelucidated processes that we normally use, are the result of a kind of 'natural selection'. It is, he says, "in the struggle for existence that the truth was won." (Hua XII, 371). The description of these natural devices is the first task of Husserl's program for elucidating them. In a second, constructive stage, the stage of justification, a "logical device, parallel to" the psychical mechanism (a *parallellaufendes logisches Verfahren*, Hua XII, 359ff), is to be developed. This is nothing other than a computer program.

But does this mean that Husserl's *Logical Investigations* belong to the project of cognitive science? One has to be careful in answering this question, since the term "intention" is ambiguous. Thus cognitivists such as Jerry Fodor use the term "intention" synonymously with "cognition". He dubs, for example, a central claim of cognitivism "intentional realism".[4] With this label he refers to a position in the discussion about the problem whether intentional sentences can be reduced to the language of other sciences or whether we need a special science of intention which is nothing other than cognitive science.[5] Since we can learn from Husserl that the basic problem of phenomenology is intentionality, we may be tempted to think that phenomenology and cognitive science are one and the same science.

The term "intention" has, however, also been used in a different sense, as, for instance, by critics of cognitive science and artificial intelligence such as John Searle.[6] The fact that Searle uses a completely different concept of intention than Fodor becomes

---

[2] E. HUSSERL, *Philosophie der Arithmetik*. In *Husserliana* 12, Den Haag: Nijhoff, 1970, 1-288.

[3] A. NEWELL and H.A. SIMON, *Human Problem Solving*, Englewood Cliffs N. J.: Prentice-Hall, 1972.

[4] J. FODOR, "Fodor's Guide to Mental Representation: the Intelligent Auntie's Vade-mecum". In *A Theory of Content and Other Essays*, Cambridge MA: MIT Press 1990, 3-29.

[5] This question, which was discussed by the Brentanian scholar Roderick Chisholm (R. CHISHOLM, *Perceiving*, Ithaca NY: Cornell University Press, 1957) and by Willard Van Orman Quine (W. V. O. QUINE, *Word and Object*, Cambridge MA: MIT-Press, 1960, § 45), leads to the label "Brentano's problem". It is crucial for the foundation of cognitive science as becomes clear by the following passage: "One may accept the Brentano thesis as showing the indispensability of intentional idioms and the importance of an autonomous science of intention, or as showing the baselessness of intentional idioms and the emptiness of a science of intention. My attitude, unlike Brentano's, is the second" (W.V.O. QUINE, *Word and Object*, 221). Cf. J. FODOR, *The Language of Thought*, Cambridge MA: Harvard University Press, 1979.

[6] J. SEARLE, "Minds, Brains, and Programs", *The Behavioral and Brain Sciences* 3, 1980: 63-73; *Intentionality*, Cambridge: Cambridge University Press, 1983; *Minds, Brains and Science*, Cambridge MA: Harvard University Press, 1984; *The Rediscovery of Mind*, Cambridge MA: MIT Press, 1992.

clear if one realizes that Searle refers with "intention" to a characteristic feature of consciousness, to which we have direct access only in a first person perspective. The cognitivist conception of cognition, in contrast, is based on a third person perspective. The cognitivist is not interested in consciousness but in an explanation of intelligent behavior, i.e., behavior which can be adopted in different contexts according to the goals the system pursues. For such explanations we need, according to cognitivism, sentences like "x believes that p" or "x desires that q".[7] Such sentences are not intended to ascribe conscious states to the system in question. Cognitivists, rather, point out that cognitions 'cross-classify' conscious and non-conscious states. This makes it possible to claim that even computers may behave intelligently without ascribing consciousness to them. In his famous thought experiment with the Chinese room Searle tries to show that the computer's faculty of symbol manipulation is not sufficient for conscious states.[8] According to Searle, this result is a decisive argument against artificial intelligence. But since cognitivists and most defenders of artificial intelligence do not claim that computers are conscious, although they insist that they have intentions, it is clear that we are confronted here with two fundamentally different concepts of intention.[9]

At first glance, it may appear that in this discussion Husserl sides with Searle, since the *Logical Investigations* introduce intentions as a feature of conscious mental states. We should not forget that Husserl abandoned the program of cognitive simulation he had defended in his earlier work, since he realized that it is not only blind symbol manipulation which results in true statements, but also symbolic knowledge. Husserl presents such a theory in his *Logical Investigations* and in which the concepts of intention and fulfillment play a central role.[10] Thus the *Logical Investigations* support the intuitions underlying Searle's thought experiment with the Chinese room: no matter how efficient blind symbol manipulation may be, it will never lead independently lead to consciousness.

Searle, however, attacks not only the project of artificial intelligence but also the project of cognitive science, which is a project studying natural intelligence.[11]

---

[7] These are called "intentional sentences" since they involve cognitive predicates such as "to believe that" or "to wish that".

[8] J. SEARLE, "Minds, Brains, and Programs". A critical discussion can be found in D. MÜNCH, "Minds, Brains, and Cognitive Science", in *Speech Acts, Meaning and Intentions. Critical Approaches to the Philosophy of John R. Searle*, edited by A. Burkhardt, Berlin: de Gruyter, 1990, 367-390; and "Intention und Kognition", in *Sprache und Denken, Language and Thought*, edited by A. Burri, Berlin: de Gruyter, 1997, 214-236.

[9] A discussion of the relation of the cognitivist concept of cognition to the phenomenological concept of intention can be found in D. MÜNCH, "Intention und Kognition"; cf. D. MÜNCH, "Kognitivismus in anthropologischer Perspektive", in *Der Mensch in der Perspektive der Kognitionswissenschaft*, edited by P. Gold and A. K. Engel, Frankfurt: Suhrkamp 1998, 17-48.

[10] Cf. D. MÜNCH, "The Early Work of Husserl and Artificial Intelligence"; Intention und Zeichen; "The Early Husserl. Forerunner and Critic of Cognitive Simulation".

[11] J. SEARLE, *Minds, Brains and Science*.

Cognitivists claim that in order to grasp higher cognitive phenomena, one needs, besides the level of intentional explanation, a level of description which uses algorithmic devices. Cognitive processes involve symbol manipulation, which can be grasped with the help of computer languages. Searle attacks this view and claims that no such symbol manipulation exists in humans' cognitive activity. Between the brain and the cognitive states there is no intermediate programming level; the brain just does the job.

In order to ascertain Husserl's position we should examine it in regard to the conception of a language of thought. This conception is important for the cognitivistic approach in cognitive science. With this conception Chomsky's first graduate student at MIT, Jerry Fodor, tries to apply insights of the Chomskyan revolution in linguistics to the philosophy of mind. Chomsky claims that having linguistic competence is nothing other than having control over the rules for generating well-formed sentences in this language. The fundamental task of linguistics consists in the reconstruction of these rules (and representing the lexicon which is used) with mathematical means. Thus the grammatical theories culminate in algorithms, which means that they are so precise that they can run on a computer. The language of thought hypothesis says that higher cognitive processes can be grasped in the same conceptual framework as language.

If we look at the Fourth Investigation we can see that Husserl is a forerunner of Chomsky. In this investigation Husserl applies the basic concepts of formal ontology which he had developed in the Third Investigation to grammar. Language is conceived as a field which is guided by purely formal rules, which has to be studied by a discipline he calls "pure grammar" (in the second edition: "purely logical grammar"). This approach has been elaborated by logicians such as Ajdukiewicz and Lesniewski to the categorial grammar.[12] This grammar has an algorithmic character, too. But Husserl does not only support a computational approach to language. Moreover, it is one of his central claims that our intentions are restricted by the laws of purely logical grammar. Thoughts which are not in accordance with these laws are nonsense, i.e., they cannot be directed towards an intentional object. Besides purely logical grammar there is also the pure logic, logic "in the pregnant sense". "The former laws guard against nonsense (*Unsinn*), the latter against formal or analytic absurditiy or countersense (*Widersinn*)". The laws of purely logical grammar allow expressions which are contradictory, such as "a wooden iron". Such an expression is not nonsense, since it entails information about the intuition which would fulfill such a symbolic intention. Pure logic is more restrictive, since it refers to the a priori forms which exclude the fulfillment of such an intention from possibility. Thus pure logic also refers to intentions and their corresponding fulfillments, i.e., to semantics, and is not restricted to the uninterpreted signs of a given calculus.

Our considerations show that one can claim that Husserl indeed shares a language of thought hypothesis. The indefinite article is used since we should be aware

---

[12] Y. BAR-HILLEL, "Husserl's Conception of a Purely Logical Grammar". *Philosophy and Phenomenological Research* 17, 1956, 362-369; J.-L. GARDIÈS, *Esquisse d'une grammaire pure*, Paris: Vrin, 1975. Engl. trans by K. Mullligan, *Rational Grammar*, Munich: Philosophia, 1985; B SMITH, *Parts and Moments*, Munich: Philosophia, 1982.

that Husserl does not defend the computational theory of representation which is part of the cognitivistic version of the language of thought hypothesis. Cognitivism, as introduced by Fodor[13] and Pylyshyn[14], claims that every cognition consists of two parts; the first is the representational content, the second is the psychological mode. The representational content is linguistically expressed by the that-clause following the intentional predicate; the psychological mode is the part which supplies the difference between "Paul believes that Husserl is a cognitive scientist" and "Paul doubts (rejects) that Husserl is a cognitive scientist". This still corresponds to a distinction Husserl made between the matter and the quality of an intentional act. But cognitivism is interested in the problem of how it is possible that an intention such as "I want to raise my arm" can cause a physical event, namely, the raising of my arm. In order to solve this mind/body problem, cognitivism offers a solution which is called the "computational theory of representation". It says that the representational content is realized in a symbol which has formal and physical aspects. An example is a group of firing neurons. Since not all neurons of that group fire and the firing occurs with a certain rate, the firing takes a form. But the neurons themselves are physical entities and the firing is a physical event. The computational theory of representation says that symbols underlying the representational content have their semantic properties—they can represent something—merely because of their form. This implies that every difference in meaning corresponds to a difference in the form of the underlying symbol. Since the symbols are at the same time physical entities, they can cause a physical event, for example, a movement of the body.

In his *Logical Investigations* Husserl is not interested in the mind/body problem and he does not consider the solution suggested by cognitivism.[15] Thus Husserl defends a language of thought hypothesis without a computational theory of representation. Nevertheless, it should be noted that Husserl's position is by no means a matter of course. In connection with his convictions about language, it follows that an explanation of high level cognitions requires a level of description which can be called the "programming level". It is true that Husserl shares with Searle the conviction that we cannot explain at this level, why intentional acts are conscious. But cognitive science is not confined to this either, since it is not conceived as a science of consciousness.[16] A computational approach is what is required. But according to Husserl a full description of high level cognitive phenomena requires such an approach. Searle, in contrast, attacks cognitive science. Thus, Husserl has in his *Logical Investigations* much

---

[13] J. FODOR, *The Language of Thought*; and *Representations: Philosophical Essays on the Foundations of Cognitive Science*, Cambridge MA: MIT Press, 1981.

[14] Z. PYLYSHYN, *Computation and Cognition. Towards a Foundation for Cognitive Science*, Cambridge MA: MIT Press, 1984.

[15] This problem belongs to genetic psychology.

[16] Cognitive science deals, of course, with conscious phenomena but it is not (primarily) interested in consciousness as such.

more in common with cognitive science than with Searle.[17]

II. PHENOMENOLOGY AND DESCRIPTIVE PSYCHOLOGY

Nevertheless we have to be careful with the claim that Husserl is a cognitive scientist. Cognitive science is an interdisciplinary project to study cognitive phenomena with empirical means. The empirical approach is essential. But in regard to experience phenomenology is not without problems. Other problems arise because of Husserl's transcendental turn which took place around 1908. The second edition of the *Logical Investigations* was revised by Husserl after his transcendental turn. It is true that it was not made a work of transcendental phenomenology but nevertheless there are some substantial changes. Thus, Husserl writes in the first edition of the *Logical Investigations*:

> Phenomenology is descriptive psychology. Therefore a critique of knowledge is essentially psychology or can, at least, only be built on the fundament of psychology. Therefore pure logic is also based on psychology – why, then, the whole argument against psychologism? (LI, 262 [Hua XIX, 24], my transl.)

In response to this objection Husserl claims:

> The necessity of such a psychological foundation of pure logic, namely of a strictly descriptive one, indicates the mutual independence of both sciences, logic and psychology. This is true because pure description is merely an initial stage (*Vorstufe*) of theory, but not theory itself. Thus one and the same region of pure description can be used as a preparation for very different theoretical sciences. Psychology as a complete science is not a fundament of pure logic, but certain classes of descriptions, which are an initial stage of the theoretical research of psychology (namely insofar as they describe the empirical objects, whose genetic relations this science intends to pursue), and which form at the same time the basis for those fundamental abstractions, in which the logician grasps with

---

[17] For Searle the concepts of background and network play an important role in his rejection of the language of thought hypothesis (*Intentionality*, chap. 5); cf. also J.R. SEARLE, *Expression and Meaning. Studies in the Theory of Speech Acts*, Cambridge: Cambridge University Press, 1979, chap. 5. These concepts can be found in Husserl as well, but it is the later Husserl who developed this concept. It should be emphasized that even the transcendental Husserl holds the view that there is a programming level, which should, of course, not be confounded with the computational theory of representation. Dreyfus has pointed out that Husserl has to be esteemed "as the father of current research in cognitive psychology and artificial intelligence." H. L. DREYFUS (ed.), *Husserl, Intentionality and Cognitive Science*, Cambridge MA.: MIT Press, 1982, 2. What strikes Dreyfus as so similar to artificial intelligence is Husserl's concept of the noema, which Husserl regards as a "strict rule (*feste Regel*) for possible syntheses." For a discussion cf.R. MCINTYRE, "Searle on Intentionality", *Inquiry* 27, 1984, 468-83.

evidence the essence of his ideal objects and relations.

This passage is not to be found in the second edition. Rather, Husserl claims: "phenomenology is *not* descriptive psychology". (LI, 261 [Hua XIX, 23]). In the "Introduction'" to his *Ideas* we read:

> In the last decade there has been much talk of phenomenology in German philosophy and psychology. In presumed agreement with the *Logical Investigations*, phenomenology is conceived as an initial stage (*Unterstufe*) of empirical psychology, as a region containing 'immanent' descriptions of psychical events (*Erlebnisse*), which – such is their understanding of this immanence—remains strictly within the framework in inner experience (*Erfahrung*). (*Ideas* I, 37-38 [Hua III/1, 3-4])

Husserl protests against this understanding of phenomenology in his *Ideas*. But if we compare the two quotations we see that Husserl's understanding of phenomenology has changed.

It is helpful to consider the change in terminology with regard to psychology. The most striking change consists in the rejection of the term "descriptive psychology" which he uses in the first edition in order to characterize phenomenology. With this term, Husserl refers to Brentano's conception of psychology. One should, however, notice that Husserl realized already in the first edition of the *Logical Investigations* that his phenomenology is not identical with Brentano's project. Thus he notes that the term "descriptive psychology" is equivocal and therefore he prefers the term "phenomenology". One argument says that "descriptive psychology" is used by some philosophers to denote "the region of scientific psychological investigations which are delineated by the methodological preference of inner experience and by the abstraction of all psychophysical explanations." (LI, 263 [Hua XIX, 24], my transl.). With this remark, Husserl refers to Brentano, who claims that inner experience has an exceptional epistemological status, a claim which Husserl rejects in the Appendix to the Sixth Investigation, "Outer and inner perception. Physical and psychical phenomena". We can further take it for granted that Husserl was aware of all the fundamental innovations he introduced in his *Logical Investigations*, for instance his concept of intention and the intentional analysis.[18]

The reason why Husserl changed the terminology becomes clear if we choose a structural approach and take into account the opposition, i.e., the terminology which Husserl uses in order to dissociate phenomenology from different psychological approaches. In the first edition Husserl uses for these non-phenomenological psychologies expressions such as "genetic-psychological" (Hua XIX, 10) he talks about a "psychophysical experiment" (Hua XIX, 16), and he refers to "physiological psychology" (Hua XIX, 17). These terms are no longer used in the second edition but

---

[18] Cf. D. MÜNCH, *Intention und Zeichen*.

are instead substituted by expressions such as "empirically-psychological" (LI, 252 [XIX, 10]), by "psychological experiment" (LI, 256 [Hua XIX, 16], my transl.) and "experimental psychology" (LI, 257 [Hua XIX, 17]).

First edition	Second edition
"genetic-psychological"	"empirical-psychological"
"psychophysical experiment"	"psychological experiment"
"physiological psychology"	"experimental psychology"

The terminology of the first edition is influenced by Brentano's and Wundt's conception of psychology. Thus the distinction between genetic and descriptive psychology is essential for the understanding of Brentano, who insists that descriptive psychology is the fundamental philosophical science.[19] He describes the different psychical elements and the possible ways of their combination. Genetic psychology, in contrast, is a causal science which studies the physiological causes of psychical phenomena. Thus, genetic psychology is not psychology proper, but psychophysics. This program has not only been formulated by the scientists who we call now psychophysicians, such as Fechner, but also by Brentano's great rival Wilhelm Wundt. Thus in his principle work *Grundzüge der Physiologischen Psychologie*[20], which appeared in the same year as Brentano's *Psychology from an empirical standpoint* (1874), Wundt formulated a program for experimental psychology.[21] Wundt points out that the psychical processes, with which we are acquainted only from inside, and from a first person perspective, cannot be made the direct object of experimental research. With the help of experiments we can only draw conclusions from outside, from a third person perspective. The reason for this is that it is essential for a scientific experiment to be in control of the different parameters and to quantitatively determine the relation between them. But this requires a third person perspective, which can direct one only to physical but not to psychical phenomena. Therefore a genuine psychological experiment is impossible. We can study experimentally only the "outer, physical conditions of inner processes".[22] One consequence is that only quite simple psychophysical processes can be studied experimentally, whereas complex cognitive processes such as thinking or speaking cannot be studied in this way. Such phenomena can be studied only by investigating the

---

[19] F. BRENTANO, *Psychologie vom empirischen Standpunkt*, Hamburg: Meiner, 1973. Engl. trans. by. L. L. McAlister, *Psychology from an Empirical Standpoint*, London: Routledge,1981.

[20] W. WUNDT, *Grundzüge der Physiologischen Psychologie*, Leipzig: Engelmann, 1874.

[21] Cf. W. MACK, "Zeichen und Audruck in der Sprachtheorie Wilhelm Wundts". *Zeitschrift für Semiotik* (Special issue: "Zeichenphilosophie im 19. Jahrhundert", edited by D. Münch) 23/1, 2001.

[22] W. WUNDT, *Grundzüge der Physiologischen Psychologie,* 5.

products of cognitive processes, namely language, myth, custom and tradition. The investigation of such products and the drawing of conclusions in regard to the underlying psychical processes is, according to Wundt, the task of folk psychology (*Völkerpsychologie*). This discipline is not an individual psychology, since these phenomena are the result of complex social interaction. Thus we have, according to Wundt, an experimental individual psychology which deals with low level psychical phenomena and a non-experimental folkpsychology which deals with high level cognitive phenomena.

In the light of this psychological context, the terminology of the first edition of the *Logical Investigations* is perfectly reasonable. Obviously Husserl refers with "genetic psychology" and "physiological psychology" to Wundt's influential experimental psychology; the term "descriptive psychology" indicates that he argues for an approach which indeed departs from Brentano's psychology in essential respects but which is in agreement with Brentano insofar as it designates a purely descriptive individual psychology, a suggestion, which Wundt rejects. Since Wundt's folk psychology, which can also be called "descriptive", is not meant by Husserl's use "descriptive psychology", one can understand it as an abbreviation for "descriptive individual (or act) psychology in line with Brentano".

The question arises why Husserl has changed his terminology for the non-phenomenological psychologies in the second edition. The passage from the "Introduction" of his *Ideas* quoted above provides an important hint since it says that phenomenology was taken up by empirical psychologists. This was the case with the Würzburg school (Külpe, Bühler, Dürr, Messer), which was actually inspired by Husserl. Most important is Karl Bühler's habilitation on 'Facts and problems concerning the psychology of cognitive processes'.[23] In this work Bühler makes clear how highly he esteems Husserl's *Logical Investigations*. Psychology, Bühler says, has neglected cognitions very badly. There is not much more to be found than occasional observations, the only exception being Lazarus and Steinthal, who applied "certain methods", which proceeded, however, from the primacy of language. This means that they did not try to develop the linguistic laws from "cognitive facts" (*Denktatsachen*) but, rather, construed the cognitive facts according to the laws governing language. Bühler contrasts this approach with a new one. "A peculiar very fruitful method has recently been developed by Husserl".[24] Bühler calls this method "transcendental", since he sees his prototype in Kant, who distinguished between logical and psychological cognitive laws. In Kant and his successors, however, there is "no connection, an incomparability" between the logical and the psychical.

> Husserl's method breaks with this view and its exceptional fertility can be taken as an indirect proof that the positive presupposition, which it contains, is right. On the basis of our investigations, which

---

[23] K. BÜHLER, "Tatsachen und Probleme zu einer Psychologie der Denkvorgänge." *Archiv für die gesamte Psychologie* IX, 1907, 297-365; XII, 1908, 1-92.

[24] K. BÜHLER, "Tatsachen und Probleme zu einer Psychologie der Denkvorgänge", 298.

have a completely different methodological foundation we claim that the correspondence which has not been tested by Husserl does indeed exist, and that it forces us to completely revise our views of the character of psychical laws.[25]

One can even show that Bühler designed his experiments according to concepts introduced by Husserl. Thus he confronted his test persons with aphorisms and asked them to report what was going on in their mind. In Husserl's terminology we can describe these experiments as an endeavor to study the process of fulfillment of an empty symbolic intention (the aphorism, which was not yet understood). It was not only Bühler who held Husserl's *Logical Investigations* in such high esteem. Thus August Messer wrote different papers on the relation between Husserl's phenomenology and psychology[26]; his *Empfindung und Denken* (1908), which has been reviewed by G. E. Moore (1910)[27], is a kind paraphrase of the *Logical Investigations*, and Otto Selz gave his habilitation lecture on *Husserl's phenomenology and its relation to the psychological statement of the problem*. The Würzburg school is of special relevance for our question concerning the relation of Husserl's *Logical Investigations* to cognitive science, since it was an important stage in the history of cognitive science and has for a long time been identified with cognitive psychology (*Denkpsychologie*). Thus Newell and Simon acknowledge that their own approach of cognitive simulation was akin to that of the Würzburg school.

With the rise of the Würzburg school at the beginning of the last century the psychological landscape changed. Now, there was an experimental individual psychology, studying high level cognitive phenomena, which was missing at around 1900, when the first edition of the *Logical Investigations* appeared. It is now interesting to see Husserl's reaction. One can describe it as the sharpest possible form of dissociation.[28] Actually this dissociation was so effective that despite the importance of the Würzburg school and its endeavor to come in contact with Husserl, they have been completely neglected in the official phenemenological tradition.[29]

The rise of the Würzburg school, which Husserl rejected, made it necessary for Husserl to renounce opposition between descriptive and genetic psychology. The effect

---

[25] K. BÜHLER, "Tatsachen und Probleme zu einer Psychologie der Denkvorgänge", 299.

[26] A. MESSER, "Über die Frage des Abhängigkeitsverhältnisses der Logik von der Psychologie. Betrachtungen im Anschluß an die 'Logischen Untersuchungen' von Edmund Husserl". *Archiv für die gesamte Psychologie* I, 1903, 527-544; "Phänomenologie in ihrem Verhältnis zur Psychologie". *Archiv für die gesamte Psychologie* XXII, 1911,117-29.

[27] A. MESSER, *Empfindung und Denken*, Leipzig, 1908; G.E. MOORE, "Review of Messer 1908." *Mind* 19, 1910, 395-409.

[28] Cf. Husserl's remarks on Külpe and Messer in his *Ideas*.

[29] In H. SPIEGELBERG'S, *The Phenomenological Movement*, Den Haag: Nijhoff,1960/82, the Würzburg School or its members (Bühler, Messer, Dürr) are not even mentioned; only Külpe is mentioned once, in context with Heidegger.

was that the meaning of the term "descriptive psychology" exploded. We saw that in the first edition this term could be conceived as an abbreviation for "descriptive individual (or act) psychology in line with Brentano" and that he could therefore be used to characterize his own approach, even though there were deep differences with Brentano. The opposition to the extremely influential Wundt made this possible, since there were, roughly, merely the two schools, that of Brentano and that of Wundt. But with the rise of the Würzburg school the situation changed. It was an individual act psychology; it was in the tradition of Brentano since it was explicitly a continuation of Husserl's own *Logical Investigations*; and it was descriptive, since the test persons had to describe their experiences. As a consequence, the meaning of the term "descriptive psychology" had to change. We can study this in the third supplement to § 6 of the introduction to the second volume, where Husserl writes that phenomenology is not descriptive psychology and continues: "Descriptive-psychological statements about perceptions, judgements, emotions, volitions, etc. are about the thus named real states of animal beings and, therefore about the reality of nature, just as descriptive statements about physical states are as a matter of course about occurrence of nature, namely about those of real nature and not about an imaginary nature."(LI, 261 [Hua XIX, 23], my transl.) According to this characterization, descriptive psychology makes statements such as "person x is at time t in cognitive state c". But this has nothing to do with descriptive psychology as introduced by Franz Brentano; it is, rather, directed against the "interrogative method" (*Ausfragemethode*), as Wundt called the approach of the Würzburg school. But what this school learned from the *Logical Investigations* was, of course, not this descriptive method, but the framework of intention and fulfillment, which Husserl developed, as we shall see below, with the help of descriptive means.

III. DESCRIPTION

The strange fate of the term "descriptive psychology" in the second edition of the *Logical Investigations* is remarkable since Husserl insisted that phenomenology remains a descriptive science. Nevertheless, he contrasts transcendental (or pure) phenomenology with the conception of descriptive psychology, mentioned above. According to Husserl, descriptive psychology is a science of *facts* as well as a science of *realities*. Pure or transcendental phenomenology, in contrast, is a science of essential being and the non-real (cf. Hua III/1, 6-7). This characterization sounds very pretentious, yet should not impress us too much, however. The question is whether it can withstand a sober analysis. In order to avoid confusion, it makes sense in a first step—and only a first step can be made in this paper—to distinguish different concepts of description which can be applied to the *Logical Investigations*.

In the Aristotelian tradition there is an old dichotomy of concrete and abstract sciences. Concrete sciences include mineralogy, botany and zoology; abstract sciences include physics and mathematics. The concrete sciences consist in the description and classification of the objects in question. The abstract sciences, in contrast, are either formal sciences such as mathematics or are interested in natural laws which make explanations possible. With the rise of modern science it became, of course, clear that the original criteria of abstract and concrete are not convincing, since concrete objects such as minerals and geological formations can also be made the object of explanatory sciences. This leads to another distinction: some sciences are descriptive, that is, they are primarily interested in classifications, while other sciences are interested in the genesis of the entities and their causes. Thus a distinction was drawn between the descriptive science of *Geognosie* on the one hand, which was conceived as the science of the structure and formation of the earth's crust, and geology on the other, which studies the origin and the causal processes which terminated in these phenomena.

This distinction was decisive for Brentano's conception of descriptive psychology, which he separates from genetic psychology. Descriptive psychology, which he also called "Psychognosie", determines the elements of psychical phenomena and their possible combinations.[30] Genetic psychology, in contrast, deals, like geology, with the causes which are relevant for the genesis of these phenomena. It is not without interest to learn that Brentano also conceived of ontology in this way. Already, in his Würzburg lectures in the late 1860s, Brentano claimed that ontology was based on descriptive psychology. Ontology itself is conceived of as a descriptive science; its main task consists in determining the different kinds of parts. The basic distinction is between *physical*, *logical* and *metaphysical* parts. Physical parts are separable, i.e., they are still concrete, like a leg of a chair, which one can saw off a chair. Husserl calls these separable parts in the third *Logical Investigations* "pieces" (*Stücke*). Logical parts are the different genera and species. Logical parts, in contrast to pieces, exist only in the mind of the beholder; they have, however, a *fundamentum in re*. Husserl deals with these kinds of parts in the Second Investigation. It is interesting to see that even in his terminology Husserl is under the influence of Brentano since he calls that which later became well-known as *Wesensanschauung* in the *Logical Investigations* "intuition of species" (*Speziesanschauung*). The metaphysical parts are Brentano's version of the Aristotelian categories[31]—the color and the extension of a thing are examples of metaphysical parts; they are neither separable nor are they merely in the mind of the beholder, like logical parts. These metaphysical parts are the source for Husserl's conception of foundation. An example is again the relation of color and extension, which are mutually founded in one another, since one cannot exist without the other. Also in this case the influence of Brentano can be noticed in his terminology, since Husserl calls such a relation a "metaphysical connection". All this is evidence that Husserl is at least to some extent a descriptive psychologist in the Brentanian sense.

An extension of this analytic approach, which goes beyond the part-whole ontology suggested by Brentano, can be found in the description of intentional acts. A basic contribution of the *Logical Investigations* to the philosophy of mind consists in

---

[30] Cf. D. MÜNCH, *Psychologie und Metaphysik. Historisch-systematische Untersuchungen zum Frühwerk Franz Brentanos*, Amsterdam: Rodopi, in preparation.

[31] Cf. D. MÜNCH, "Franz Brentanos Reform der Kategorienlehre". In *Sign Processes in Complex Systems. Proceedings of 7th International Congress of the IASS-AIS*, edited by W. Schmitz, 2000.

the insight that intentional acts are directed towards something "outside" of the mind. With this claim Husserl attacks the container theory of mind which was predominant in empirical approaches. The classical model says that we receive sensations from the outside world, which sensations are in turn the object of internal processing. According to the standard approach, this processing is performed by the mechanism of associations which lead to higher level cognitions, such as abstract or general concepts, which are in turn the building blocks for other cognitive processes. The important point is that all the psychical processes are internal and that there is no way out. Husserl, however, shows that our consciousness is something completely different. Normally we are directed towards objects or states of affairs which do not belong to the psychical container. If we see, for instance, a house, then we are directed towards the real thing made out of bricks or concrete in which humans are living. And it is obvious that the object about which we have this perception is something other than a complex of sensation. The same is true if we refer to an entity which is not intuitively presented, as, for instance, the Moscow television tower. Things happen with the intended object—it lights up, for instance—which are not, and cannot be, true of the immanent content of our psychical acts. This example shows that intentional acts transcend the realm of the immanent. Husserl further shows that we can refer with different acts to one and the same object. The same person can be perceived with different senses and from different angles, which is not true of the immanent content. Moreover, it is possible to refer, with different symbolic intentions founded in different definite descriptions, to the same thing. Thus we can intend a building as the house in which Mr. Brown lives or as the house with the dark green facade.

Such a kind of analysis can be understood as a kind of description. As a good Aristotelian Husserl teaches us differences; therefore he presents us with examples which have to be intuited, in order to discover the different parts which are relevant. One should notice that such descriptions, although they are founded in the intuition of concrete examples, are directed towards the general. The object or state of affairs which functions as the intuitive basis for such a generalizing abstraction is not necessarily a reality which actually exists.

This descriptive approach made the foundation of another kind of description possible. It is the *intentional analysis*, which is based on the concept of intention and fulfillment and the interior content that makes a correlation between them. Husserl shows that there are different kinds of intentional acts. The basic distinction is that between significant or symbolic intention (both terms are used synonymously in the *Logical Investigations*) on the one hand and the intuitive intention on the other. In intuitive intentions the intended object or state of affairs is either directly present or is presented in an analogue form, i.e., in the form of imagination, remembrance or picture. Symbolic intentions, in contrast, are lacking this intuitive character, that is, they are "empty". All intentions which are based on linguistic expressions are such symbolic intentions. Husserl points out that there is an internal relation between signification and intuition, insofar as every signification intends in a certain sense an intuition, which functions as a fulfillment. In more modern terminology, that used by Searle, one can say that the signification contains the condition of satisfaction (fulfillment). His theory of symbolic knowledge, which Husserl presents in his *Logical Investigations*, is based on this idea. It says that knowledge is nothing other than a fulfilled symbolic intention.

The correlation between intention and fulfillment makes a special intentional analysis possible. If we want to make clear the meaning of a symbolic intention we have to study what would count as a fulfillment of such an intention and whether there are typical structures in the course of the fulfilling intuitive process. Thus, if we want to elucidate the concept of a thing, we have to describe regularities in the course of intuition. We can go around and view it from different angles, and during this process the gaining of a new perspective corresponds to a loss of other perspectives, and so on. Obviously this intentional analysis is descriptive in character, although not in the Brentanian sense, and it was this concept which inspired the Würzburg school.

There is a further concept of description applicable to the *Logical Investigations*. It is the concept of functional description which is used by designers.[32] Such descriptions specify what a system or a part of a system does, without specifying the way in which the system does it. Moreover, such a description does not necessarily involve the existence of that machine. In contrast, it is normally the case that the machine does not yet exist, the description of the machine is prior to the actual instantiation of the machine.

It is not difficult to see that this concept of a functional description can be applied to Husserl's *Logical Investigations* as well. Consider, for instance, Husserl's characterization of the act and the act matter. The act is introduced by Husserl as a function which endows a given complex of sensations with meaning, transforming it into an intention, which is directed towards an object or state of affairs. The act matter is, just as Frege's "sense", that part of the act, which fixes the direction towards the object. These are functional descriptions which say nothing about the way in which the task in question is performed. Moreover, the description is not restricted to a certain kind of contingent entity, which performs the act; it can, at least in principle, be performed by angels, humans and (perhaps) by some machines.

IV. SUMMARY

Our considerations show that Husserl's *Logical Investigations* are much less anti-empirical than the statements which Husserl made after his transcendental turn suggest. It is true, of course, that Husserl never conceived phenomenology as an experimental psychology and that he is not interested—at least not during his professional period as a phenomenologist—in the experiences that any real person has at a certain time. We do, however, have to distinguish the question of whether phenomenology itself is empirical psychology from the question of whether phenomenology is an integral part of a greater project which studies cognitive phenomena empirically. In regard to this second question the answer has to be affirmative. As we have seen, Husserl claims in

---

[32] Cf. H. SIMON, *The Sciences of the Artificial*, Cambridge MA: MIT Press, 1969.

the first edition that phenomenology is the initial stage in the study of cognitive phenomena. He points out that phenomenology "serves as the preparation of psychology as an empirical science. It analyzes and describes (especially as phenomenology of thinking and cognition) the experiences of presentation, judgment, and knowledge, which find their genetic explanation in psychology, their investigation according to empirical-lawful relations." (LI, 249 [Hua XIX, 7], my transl.). And further, we have seen that he actually developed with the concepts of intention and fulfillment an approach which is, to use Bühler's words, "very fruitful" for empirical cognitive studies. And we can assume that further study of the *Logical Investigations* will detect an even greater relevance for the project of cognitive science.

One should also be aware of the fact that phenomenology, in turn, can profit from the empirical sciences belonging to the project of cognitive science. This is true, because one can derive from eidetic statements predictions about facts. If there is, for instance, a purely logical grammar, we can expect that its laws lead to the hypothesis that there are language universals, which are about real languages. Every sober philosopher would certainly agree that empirical findings are therefore relevant for eidetic sciences. Only a Hegelian would object to findings which contradict the predictions: 'the worse for reality'. Around 1900 Husserl was obviously convinced that his different kinds of description were adequate without taking into account empirical findings, but he rejected the claim of infallibility which can be found in Brentano's descriptive psychology. Thus we are on solid ground when we read the *Logical Investigations* today, a hundred years after their first publication conceiving them as belonging to cognitive science, i.e., to a project which studies empirically cognitive phenomena. The studies of different cultures, of the cognitive development of children and of pathological cases shall at least in principle confront the phenomenologist with new phenomena—and, indeed, they do.[33] But if this is true, Husserl's transcendental turn appears in a new light. In his early work, Husserl belongs to the Aristotelian tradition which conceives of philosophy as an empirical enterprise. In the first edition of his *Logical Investigations*, Husserl confessed to belonging to this tradition, into which Friedrich Trendelenburg and Franz Brentano had injected new life,[34] when he called phenomenology "descriptive psychology". The transcendental turn, however, locks phenomenology up in the ivory tower of transcendental philosophy, which makes impossible a confrontation with the findings of empirical sciences, which could excite the inmate too much. This remark should not detain anyone from an endeavour which tries to make use of Husserl's later phenomenology, such as his genetic phenomenology, in relation to cognitive science. But one should be aware that such an endeavour is probably not possible strictly within the framework of transcendental phenomenology. For Husserl's violent exclusion of phenomenology from empirical sciences, one cannot

---

[33] A famous example for a phenomenologist who shares the same view is Merleau-Ponty.

[34] For a presentation of this tradition cf. D. Münch, "Zeichenphilosophie und ihre aristotelischen Wurzeln". *Zeitschrift für Semiotik* (*Special issue: Zeichenphilosophie*, edited by D. Münch) 22/3-4, 2000, and D. Münch (ed.), *Zeichenphilosophie im 19. Jahrhundert* (*Special issue of the Zeitschrift für Semiotik*) 23/1, 2001.

find a genuine philosophical reason, but merely extra-philosophical motivations which must be studied by a sociology of philosophy.[35]

---

[35] Such an explanation for Husserl's transcendental turn, which takes into account extra-philosophical motivations, can be found in D. Münch, "Edmund Husserl und die Würzburger Schule". *Brentano Studien* 7, 1997, 89-122; "Die mannigfachen Beziehungen zwischen Philosophie und Psychologie. Das Verhältnis Edmund Husserls zur Würzburger Schule in philosophie-, psychologie- und institutionengeschichtlicher Perspektive", in *Psychologiegeschichte – Beziehungen zu Philosophie und Grenzgebiete*, edited by J. Jahnke, J. Fahrenberg, R. Stegie and E. Bauer, Munich: Profil, 1998, 318-345; and "Il contesto della svolta trascendentale di Husserl", in *Il realismo fenomenologico. La fenomenologia dei circoli di Monaco e Gottinga*, edited by S. Besoli, Quodlibet Macerata, 2000.

Appendix

DORION CAIRNS

THE FIRST MOTIVATION OF TRANSCENDENTAL EPOCHÉ

Edited by Lester Embree, F. Kersten, and Richard M. Zaner[1]

Husserl's philosophical thinking was largely motivated by two antipathies: One was an aversion to obscurity in concepts, in propositions, in theories. The other was an aversion to beliefs that he had not thoroughly justified by his own observations. As long as their material content remained obscure, the first antipathy extended even to concepts, propositions, and theories whose formal logical structures were perfectly distinct and evidently consistent. The second antipathy extended to all beliefs not thoroughly justified by his own observation, no matter how successful the practice based on them might be, and no matter how consonant the beliefs themselves might be with commonly accepted opinions.

Naturally, the positive counterpart of these dislikes was a desire to see everything for himself, to ground all his philosophical beliefs on his own adequate insight, and to use words in philosophical discourse to express only clear significations that he himself had formed on the basis of original observation and analysis of what he himself perceived.

There is a striking disparity between Husserl's style of thinking and that of the typical mathematician-turned-philosopher. Reading his earliest publication, the *Philosophie der Arithmetik* (1891), we ask how someone who started as a mathematician ever turned to producing something of this kind—or, more wisely, we ask how someone to whom this manner of inquiry and *this* ideal of demonstration are patently congenial ever happened to follow the path of mathematical analysis through to the doctorate and a place as assistant to Karl Weierstrass. A partial answer is suggested by Husserl's much later characterization of that great mathematician as the man who finally cleared away the old obscure manner of speaking about "infinitesimals" and substituted concepts based on clear and distinct insights.[2] It is likely that the young Husserl was drawn to pure mathematics less by its formal distinctness and consistency,

---

[1] This previously unpublished MS. contains the result of reflection over some twenty years by Dorion Cairns (1901-1973) on the actual motivation that led his teacher, Edmund Husserl, to perform the transcendental phenomenological *epoché* and reduction for the first time. The MS. is pp. 039436-039468 in the Cairns Nachlass held in Archival Repository of the Center for Advanced Research in Phenomenology, Inc. at the University of Memphis. In what seems a recasting of the first three pages there occurs the handwritten note: "This is rather good. Apparently it was written in 1938. Typed later. D.C. Oct 4, 1957." It thus stems from the thinking Cairns did at the time of Husserl's death about the significance of the phenomenologist's life and work. Some changes were no doubt made whenever the MS was typed and there are also some handwritten changes on the typescript, perhaps also made in 1957. The MS has been transcribed by Mr. S. J. Julian. We have added the title and the section titles and made some minor stylistic changes and also substituted "mental process" for "subjective process" throughout in order to conform to Cairns's final translation usage. *The Editors.*

[2] Cairns's footnote: O. BECKER, "Die Philosophie Edmund Husserls," *Kant-Studien*, Bd. XXXV, Heft 2/3, 1930, 119.

and less by the power of its symbolic-deductive technique, than by the superior clarity of what he unfashionably called its "insights."

On the other hand, it is more likely that the apparent *lack* of clear insights in philosophy had deterred him from starting as a philosopher. In 1919, Husserl wrote in appreciation of Franz Brentano:

> At a time when my philosophical interests were increasing and I was hesitant whether I should stick to mathematics as a calling or devote myself wholly to philosophy, Brentano's lectures turned the scales. ... From his lectures I first derived the conviction which gave me the courage to choose philosophy as a life calling—the conviction, namely, that philosophy too is a field of serious work, that it can be treated in the spirit of strictest science and therefore must be so treated. The pure objectivity with which Brentano went to the heart of all problems, his critical treatment of them, his dialectical evaluation of the different possible arguments, his analysis of equivocations, the manner in which he traced all philosophical concepts to their primal source in intuition—all this filled me with admiration and confidence.[3]

This passage develops the same motif that was to reappear briefly in his already cited characterization of Weierstrass: insight, the removal of obscurity and equivocation, the tracing of concepts to their primal source in intuition. These are the features that, even then, made mathematics seem to Husserl worthy of the name "science," the features that he had vainly sought in philosophy. And when, in the context from which I just now quoted, Husserl expresses a passing criticism of Brentano, it is an objection to what, I dare say, are the sins that most easily beset the *mathematically* inclined philosopher: excessive haste in passing from intuition to sharply defined concepts, a predilection for systematic constructs, and a tendency to rely on arguments to justify his choosing among a number of equally self-consistent "solutions" to a philosophical problem.

The demand that all one's philosophical beliefs be *completely* justified by intuition, by insight, is one that can never be satisfied. In a letter to the present writer, which is additional testimony to the nature of his initial philosophical motive and ideal, Husserl once described his early efforts to fulfill that demand as utterly frustrated.

> I was very late [he continued] in recognizing that my own failure was also the failure of all contemporary philosophy. At first I had inevitably attributed the obscurity and the pseudo-scientific character of the latter to my own incompetence.... I then decided to renounce

---

[3] E. HUSSERL, "Erinnerung an Franz Brentano," 153f, in O. KRAUS, *Franz Brentano: Zur Kenntnis seines Lebens und seiner Lehre. Mit Beiträgen von Carl Stumpf und Edmund Husserl*, München: C.H. Beck, 1919. Cairns's translation.

every great goal in my philosophical labors and be happy if only, here and there in the dark unstable swamp, I could find by my efforts one smallest bit of solid ground on which I could really stand. I said to myself, "I will accept as valid nothing but what I can repeatedly grasp as something that is itself given to me." And so I lived, from despair to despair, until, in my fourteen years . . . . at Halle, I finally made a beginning.[4]

Husserl's endeavor to establish at least something in a manner satisfactory to his desire for perfectly insightful belief led him, in fact, through obscurities and confusions to a clear paradox—a paradox that, as I shall attempt to show, could be overcome only by the eventual establishment of what he was to call a "transcendental-phenomenological" position.

I. THE *DE FACTO* COURSE OF HUSSERL'S THOUGHT IN *PHILOSOPHIE DER ARITHMETIK*

The task that Husserl set himself in his *Habilitationsschrift* of 1887,[5] which became the nucleus of his initial publication—the first and, as it proved, the only volume of his *Philosophie der Arithmetik* (1891)—can be described in terms borrowed from his already quoted remarks about Weierstrass and Brentano. As Weierstrass had done away with the obscure manner of speaking of the infinitesimal, so Husserl was trying to dispel the less obvious obscurity that besets the senses expressed by the words "many," "two," "number," "something," "one." And, as though his procedure were a matter of course, Husserl sought, like Brentano, to trace those senses "back to their source in something that is itself seen." His presupposition was that even so primitive and emptily formal and structureless a concept as *something*, or *anything whatever*, must have been derived initially from a presentive consciousness of particular affairs as evidently *somethings*—must have as its ultimate and validating basis, the observing of some characteristic that is presented when an affair is clearly itself presented *as* at least a something or other. By actively re-producing the sense *something*, which we now accept passively along with the word "something," and by critically observing this reproductive process, the young Husserl intended to assure the clear genuineness or legitimacy of the concept and to fix the sense that the word should thenceforth express when he used it. Thus, from the start, his attempt to "clarify concepts," as he then phrased it, was primarily an attempt to see, to grasp, an itself-presented affair to which the ordinarily vague concept in question manifestly applies. Once he had evidently grasped such an example, his next task was to isolate the particular presented determinations by virtue of which the presented affair falls under that "concept." He attacked this problem by a

---

[4] E. HUSSERL, *Briefwechsel*, ed. by K. Schuhmann in collaboration with E. Schuhmann, Dordrecht: Kluwer Academic Publishers, 1994, IV, 21f. Translated by Cairns.

[5] E. HUSSERL, *Philosophie der Arithmetik. Mit ergänzenden Texten* (1890-1901), ed. by L. Eley (Hua XII), 289-338.

method of varying the exemplificatory affair as widely, and in as many dimensions, as possible while still keeping it plainly an affair to which the concept applies.

In his *Philosophie der Arithmetik* this method, which he later elaborated critically and referred to as "the method of free variation," was used uncritically, without any explicit and clear methodological understanding. And the actual results are, on the whole, far from satisfactory. The book leaves the critical reader uncomfortably aware of ten newly discovered obscurities for every old obscurity cleared away. Indeed, it was these newly discovered obscurities, and his downright mistakes in analysis, that drove the author on his way.

Husserl presupposed that we have not only number-*symbols* and *words*, but also familiar, more or less obscure, number-*concepts*, expressed by number-words. He also presupposed that, e.g., the concept of *manyness* (or *plurality*) and the concepts of the smaller cardinal numbers were initially produced for each of us by a mental process of so-called "abstracting," which had, as its concrete basis, collections of determinate objects—collections that were not merely meant but were themselves given: in that *each* member of a collection was intended particularly, and *all* the members were grasped collectively. (The problem of how the concept *manyness* is applied to groups too large to be grasped in that fashion is dealt with later in the book.) The initial problem was formulated substantially as follows: What determination in a presented collection of separately and collectively intended affairs is retained, and what determinations are abstracted from, when the concept *manyness* (*plurality*) is produced? What determination, in other words, is necessarily present in any particular example of directly and clearly presented manyness?

Obviously, it is not a determination present in *each* of intended members, severally. Rather, their *connexion*, to make up a whole of the particular kind called "a many," must be the immediate basis for abstracting the so-called concept, *manyness*. In general, one kind of "whole" (in the broadest sense) differs from another according to the nature of the connexions uniting their "parts" (again in the broadest sense). The problem, then, was to discover the *kind of connexion* that unites the parts or members of any whole that is directly and clearly intended as "a many."

Now the author of the *Philosophie der Arithmetik* maintained that the class of wholes, or "relational complexes," has two main subdivisions. One subdivision is made up of those relational complexes which are such that the nature of the complex depends on the several natures of the related parts—for example, complexes the members of which are related as similar (or as different) in intensity; or again, complexes in which an example of color is related to an example of spatial extension, which the color covers; or yet again, the complex determined by the relationship of a *generic* "concept" to a subordinate *specific* "concept." He called the wholes within this subdivision "primary relational complexes."

In the other subdivision, so he maintained, we find those relational complexes the members of which are interrelated by virtue of a unitary psychic *act* directed to each and to all of them. For example, regardless of any primary relational complexes in which they may also unite, *A* and *B* make up what may be called a "psychic relational complex" if I *will A* for the sake of *B*, or if I infer *A* from *B*, or even if I merely *think A* and *B* together.

By paying attention to the related affairs themselves, one can find their *primary* relatedness. On the other hand, so the author (mistakenly) says, the "psychic" relatedness of the members of a psychic relational complex can be found only by attending to the psychic *act* by virtue of which they make up that complex. He goes on to say that *collective combination* is a kind of "psychic," not a "primary," collection. The parts or members of a collection, qua collection, are combined only by the psychic act that, so to speak, mentally discriminates them and holds them together. On the other hand, the *spatial* relational complex made up of the petals of a rose, for example, is a primary complex. So too is the peculiar nexus made up of the individual hue of a petal and its individual surface. One may have discriminated two petals from one another, i.e., paid attention to each separately: one may also have discriminated the hue and the surface of a petal from one another. But then a further act must be performed in order to make the collection, *this petal and that petal*, or the *collection, this petal and the hue of that petal*:

> A collection is formed in that a unitary interest and, in and with it, a unitary attention at one and the same time select and unite the different contents. Collective connexion can therefore be grasped only by reflection on the psychic act by which the collection is formed.... If we ask, for example, wherein lies the connexion when we think of redness, the moon, and Napoleon, we get the answer that it lies solely in that we think these objects together—that we think them in one act. (Hua XII, 74)

More precisely, the *grasping* of each of the several affairs is a particular psychic act; and they are then *collected* by another psychic act, which includes the particular acts of grasping each severally. When I "think the concept" *manyness* or *plurality* clearly and directly, I am conscious also of some *concrete collection*, actively made by me in this manner; and, from this concrete collection, in the phraseology of the *Philosophie der Arithmetik*, I "abstract the concept" *manyness* by disregarding the specific determinations of the collected affairs and considering only their collective connexion—that is to say, I consider the affairs only as distinguished and collected Somethings.

Accordingly, the concept *manyness* contains, in and with the concept *collective combination*, the concept *something*. Everything thought of is *ipso facto* a particular something; and we derive the universal concept *something*, so the author (again mistakenly) maintains, by reflecting on the psychic act of thinking, or intending, an object. There is nothing in the affairs themselves, no common primary characteristic, that makes them somethings, in the way that all examples of color are colors by virtue by virtue of their primary content. The somethingness in a concrete something is, in other words, not an inherent but a relative determination and can be grasped, not in grasping the affair *per se*, but only in grasping the psychic act related to it as an intending of it.

And thus the concepts something, one, many, two, three, and number are not concepts or affairs as belonging to a particular genus or species. They are, on the contrary, all-embracing form-concepts; and, so the author of the *Philosophie der Arithmetik* says, their all-embracingness finds its simple explanation in the fact that they arise in the course of *reflection on psychic acts* that can be practiced on affairs of all generic and specific kinds, without exception.

But the author was not long in discovering some of the disquieting implications of these doctrines. Consistency demands an analogous theory of all other form-concepts. It demands, for example, the theory that the formal-logical structure of a fact, or of a proposition, is grasped by reflecting on the *psychic act* of judging, and that the logical structure of a deductive proof is grasped by reflecting on the *psychic act* of proving or inferring. But such theories are incompatible with the plain sense of the statements making up formal logic and formal mathematics. Clearly such statements are about *objective* forms and relations, not about the forms of subjective acts of, e.g., judging and inferring. But, if that is the case, must not the like be true of statements about the forms of collections?[6]

II. *LOGISCHE UNTERSUCHUNGEN* AND *VORLESUNGEN ZUR PHÄNOMENOLOGIE DES INNEREN ZEITBEWUßTSEINS*

Husserl's next published work, the *Prolegomena zur reinen Logik* (1900), is an unambiguous defense of the objectivity of the forms that are the subject-matter of pure logic. According to the doctrine now developed, all the form-concepts which, in the *Philosophie der Arithmetik*, were said to have their source in reflections on psychic acts, are forms of thoroughly objective affairs.

But, although Husserl abandons the earlier doctrine, he does not abandon his initial approach to the problem. Rather, he maintains, in effect, that, in his early observations he had overlooked some subtle, but crucial, differences, which are observably *there*. He still maintains that subjective acts of intending affairs separately and taking them together produce collections. He still maintains that it is only on the basis of such acts that one can grasp a concrete plurality as such. The novelty of his *later* doctrine is his contention that the act of collecting not only has its own subjective *and*-form but also produces an objective *and*-form: The *and* in the complex *A-and-B* is this (subjectively produced) objective *and*; it is not the *and* which is the inherent moment in the complex *psychic* act of collectively "combining" *A* and *B*. As the author of the *Philosophie der Arithmetik*, he had failed to distinguish the two *and*-forms, because they are quite analogous and always present together. And, in like manner, the later Husserl still maintains that a Something is a Something by virtue of being actively intended. He no longer says, however, that grasping the somethingness of something is

---

[6] On the margin of the typescript here Cairns wrote: "Elaborate further!"

grasping an abstracted moment of the active intending. His later view is that the (subjectively produced) something-form is no less objective than the "primary content."

But it was many years before all such distinctions between real determinations of mental processes, on the one hand, were clearly and steadily seen by Husserl. In the first edition of his *Logische Untersuchungen*, he still confused them from time to time. It seems that, when writing the *Logische Untersuchungen*, he *did* see clearly that, e.g., the propositional and ontological and-forms are not real determinations of the subjective acts of conjoining concepts or objects. On the other hand, he seems to have thought at times that such "categorial" forms, as ideal objects, are grasped on the basis of a consciousness of "the categorizing" acts—as though somehow these acts included in themselves the intended categorial complexes (the intended collections, propositions, states of affairs, etc.) as inherent real components.

Such confusion was favored by his terminology. The misleadingly ambiguous word "*Inhalt*" ("content") is still used in the *Logische Untersuchungen* in contexts where the later Husserl (as he in fact said) would have used "*Gegenstand*" ("object"). But, even while these and other confusions between what is "really" or inherently part of the stream of consciousness and what lies on the side of what are essentially the objects of consciousness were being cleared up—nay, largely because they *were* being cleared up—the enterprise begun in the *Philosophie der Arithmetik* and continued in the *Logische Untersuchungen* was becoming more *clearly* paradoxical. It had been announced as a "psychological" enterprise; and, to be sure, its psychological nature seemed plain enough, even after confusions and errors in the earlier results had been removed. For, whether the particular somethings, the particular collections of somethings, etc., were conceived (quite obscurely and ambiguously) as the objects of subjective acts, they were conceived as essentially *relative to* consciousness. And similarly, as the continued recurrence of the ambiguous word *Begriff* (concept) indicates, *something, many, one*, etc., were in fact considered only as *intended* universals. In their case a double, even a triple, subjectivism was involved: They were considered as (1) the *subjectively intended* universal forms (2) exemplified in *subjectively intended* complexes; and (3) these complexes, in turn, were considered as affairs that had been produced for consciousness by the latter's spontaneous activities.

And yet Husserl's evident *purpose* in the *Philosophie der Arithmetik* was to clear up the nature of plurality, number, something, etc., as formal categories of the possibly existent. Though announced and carried out as psychological inquiries—inquiries, that is to say, concerning the nature of what exists in one *specific* and restricted field of being, namely, the psychic field—the author's labors were intended to bear *universal* ontological fruits. If he persists in taking their actual fruits as universal ontology, as metaphysics, is he not committed to an absurd subjective idealism? Is he not maintaining, in effect, that, e.g., anything that is actually or possibly *anything whatever*, anything that is possibly *something*, can exist as something only thanks to subjective mental acts: which—in turn, must be *something*, and moreover something specific? Either the theme and the significance of the analyses are confined to human minds and what they produce as objects for themselves, or else analyses, will all their eventual subtleties and genuine insights, are, if taken as universal philosophy, committed to the absurdity of making the whole universe depend for its existence and its nature upon the existence and nature of a special class of processes (namely, mental processes) within the universe.

Far from rescuing the philosophical sense of phenomenology from this absurdity, the writer of the *Logische Untersuchungen* attempted to avoid the whole issue; but at the same time he actually made it more acute. He refers to propositions and facts, and to the ideal formal structures exemplified by them, as existing in themselves; he speaks in the same fashion of generic and specific universals and the materially determinate entities that exemplify them. And yet, in his actual analyses, objects are considered only qua intentional objects of mental processes. Their very *An-sich-sein* is actually investigated only as an intended *An-sich-sein*: One observable intrinsic characteristic of certain mental processes is that they intend objects as outside the stream of consciousness. Furthermore, some of these intentive processes are intrinsically processes of being conscious of objects as themselves given—themselves presented, so to speak, "in person"—while others are processes of intending objects as they were emptily, as not presented (though perhaps as capable of becoming presented). Sometimes what is intrinsically a presentative consciousness is also intrinsically a consciousness of its intended object as identical with a previously intended object; and, in that case, it is intrinsically either a confirming or a canceling of the sense imputed to the object in the previous act. Presentative consciousness, "seeing," the consciousness of an intended object as itself given, *ursprüngliche Evidenz*—all these are roughly equivalent terms—does not take one beyond that *of* which the consciousness is intrinsically a consciousness.

The tacit policy of the author of the *Logische Untersuchungen* (in the first edition) prevents both an unambiguous affirmation and an unambiguous denial that things exist, and are what they are, independent of consciousness. For the time being, at least the disquieting evidence that at least the *formal* structure of all objects of consciousness is generated by consciousness before it is evidently there to present itself—this never repudiated result of the *Philosophie der Arithmetik* —is allowed to drop from sight, at least from the reader's sight. The author's unexpressed position seems to be this: Whether or not there are affairs that exist *independently* of my consciousness, I am conscious of objects as not being *real components* of my mind, as not being really immanent in my psychic processes— this, to say the least, is the sense that objects have for me when I intend them and, in particular, when I am conscious of them as presented. Moreover, objects do have for me the sense that I mean them as having, and seeing does function as fulfilling empty intentions. Without raising the question of whether the "outside" world is essentially, or only contingently, an object of consciousness, I can legitimately consider outside objects (of my consciousness) in their status *as* objects of my consciousness, as what, to say the least, I do intend and *as* what on occasion, I do see as there.

I can observe, for example, how, in one mental process, I can be conscious of something as identical with what I remember being conscious of in *another* mental process. Or I can observe how, from phase to phase of one continuing mental process, I am *continuously* conscious of something as self-identical—perhaps itself presented as self-identical throughout the successive phases of my consciousness of it. Without asking what identity night be *apart* from consciousness of identity, I can at least ask what this identity-*for-consciousness*—this "intentional" identity—is, and I can ask, correlatively, what the consciousness of this identity is. I can ask, more particularly, about the nature of a consciousness of objective identity as an *itself-given* identity and not as a merely supposed identity.

I can also inquire about what I am *conscious of as* material things, without raising the issue of whether material things exist independently of my consciousness. I can inquire into the various manners in which I can be conscious of "something" as "an identical individual stone," let us say,—for example, how I can be aware of "it" in an act of remembering it and of how I can also be aware of "it" in an act of expecting "it" as something to be perceived under such and such conditions. I can analyze the sense of such an intentional object as presented "in person," visually or tactually, I can describe how, in seeing "it" and touching "it," I am aware of the object seen as identical with the object touched, or how, in merely seeing it, I am aware of (I intend) it as having unseen, unpresented, determinations, which could be presented in other acts of seeing or of tactual or auditory perceiving, etc.

Moreover, and still without any position concerning the actual or possible existence of anything independent of my consciousness, I can examine the way in which my opinions are confirmed or canceled by consciousness of things as themselves presented. I need not *ask* whether, in seeing what I am conscious of as "a stone" I am seeing an independent entity. Still less need I take a *position* relative to that old issue. I need not ask whether sensuous perceiving or any other type of consciousness always, or sometimes, deceives about some thing-in-itself. I can still observe that sometimes I *see* that what I take to be something incompatible with something else that I *believed* in; and I can observe that, quite universally, even seeing has for me the sense of being open to confirmation and cancellation by more seeing.

Whether the first edition of the *Logische Untersuchungen* be viewed from the standpoint of naïve common sense, from the standpoint of an absolute objectivistic metaphysics, or from the standpoint of Husserl's later, so-called transcendental phenomenology, one must, I believe, consider it a merit that Husserl did not assert that those so-called "phenomenological" analyses of consciousness with respect to its really immanent determinations and its intentional objects as intended and (in some cases) presented, have metaphysical significance. The apparent conflict between two fundamental insights is not denied. At most, the role of consciousness as necessary condition for the thereness of objects for consciousness[7] is not made a central theme in the *Logische Untersuchungen*, as it had become a decade earlier and was to be again in all Husserl's subsequent works.

At the same time, it is not surprising that, if this conflict remained present, though unthematic, those persons who sought consistency before they sought truth

---

[7] Cairns's handwritten note on the margin about here: "Restate!"

should be in no position to assimilate both respects of the *Logische Untersuchungen*. It is not surprising, in other words, that the early so-called phenomenological school was roughly divided into those who used the method of straightforward description of intentional objects as themselves given, and developed thereby an objective ontology, to which they then dogmatically ascribed universal significance for what exists, and on the other hand, those who, mindful of the fact that even self-given objects are intentional objects, developed an intentional psychology without metaphysical claims. If anyone took over both these aspects, he took over with them Husserl's still unresolved problem.

For Husserl himself, a way to surmount the problem was opened up by his analyses of the consciousness of so-called internal time, that is, the intrinsic temporal form which the stream of conscious processes and really immanent sensuous data itself has, regardless of the additional fact that it is also a process self-intended as *in* objective time. Especially illuminating was his analysis of the manner in which the receding past phases of the flux of really immanent intending and data are continually intended in the present—as identified intentional objects of a growing and steadily modified continuum of intendings or, as Husserl called them specifically, retentions. This view of the immanent temporal form of the stream of consciousness, as itself a subjectively constituted (produced or generated) result of intentionality, paved the way for the view that the status of consciousness as a process in objective time, along with other objective processes, is also a "constituted" derivative status, a derivative but valid sense that consciousness necessarily has for itself, a necessary reflexive result of its more fundamental nature of intending "a world" as outside itself.

Whether this highly unconventional view is more than the illusion it must seem to be at first is a question that lies beyond the scope of this paper. In any case, it enabled Husserl to reconcile other, apparently incompatible, views. The view that mental processes, in producing for themselves their intentional objects, are producing the world of existing objects, could not be maintained without the absurdity involved when mental processes, *as* productive of their intentional objects, are assumed to be already worldly objects among others. On the other hand, the fear that knowledge of subjectively constituted objects-for-consciousness and knowledge of subjectively constituted categorial forms of such objects is not knowledge of what exists and of the forms of what exists—this fear is dispelled; and reflective analyses of the manner in which one builds up an intended world for oneself, may be accorded the philosophic, the metaphysical, significance of an analysis of the manner in which the world itself (the only world one has) is itself produced.

It is hard to see how otherwise Husserl's principle that beliefs are philosophically justified only when based purely on observation of what is itself given could be reconciled with the evident results of his inquiries into the nature of what is itself given. Already, as we have said, in the *Philosophie der Arithmetik*, it had become plain that the given *formal* structure of objects of consciousness is produced by subjective activity. Objects do not swim into one's ken for the first time as already formally related; they are given their formal-objective relational structure by observable acts of relating them. For a purely passive consciousness— if we allow ourselves that fiction—there would be no "thises" and no "thats," no "pluralities," and no "facts" with syntactical structures. The *Vorlesungen zur Phänomenologie des inneren Zeitbewusstseins* had brought out, however, that even the process-form of consciousness itself is not an ultimate datum, but a product of a more fundamental passive intentional synthesis, and that, accordingly, even the most primitive raw material for active categorizing is the product of intentional synthesis. Seeing, as the process that validates belief, must be a seeing of produced intentional objects of consciousness, since that is the only kind of objects that can be there for us to see. Nothing can impinge on consciousness as so to speak, ready made, from outside.

III. SIGNIFICANCE OF THE *DE FACTO* COURSE OF HUSSERL'S THOUGHT FOR THE SELF-CONSCIOUS EXERCISE OF TRANSCENDENTAL PHENOMENOLOGICAL *EPOCHÉ*

Husserl's transcendental idealism was not something extraneous, added to an already consistent body of thought. Rather it was, I think, the necessary outcome, if his phenomenology was to have both a consistent and a philosophical significance. It was the only way of surmounting a problem that was inevitable from the start, a problem that became explicit for Husserl as soon as he tried to make clear to himself the significance of such analyses as he had actually performed.

These analyses were, as I have said, actually analyses of mental processes and of the intentional objects of mental processes, purely *as* intentional, i.e., as what is intended in mental processes, the latter being what they observably are, *per se.*

Parenthetically, I may remark that one completely misinterprets these analyses if one understands them as presupposing a relation between an existent mental process, on the one hand, and, on the other hand, a coordinate ready-made object that happens on occasion to become incidentally an objects an object of consciousness. Husserl's attitude and his problems are not those of philosophers who start by assuming, reasonably enough: Here are conscious process, on the one hand, and things, on the other hand; in general, things and processes are related, and in particular organisms or their minds "take account" other things—they perceive them, remember them, like them, etc., under certain circumstances. Husserl starts by saying: Here at least is my consciousness, and regardless of whether anything else exists, my consciousness exists and is intrinsically an intending, sometimes a seeing-intending of objects *as* outside it, *as* identical, *as* existent, *as* unitary, *as* many, etc.

If we conceive a purely descriptive psychology broadly enough to include description not only of the real contents of the stream of mental processes, but also of the objects they intend—descriptions of these objects purely *qua* intended—then obviously *all* the analyses in question were contributions to such a pure descriptive psychology. This is true even of these analyses which have as their theme the intentional objects of mental processes which are observably, and *per se*, processes of being consciousness of intended objects as *themselves given*. In describing "the object" as itself given in such, so-called "evident," processes, one is not describing the object as though it were something apart from these processes. One's *real* datum is the mental process which is descriptively a *consciousness of* an object as "itself-given" and as presenting the characteristics set forth in the description. In other words, one is describing the evident *objective sense* of the intentional object, as the latter is interested in an evidential act.

On the other hand, as I have said, the initial dominant purpose of Husserl's investigations was not to develop a purely descriptive psychology, simply for the sake of knowing more *about the psyche*. He undertook such investigations as a means to the critical justification of all alleged knowledge, including knowledge of *other entities besides* the psychic.

He was convinced from the start that *any* opinion about *anything* would have to square with what the thing is seen to be when it is itself given. Thus "evidentness," the actual givenness of what is intended, was from the start conceived as containing the norm for belief about anything.

Here, then, was a difficulty: In order to test an opinion, one had to bring the objects of opinion to self-givenness and then examine not only the given object, straightforwardly, naïvely, but also the evidentness, the givenness, of the object. But the latter examination, as we have said, brought out characteristics of the given object, not as an independent entity, but as a "sense" intended in a mental process.

What justification is there for presuming that, when a subjective act is descriptively a consciousness of an object as "itself presented" and as presented with the qualities ascribed to it—then the object is a genuine entity and *has* the qualities it is intended as having?

The problem is acute because one's stream of psychic processes are, as a matter of course, taken to be a process in the world, along with a great many other things, the existence and essential nature of which does not depend on the existence of one's human mind.

We all have this undoubted belief about things, but now when we come to examine the evidence for this belief, we seem to discover only that some *mental processes* are descriptively processes of being aware of this or that as itself given, with such and such properties.

The[8] problem was even more acute, however, because, as the inquiries of the *Philosophie der Arithmetik* had already shown, the *categorial forms* of intended objects are *produced* by subjective activities. That an object is "something or other," that it is "one," that two objects are "two," etc. for a conscious subject,— these facts seemed to be owing to the fact that objects are *actively* grasped, distinguished, and collected. Only because these processes have taken place does one have the basis for "abstracting" the universal forms "something or other," "two," "three," etc.

By ascribing to consciousness a dual status primarily as *over against* the whole world and producing it and only secondarily though veritably as a process in the world, Husserl's transcendental idealism–whatever its truth value—seemed to enable him to do justice, on the one hand, to the results of his "constitutional" analyses and, on the

---

[8] Cairns's marginal note: "Skip?"

other hand, to the indubitable fact that consciousness is also essentially the consciousness belonging to animals in the world, and coordinate with other things in it.

This doctrine is a matter of insight, not speculation—but that would take too long to develop here.

INDEX

Ajdukiewicz, K. 16, 203
Albott, C.S.R. 29
Aquinas, Th. 81
Aristotle, 41f, 48, 56f, 79-92, 199
Arnauld, A. 79ff, 92
Austin, J. 43
Bacon, F. 88
Bar-Hillel, Y. 203
Becker, O. 219
Benoist, J. 44, 93, 94, 99-108, 152
Bergson, H. 70
Berkeley, G. 155
Bernet, R. 114, 141, 151, 192, 196
Bloom, P. 172f, 175
Bolzano, B. 41ff, 46ff, 53ff, 60, 74
Bort, K. 128
Brand, G. 104
Brentano, F. 24, 44, 46, 81ff, 89f, 200f, 206ff, 210ff, 214f, 220f
Brogaard, B. 9, 167
Bühler, K. 208ff, 214
Bundgaard, P. 161
Burkhardt, A. 49
Buzetti, D. 44
Cantor, G. 57f
Cardan, G. 159
Carnap. R. 52
Chisholm, R. 201
Chomsky, N. 203
Church, A. 73f
Churchill, W. 171
Claesges, U. 143
Colin, A. 185
Cornelius, H. 102
Daubert, J. 16, 112
Davidson, D. 72f, 76, 79
De Boer, T. 103, 106, 194
Depraz, N. 192
Derrida, J. 16
Descartes, R. 70, 88f
Destutt de Tracy, A.L.C. 42
Dilthey, W. 15, 70
Dodd, J. 125
Dreyfus, H.L. 205
Drummond, J. 84, 86, 192

Dürr, E. 208f
Eco, U. 16
Eisler, R. 113
Embree, L. 219
Fauconnier, G. 161
Fechner, G.T. 207
Ferriani, M. 44
Findlay, J. 21, 23, 25, 28, 95
Fine, K. 57
Fink, E. 107, 112, 186, 188
Fischer, A. 113
Fish, S. 76
Fodor, J. 201, 203f
Frege, G. 32f, 41-47, 52, 54f, 57f, 60, 62, 73f, 213
Galileo 70
Gardiès, J.-L. 203
Geiger, M. 16
Gell-Mann, M. 147
Gödel, K. 52, 54
Goethe, J.W. von 158f
Hanna, R. 32
Hart, J.G. 104
Hartmann, N. 188
Heidegger, M. 16, 80, 86, 88f, 100f, 103, 128, 209
Held, K. 143
Hering, J. 73
Hill, C.O. 58
Hintikka, J. 52
Hjelms, E. 9
Hjelmslev, L. 16
Hobbes, T. 70, 80, 82, 85f
Hocking, W.E. 5
Hofstadter, D. 159
Holenstein, E. 166
Hume, D. 71ff, 75, 85f, 155
IJsseling, S. 46
Ingarden, R. 16, 151
Iser, W. 16
Jakobson, R. 16
Jauss, H.-R. 16
Julian, S.J. 219
Kant, I. 54, 70, 72f, 74ff, 83, 94, 96, 149, 187, 208
Kaplan, D. 52

Keizer, M. de 9
Kern, I. 141, 189, 192
Kersten, F. 219
Koffka, K. 166
Koyré, A. 185
Kraus, O. 220
Kripke, S. 52
Külpe, O. 208
Künne, W. 42
Lakoff, G. 147, 156, 167
Landgrebe, L. 107, 113, 122
Lazarus, M. 208
Leibniz, G.W. 20, 58
Lesniewski, S. 16, 203
Levinas, E. 95, 185
Lipps, Th. 15, 16
Locke, J. 70, 73f, 83, 86, 155, 160, 164, 166
Lohmar, D. 151, 157
Lotze, H. 20, 74, 94
Luft, S. 29
Mach, E. 15
Mack, W. 207
McIntyre, R. 58, 60, 63, 192, 205
Mahoney, M.S. 87
Malebranche, N. 79ff, 92
Marbach, E. 141
Martin, B. 147
Martin-Löf, P. 58
Meinong, A. 166
Melle, U. 46, 152. 180
Mensch, J.R. 189
Merleau-Ponty, M. 104, 214
Messer, A. 208ff
Mill, J.S. 190
Miller, J.P. 88
Mohanty, J.N. 33, 52, 141, 192, 194
Moore, G.E. 209
Münch, D. 128, 152
Nagel, T. 91
Napoleon, 144, 223
Natorp, P. 15, 74, 103
Nef, F. 42
Nenon, T. 129
Newell, A. 201, 209
Nietzsche, F. 72, 86
Østergaard, S. 161
Palagyi, M. 74

Parret, H. 49
Peiffer, G. 185
Peirce, C.S. 147-67
Peruzzi, A. 147, 167
Petitot, J. 165f
Petruzella, G. 9
Plato 74, 85, 199
Popper, K. 188
Putnam, H. 73
Pylyshyn, Z. 204
Quine, W.v.O. 52, 54, 59, 75, 201
Reinach, A. 16, 49
Riemann, B. 88
Rorty, R. 72f, 76f
Rosado Haddock, G.E. 128
Rosen, S. 82, 86
Roy, J.-M. 155
Russell, B. 16, 52, 73
Sartre, J.-P. 16, 71
Saussure, F. de 173
Schopenhauer, A. 28
Schuhmann, K. 157
Schuppe, W. 15
Schütz, A. 186
Searle, J. 49, 201-5, 212
Seebohm, T.M. 128, 142, 151
Sellars, W. 75
Selz, O. 209
Siebel, M. 42
Sigwart, C. 33
Simon, H. 201, 209, 213
Simons, P. 53, 57f
Sinigalia, C. 114
Smith, B. 44, 49, 53, 147, 154, 167, 203
Smith, D.W. 192
Smith, J.A. 85
Socrates 199
Sokolowski, R. 80f, 83, 86, 90f, 128, 150f, 153, 194
Soldati, G. 128
Spet, G. 16, 113
Spiegelberg, H. 70, 73, 209
Stein, E. 16, 113, 116
Steinthal, H. 208
Ströker, E. 138, 151
Stumpf, C. 15
Taminiaux, J. 86

Tarski, A. 52, 54, 61
Textor, M. 42
Tieszen, R. 58
Trendelenburg, F. 214
Twardowski, K. 96
Vaihinger, H. 115
Vico, G. 86
Volkelt, J. 187f, 191
Ward, J. 188
Weierstrass, K. 219ff
Wenders, W. 52
Wertheimer, M. 16
Whitehead, A. 52, 70f
Wittgenstein, L. 60, 62, 73, 104
Willard, D. 19, 52, 128, 153
Wundt, W. 15, 207ff
Yolton, J.W. 79
Zahavi, D. 65, 167, 189, 192

Phaenomenologica

1. E. Fink: *Sein, Wahrheit, Welt.* Vor-Fragen zum Problem des Phänomen-Begriffs. 1958
ISBN 90-247-0234-8
2. H.L. van Breda and J. Taminiaux (eds.): *Husserl et la pensée moderne / Husserl und das Denken der Neuzeit.* Actes du deuxième Colloque International de Phénoménologie / Akten des zweiten Internationalen Phänomenologischen Kolloquiums (Krefeld, 1.–3. Nov. 1956). 1959
ISBN 90-247-0235-8
3. J.-C. Piguet: *De l'esthétique à la métaphysique.* 1959   ISBN 90-247-0236-4
4. *E. Husserl: 1850–1959.* Recueil commémoratif publié à l'occasion du centenaire de la naissance du philosophe. 1959   ISBN 90-247-0237-2
5/6. H. Spiegelberg: *The Phenomenological Movement.* A Historical Introduction. 3rd revised ed. with the collaboration of Karl Schuhmann. 1982   ISBN Hb: 90-247-2577-1; Pb: 90-247-2535-6
7. A. Roth: *Edmund Husserls ethische Untersuchungen.* Dargestellt anhand seiner Vorlesungsmanuskripte. 1960   ISBN 90-247-0241-0
8. E. Levinas: *Totalité et infini.* Essai sur l'extériorité. 4th ed., 4th printing 1984
ISBN Hb: 90-247-5105-5; Pb: 90-247-2971-8
9. A. de Waelhens: *La philosophie et les expériences naturelles.* 1961   ISBN 90-247-0243-7
10. L. Eley: *Die Krise des Apriori in der transzendentalen Phänomenologie Edmund Husserls.* 1962
ISBN 90-247-0244-5
11. A. Schutz: *Collected Papers, I.* The Problem of Social Reality. Edited and introduced by M. Natanson. 1962; 5th printing: 1982   ISBN Hb: 90-247-5089-X; Pb: 90-247-3046-5
Collected Papers, II *see* below under Volume 15
Collected Papers, III *see* below under Volume 22
Collected Papers, IV *see* below under Volume 136
12. J.M. Broekman: *Phänomenologie und Egologie.* Faktisches und transzendentales Ego bei Edmund Husserl. 1963   ISBN 90-247-0245-3
13. W.J. Richardson: *Heidegger. Through Phenomenology to Thought.* Preface by Martin Heidegger. 1963; 3rd printing: 1974   ISBN 90-247-02461-1
14. J.N. Mohanty: *Edmund Husserl's Theory of Meaning.* 1964; reprint: 1969   ISBN 90-247-0247-X
15. A. Schutz: *Collected Papers, II.* Studies in Social Theory. Edited and introduced by A. Brodersen. 1964; reprint: 1977   ISBN 90-247-0248-8
16. I. Kern: *Husserl und Kant.* Eine Untersuchung über Husserls Verhältnis zu Kant und zum Neukantianismus. 1964; reprint: 1984   ISBN 90-247-0249-6
17. R.M. Zaner: *The Problem of Embodiment.* Some Contributions to a Phenomenology of the Body. 1964; reprint: 1971   ISBN 90-247-5093-8
18. R. Sokolowski: *The Formation of Husserl's Concept of Constitution.* 1964; reprint: 1970
ISBN 90-247-5086-5
19. U. Claesges: *Edmund Husserls Theorie der Raumkonstitution.* 1964   ISBN 90-247-0251-8
20. M. Dufrenne: *Jalons.* 1966   ISBN 90-247-0252-6
21. E. Fink: *Studien zur Phänomenologie, 1930–1939.* 1966   ISBN 90-247-0253-4
22. A. Schutz: *Collected Papers, III.* Studies in Phenomenological Philosophy. Edited by I. Schutz. With an introduction by Aaron Gurwitsch. 1966; reprint: 1975   ISBN 90-247-5090-3
23. K. Held: *Lebendige Gegenwart.* Die Frage nach der Seinsweise des transzendentalen Ich bei Edmund Husserl, entwickelt am Leitfaden der Zeitproblematik. 1966   ISBN 90-247-0254-2
24. O. Laffoucrière: *Le destin de la pensée et 'La Mort de Dieu' selon Heidegger.* 1968
ISBN 90-247-0255-0
25. E. Husserl: *Briefe an Roman Ingarden.* Mit Erläuterungen und Erinnerungen an Husserl. Hrsg. von R. Ingarden. 1968   ISBN Hb: 90-247-0257-7; Pb: 90-247-0256-9
26. R. Boehm: *Vom Gesichtspunkt der Phänomenologie* (I). Husserl-Studien. 1968
ISBN Hb: 90-247-0259-3; Pb: 90-247-0258-5
For *Band II see* below under Volume 83

Phaenomenologica

27. T. Conrad: *Zur Wesenslehre des psychischen Lebens und Erlebens.* Mit einem Geleitwort von H.L. van Breda. 1968   ISBN 90-247-0260-7
28. W. Biemel: *Philosophische Analysen zur Kunst der Gegenwart.* 1969
     ISBN Hb: 90-247-0263-1; Pb: 90-247-0262-3
29. G. Thinès: *La problématique de la psychologie.* 1968
     ISBN Hb: 90-247-0265-8; Pb: 90-247-0264-X
30. D. Sinha: *Studies in Phenomenology.* 1969   ISBN Hb: 90-247-0267-4; Pb: 90-247-0266-6
31. L. Eley: *Metakritik der formalen Logik.* Sinnliche Gewissheit als Horizont der Aussagenlogik und elementaren Prädikatenlogik. 1969   ISBN Hb: 90-247-0269-0; Pb: 90-247-0268-2
32. M.S. Frings: *Person und Dasein.* Zur Frage der Ontologie des Wertseins. 1969
     ISBN Hb: 90-247-0271-2; Pb: 90-247-0270-4
33. A. Rosales: *Transzendenz und Differenz.* Ein Beitrag zum Problem der ontologischen Differenz beim frühen Heidegger. 1970   ISBN 90-247-0272-0
34. M.M. Saraiva: *L'imagination selon Husserl.* 1970   ISBN 90-247-0273-9
35. P. Janssen: *Geschichte und Lebenswelt.* Ein Beitrag zur Diskussion von Husserls Spätwerk. 1970
     ISBN 90-247-0274-7
36. W. Marx: *Vernunft und Welt.* Zwischen Tradition und anderem Anfang. 1970
     ISBN 90-247-5042-3
37. J.N. Mohanty: *Phenomenology and Ontology.* 1970   ISBN 90-247-5053-9
38. A. Aguirre: *Genetische Phänomenologie und Reduktion.* Zur Letztbegründung der Wissenschaft aus der radikalen Skepsis im Denken E. Husserl. 1970   ISBN 90-247-5025-3
39. T.F. Geraets: *Vers une nouvelle philosophie transcendentale.* La genèse de la philosophie de Maurice Merleau-Ponty jusqu'à la 'Phénoménologie de la perception.' Préface par E. Levinas. 1971   ISBN 90-247-5024-5
40. H. Declève: *Heidegger et Kant.* 1970   ISBN 90-247-5016-4
41. B. Waldenfels: *Das Zwischenreich des Dialogs.* Sozialphilosophische Untersuchungen in Anschluss an Edmund Husserl. 1971   ISBN 90-247-5072-5
42. K. Schuhmann: *Die Fundamentalbetrachtung der Phänomenologie.* Zum Weltproblem in der Philosophie Edmund Husserls. 1971   ISBN 90-247-5121-7
43. K. Goldstein: *Selected Papers/Ausgewählte Schriften.* Edited by A. Gurwitsch, E.M. Goldstein Haudek and W.E. Haudek. Introduction by A. Gurwitsch. 1971   ISBN 90-247-5047-4
44. E. Holenstein: *Phänomenologie der Assoziation.* Zu Struktur und Funktion eines Grundprinzips der passiven Genesis bei E. Husserl. 1972   ISBN 90-247-1175-4
45. F. Hammer: *Theonome Anthropologie?* Max Schelers Menschenbild und seine Grenzen. 1972
     ISBN 90-247-1186-X
46. A. Pažanin: *Wissenschaft und Geschichte in der Phänomenologie Edmund Husserls.* 1972
     ISBN 90-247-1194-0
47. G.A. de Almeida: *Sinn und Inhalt in der genetischen Phänomenologie E. Husserls.* 1972
     ISBN 90-247-1318-8
48. J. Rolland de Renéville: *Aventure de l'absolu.* 1972   ISBN 90-247-1319-6
49. U. Claesges und K. Held (eds.): *Perspektiven transzendental-phänomenologischer Forschung.* Für Ludwig Landgrebe zum 70. Geburtstag von seiner Kölner Schülern. 1972   ISBN 90-247-1313-7
50. F. Kersten and R. Zaner (eds.): *Phenomenology: Continuation and Criticism.* Essays in Memory of Dorion Cairns. 1973   ISBN 90-247-1302-1
51. W. Biemel (ed.): *Phänomenologie Heute.* Festschrift für Ludwig Landgrebe. 1972
     ISBN 90-247-1336-6
52. D. Souche-Dagues: *Le développement de l'intentionnalité dans la phénoménologie husserlienne.* 1972   ISBN 90-247-1354-4
53. B. Rang: *Kausalität und Motivation.* Untersuchungen zum Verhältnis von Perspektivität und Objektivität in der Phänomenologie Edmund Husserls. 1973   ISBN 90-247-1353-6
54. E. Levinas: *Autrement qu'être ou au-delà de l'essence.* 2nd. ed.: 1978   ISBN 90-247-2030-3
55. D. Cairns: *Guide for Translating Husserl.* 1973   ISBN Pb: 90-247-1452-4

Phaenomenologica

56. K. Schuhmann: *Die Dialektik der Phänomenologie, I.* Husserl über Pfänder. 1973
ISBN 90-247-1316-1
57. K. Schuhmann: *Die Dialektik der Phänomenologie, II.* Reine Phänomenologie und phänomenologische Philosophie. Historisch-analytische Monographie über Husserls 'Ideen I'. 1973
ISBN 90-247-1307-2
58. R. Williame: *Les fondements phénoménologiques de la sociologie compréhensive: Alfred Schutz et Max Weber.* 1973
ISBN 90-247-1531-8
59. E. Marbach: *Das Problem des Ich in der Phänomenologie Husserls.* 1974   ISBN 90-247-1587-3
60. R. Stevens: *James and Husserl: The Foundations of Meaning.* 1974   ISBN 90-247-1631-4
61. H.L. van Breda (ed.): *Vérité et Vérification / Wahrheit und Verifikation.* Actes du quatrième Colloque International de Phénoménologie / Akten des vierten Internationalen Kolloquiums für Phänomenologie (Schwabisch Hall, Baden-Württemberg, 8.–11. September 1969). 1974
ISBN 90-247-1702-7
62. Ph.J. Bossert (ed.): *Phenomenological Perspectives.* Historical and Systematic Essays in Honor of Herbert Spiegelberg. 1975.
ISBN 90-247-1701-9
63. H. Spiegelberg: *Doing Phenomenology.* Essays on and in Phenomenology. 1975
ISBN 90-247-1725-6
64. R. Ingarden: *On the Motives which Led Husserl to Transcendental Idealism.* 1975
ISBN 90-247-1751-5
65. H. Kuhn, E. Avé-Lallemant and R. Gladiator (eds.): *Die Münchener Phänomenologie.* Vorträge des Internationalen Kongresses in München (13.–18. April 1971). 1975   ISBN 90-247-1740-X
66. D. Cairns: *Conversations with Husserl and Fink.* Edited by the Husserl-Archives in Louvain. With a foreword by R.M. Zaner. 1975
ISBN 90-247-1793-0
67. G. Hoyos Vásquez: *Intentionalität als Verantwortung.* Geschichtsteleologie und Teleologie der Intentionalität bei Husserl. 1976
ISBN 90-247-1794-9
68. J. Patočka: *Le monde naturel comme problème philosophique.* 1976   ISBN 90-247-1795-7
69. W.W. Fuchs: *Phenomenology and the Metaphysics of Presence.* An Essay in the Philosophy of Edmund Husserl. 1976
ISBN 90-247-1822-8
70. S. Cunningham: *Language and the Phenomenological Reductions of Edmund Husserl.* 1976
ISBN 90-247-1823-6
71. G.C. Moneta: *On Identity.* A Study in Genetic Phenomenology. 1976   ISBN 90-247-1860-0
72. W. Biemel und das Husserl-Archiv zu Löwen (eds.): *Die Welt des Menschen – Die Welt der Philosophie.* Festschrift für Jan Patočka. 1976
ISBN 90-247-1899-6
73. M. Richir: *Au-delà du renversement copernicien.* La question de la phénoménologie et son fondement. 1976
ISBN 90-247-1903-8
74. H. Mongis: *Heidegger et la critique de la notion de valeur.* La destruction de la fondation métaphysique. Lettre-préface de Martin Heidegger. 1976
ISBN 90-247-1904-6
75. J. Taminiaux: *Le regard et l'excédent.* 1977
ISBN 90-247-2028-1
76. Th. de Boer: *The Development of Husserl's Thought.* 1978
ISBN Hb: 90-247-2039-7; Pb: 90-247-2124-5
77. R.R. Cox: *Schutz's Theory of Relevance.* A Phenomenological Critique. 1978
ISBN 90-247-2041-9
78. S. Strasser: *Jenseits von Sein und Zeit.* Eine Einführung in Emmanuel Levinas' Philosophie. 1978
ISBN 90-247-2068-0
79. R.T. Murphy: *Hume and Husserl.* Towards Radical Subjectivism. 1980   ISBN 90-247-2172-5
80. H. Spiegelberg: *The Context of the Phenomenological Movement.* 1981   ISBN 90-247-2392-2
81. J.R. Mensch: *The Question of Being in Husserl's Logical Investigations.* 1981
ISBN 90-247-2413-9
82. J. Loscerbo: *Being and Technology.* A Study in the Philosophy of Martin Heidegger. 1981
ISBN 90-247-2411-2
83. R. Boehm: *Vom Gesichtspunkt der Phänomenologie II.* Studien zur Phänomenologie der Epoché. 1981
ISBN 90-247-2415-5

Phaenomenologica

84. H. Spiegelberg and E. Avé-Lallemant (eds.): *Pfänder-Studien.* 1982 ISBN 90-247-2490-2
85. S. Valdinoci: *Les fondements de la phénoménologie husserlienne.* 1982 ISBN 90-247-2504-6
86. I. Yamaguchi: *Passive Synthesis und Intersubjektivität bei Edmund Husserl.* 1982
ISBN 90-247-2505-4
87. J. Libertson: *Proximity.* Levinas, Blanchot, Bataille and Communication. 1982
ISBN 90-247-2506-2
88. D. Welton: *The Origins of Meaning.* A Critical Study of the Thresholds of Husserlian Phenomenology. 1983 ISBN 90-247-2618-2
89. W.R. McKenna: *Husserl's 'Introductions to Phenomenology'.* Interpretation and Critique. 1982
ISBN 90-247-2665-4
90. J.P. Miller: *Numbers in Presence and Absence.* A Study of Husserl's Philosophy of Mathematics. 1982 ISBN 90-247-2709-X
91. U. Melle: *Das Wahrnehmungsproblem und seine Verwandlung in phänomenologischer Einstellung.* Untersuchungen zu den phänomenologischen Wahrnehmungstheorien von Husserl, Gurwitsch und Merleau-Ponty. 1983 ISBN 90-247-2761-8
92. W.S. Hamrick (ed.): *Phenomenology in Practice and Theory.* Essays for Herbert Spiegelberg. 1984
ISBN 90-247-2926-2
93. H. Reiner: *Duty and Inclination.* The Fundamentals of Morality Discussed and Redefined with Special Regard to Kant and Schiller. 1983 ISBN 90-247-2818-6
94. M.J. Harney: *Intentionality, Sense and the Mind.* 1984 ISBN 90-247-2891-6
95. Kah Kyung Cho (ed.): *Philosophy and Science in Phenomenological Perspective.* 1984
ISBN 90-247-2922-X
96. A. Lingis: *Phenomenological Explanations.* 1986 ISBN Hb: 90-247-3332-4; Pb: 90-247-3333-2
97. N. Rotenstreich: *Reflection and Action.* 1985 ISBN Hb: 90-247-2969-6; Pb: 90-247-3128-3
98. J.N. Mohanty: *The Possibility of Transcendental Philosophy.* 1985
ISBN Hb: 90-247-2991-2; Pb: 90-247-3146-1
99. J.J. Kockelmans: *Heidegger on Art and Art Works.* 1985 ISBN 90-247-3102-X
100. E. Lévinas: *Collected Philosophical Papers.* 1987
ISBN Hb: 90-247-3272-7; Pb: 90-247-3395-2
101. R. Regvald: *Heidegger et le problème du néant.* 1986 ISBN 90-247-3388-X
102. J.A. Barash: *Martin Heidegger and the Problem of Historical Meaning.* 1987
ISBN 90-247-3493-2
103. J.J. Kockelmans (ed.): *Phenomenological Psychology.* The Dutch School. 1987
ISBN 90-247-3501-7
104. W.S. Hamrick: *An Existential Phenomenology of Law: Maurice Merleau-Ponty.* 1987
ISBN 90-247-3520-3
105. J.C. Sallis, G. Moneta and J. Taminiaux (eds.): *The Collegium Phaenomenologicum. The First Ten Years.* 1988 ISBN 90-247-3709-5
106. D. Carr: *Interpreting Husserl.* Critical and Comparative Studies. 1987. ISBN 90-247-3505-X
107. G. Heffernan: *Isagoge in die phänomenologische Apophantik.* Eine Einführung in die phänomenologische Urteilslogik durch die Auslegung des Textes der *Formalen und transzendenten Logik* von Edmund Husserl. 1989 ISBN 90-247-3710-9
108. F. Volpi, J.-F. Mattéi, Th. Sheenan, J.-F. Courtine, J. Taminiaux, J. Sallis, D. Janicaud, A.L. Kelkel, R. Bernet, R. Brisart, K. Held, M. Haar et S. IJsseling: *Heidegger et l'idée de la phénoménologie.* 1988 ISBN 90-247-3586-6
109. C. Singevin: *Dramaturgie de l'esprit.* 1988 ISBN 90-247-3557-2
110. J. Patočka: *Le monde naturel et le mouvement de l'existence humaine.* 1988 ISBN 90-247-3577-7
111. K.-H. Lembeck: *Gegenstand Geschichte.* Geschichtswissenschaft in Husserls Phänomenologie. 1988 ISBN 90-247-3635-8
112. J.K. Cooper-Wiele: *The Totalizing Act.* Key to Husserl's Early Philosophy. 1989
ISBN 0-7923-0077-7

Phaenomenologica

113. S. Valdinoci: *Le principe d'existence*. Un devenir psychiatrique de la phénoménologie. 1989
ISBN 0-7923-0125-0
114. D. Lohmar: *Phänomenologie der Mathematik*. 1989   ISBN 0-7923-0187-0
115. S. IJsseling (Hrsgb.): *Husserl-Ausgabe und Husserl-Forschung*. 1990   ISBN 0-7923-0372-5
116. R. Cobb-Stevens: *Husserl and Analytic Philosophy*. 1990   ISBN 0-7923-0467-5
117. R. Klockenbusch: *Husserl und Cohn*. Widerspruch, Reflexion und Telos in Phänomenologie und Dialektik. 1989
ISBN 0-7923-0515-9
118. S. Vaitkus: *How is Society Possible?* Intersubjectivity and the Fiduciary Attitude as Problems of the Social Group in Mead, Gurwitsch, and Schutz. 1991   ISBN 0-7923-0820-4
119. C. Macann: *Presence and Coincidence*. The Transformation of Transcendental into Ontological Phenomenology. 1991
ISBN 0-7923-0923-5
120. G. Shpet: *Appearance and Sense*. Phenomenology as the Fundamental Science and Its Problems. Translated from Russian by Th. Nemeth. 1991   ISBN 0-7923-1098-5
121. B. Stevens: *L'apprentissage des signes*. Lecture de Paul Ricœur. 1991   ISBN 0-7923-1244-9
122. G. Soffer: *Husserl and the Question of Relativism*. 1991   ISBN 0-7923-1291-0
123. G. Römpp: *Husserls Phänomenologie der Intersubjektivität*. Und Ihre Bedeutung für eine Theorie intersubjektiver Objektivität und die Konzeption einer phänomenologischen Philosophie. 1991
ISBN 0-7923-1361-5
124. S. Strasser: *Welt im Widerspruch*. Gedanken zu einer Phänomenologie als ethischer Fundamentalphilosophie. 1991   ISBN Hb: 0-7923-1404-2; Pb: 0-7923-1551-0
125. R.P. Buckley: *Husserl, Heidegger and the Crisis of Philosophical Responsibility*. 1992
ISBN 0-7923-1633-9
126. J.G. Hart: *The Person and the Common Life*. Studies in a Husserlian Social Ethics. 1992
ISBN 0-7923-1724-6
127. P. van Tongeren, P. Sars, C. Bremmers and K. Boey (eds.): *Eros and Eris*. Contributions to a Hermeneutical Phenomenology. Liber Amicorum for Adriaan Peperzak. 1992
ISBN 0-7923-1917-6
128. Nam-In Lee: *Edmund Husserls Phänomenologie der Instinkte*. 1993   ISBN 0-7923-2041-7
129. P. Burke and J. Van der Veken (eds.): *Merleau-Ponty in Contemporary Perspective*. 1993
ISBN 0-7923-2142-1
130. G. Haefliger: *Über Existenz: Die Ontologie Roman Ingardens*. 1994   ISBN 0-7923-2227-4
131. J. Lampert: *Synthesis and Backward Reference in Husserl's* Logical Investigations. 1995
ISBN 0-7923-3105-2
132. J.M. DuBois: *Judgment and Sachverhalt*. An Introduction to Adolf Reinach's Phenomenological Realism. 1995
ISBN 0-7923-3519-8
133. B.E. Babich (ed.): *From Phenomenology to Thought, Errancy, and Desire*. Essays in Honor of William J. Richardson, S.J. 1995
ISBN 0-7923-3567-8
134. M. Dupuis: *Pronoms et visages*. Lecture d'Emmanuel Levinas. 1996
ISBN Hb: 0-7923-3655-0; Pb 0-7923-3994-0
135. D. Zahavi: *Husserl und die transzendentale Intersubjektivität*. Eine Antwort auf die sprachpragmatische Kritik. 1996
ISBN 0-7923-3713-1
136. A. Schutz: *Collected Papers, IV*. Edited with preface and notes by H. Wagner and G. Psathas, in collaboration with F. Kersten. 1996
ISBN 0-7923-3760-3
137. P. Kontos: *D'une phénomologie de la perception chez Heidegger*. 1996 ISBN 0-7923-3776-X
138. F. Kuster: *Wege der Verantwortung*. Husserls Phänomenologie als Gang durch die Faktizität. 1996
ISBN 0-7923-3916-9
139. C. Beyer: *Von Bolzano zu Husserl*. Eine Untersuchung über den Ursprung der phänomenologischen Bedeutungslehre. 1996
ISBN 0-7923-4050-7
140. J. Dodd: *Idealism and Corporeity*. An Essay on the Problem of the Body in Husserl's Phenomenology. 1997
ISBN 0-7923-4400-6
141. E. Kelly: *Structure and Diversity*. Studies in the Phenomenological Philosophy of Max Scheler. 1997
ISBN 0-7923-4492-8

Phaenomenologica

142. J. Cavallin: *Content and Object*. Husserl, Twardowski and Psychologism. 1997
 ISBN 0-7923-4734-X
143. H.P. Steeves: *Founding Community*. A Phenomenological-Ethical Inquiry. 1997
 ISBN 0-7923-4798-6
144. M. Sawicki: *Body, Text, and Science*. The Literacy of Investigative Practices and the Phenomenology of Edith Stein. 1997 ISBN 0-7923-4759-5; Pb: 1-4020-0262-9
145. O.K. Wiegand: *Interpretationen der Modallogik*. Ein Beitrag zur phänomenologischen Wissenschaftstheorie. 1998 ISBN 0-7923-4809-5
146. P. Marrati-Guénoun: *La genèse et la trace*. Derrida lecteur de Husserl et Heidegger. 1998
 ISBN 0-7923-4969-5
147. D. Lohmar: *Erfahrung und kategoriales Denken*. 1998 ISBN 0-7923-5117-7
148. N. Depraz and D. Zahavi (eds.): *Alterity and Facticity*. New Perspectives on Husserl. 1998
 ISBN 0-7923-5187-8
149. E. Øverenget: *Seeing the Self*. Heidegger on Subjectivity. 1998
 ISBN Hb: 0-7923-5219-X; Pb: 1-4020-0259-9
150. R.D. Rollinger: *Husserls Position in the School of Brentano*. 1999 ISBN 0-7923-5684-5
151. A. Chrudzimski: *Die Erkenntnistheorie von Roman Ingarden*. 1999 ISBN 0-7923-5688-8
152. B. Bergo: *Levinas Between Ethics and Politics*. For the Beauty that Adorns the Earth. 1999
 ISBN 0-7923-5694-2
153. L. Ni: *Seinsglaube in der Phänomenologie Edmund Husserls*. 1999 ISBN 0-7923-5779-5
154. E. Feron: *Phénoménologie de la mort*. Sur les traces de Levinas. 1999 ISBN 0-7923-5935-6
155. R. Visker: *Truth and Singularity*. Taking Foucault into Phenomenology. 1999
 ISBN Hb: 0-7923-5985-2; Pb: 0-7923-6397-3
156. E.E. Kleist: *Judging Appearances*. A Phenomenological Study of the Kantian *sensus communis*. 2000 ISBN Hb: 0-7923-6310-8; Pb: 1-4020-0258-0
157. D. Pradelle: *L'archéologie du monde*. Constitution de l'espace, idéalisme et intuitionnisme chez Husserl. 2000 ISBN 0-7923-6313-2
158. H.B. Schmid: *Subjekt, System, Diskurs*. Edmund Husserls Begriff transzendentaler Subjektivität in sozialtheoretischen Bezügen. 2000 ISBN 0-7923-6424-4
159. A. Chrudzimski: *Intentionalitätstheorie beim frühen Brentano*. 2001 ISBN 0-7923-6860-6
160. N. Depraz: *Lucidité du corps*. De l'empirisme transcendantal en phénoménologie. 2001
 ISBN 0-7923-6977-7
161. T. Kortooms: *Phenomenology of Time*. Edmund Husserl's Analysis of Time-Consciousness. 2001
 ISBN 1-4020-0121-5
162. R. Boehm: *Topik*. 2002 ISBN 1-4020-0629-2
163. A. Chernyakov: *The Ontology of Time*. Being and Time in the Philosophies of Aristotle, Husserl and Heidegger. 2002 ISBN 1-4020-0682-9
164. D. Zahavi and F. Stjernfelt (eds.): *One Hundred Years of Phenomenology*. Husserl' Logical Investigations Revisited. 2002 ISBN 1-4020-0700-0
165. B. Ferreira: *Stimmung bei Heidegger*. Das Phänomen der Stimmung im Kontext von Heideggers Existenzialanalyse des Daseins. 2002 ISBN 1-4020-0701-9

Previous volumes are still available

Further information about *Phenomenology* publications are available on request

Kluwer Academic Publishers – Dordrecht / Boston / London